Women in the Hindu World

THE OXFORD CENTRE FOR HINDU STUDIES
MANDALA PUBLISHING SERIES

The Oxford Centre for Hindu Studies Mandala Publishing Series offers authoritative yet accessible introductions to a wide range of subjects in Hindu Studies. Each book in the series aims to present its subject matter in a form that is engaging and readily comprehensible to persons of all backgrounds—academic or otherwise—without compromising scholarly rigor. The series thus bridges the divide between academic and popular writing by preserving and utilising the best elements of both.

WOMEN IN THE HINDU WORLD

Mandakranta Bose

MANDALA
San Rafael Los Angeles London

CONTENTS

Acknowledgements
vii

Introduction
1

I. Divinity and Femininity
7

II. Women and Sacred Knowledge
51

III. Regulating Women's Lives:
Scriptures and Injunctions
81

IV. A Room of Their Own:
Women's Writings
125

V. Women at Worship
163

VI. Women, Art, and Religion
197

ACKNOWLEDGEMENTS

My thanks for the discussion in the pages that follow go first to the Oxford Centre for Hindu Studies, not only for encouraging me to undertake it, but also for providing me with resources to carry it out. A very valuable part of the Centre's assistance has been the critical oversight of the chapters by Nicholas Sutton, the editorial work of Lucian Wong, and the organisational support of Lal Krishna. I am indebted too in clarifying my ideas here, as in all my efforts to understand Hinduism, to conversations with Professor Gavin Flood, Academic Director of the Centre, and to Bjarne Wernicke-Olesen, as also to several students and visiting scholars at the Centre in Trinity Term and Summer 2019. To Nandana Nagaraj, my thanks are due not only for her help with countless practical matters, but also for sharing with me her knowledge of worship practices. As for Shaunaka Rishi, the Administrative Director of OCHS, I shall say no more than that he has stood by me as a dear friend for many years now and has let me share his hopes for Hindu Studies in Oxford. In presenting my ideas and arguments here, I have drawn upon exchanges with my students at the University of British Columbia, learning through the years the art of clarity in word and thought. I have also gratefully benefited from the feedback of the anonymous reader of the book. To my husband Tirthankar Bose, my debts shall remain ever unpaid.

Introduction

This short study aims at introducing the reader to the challenging notion of womanhood in Hindu religious culture, including its formative influence on women's situation in social life. Divided into seven related chapters following this Introduction, this monograph aims at encouraging reading and self-directed reflection, reinforced by a list of suggested reading material. The chapters proceed both historically and thematically, covering abstract philosophical ideas as well as concrete worldly conditions, from the earliest stages of Hindu society to the present, marking through time the evolving conception of women, their religious roles, and their social status as derived from Hindu philosophical thought. A theme followed through this monograph will be the paradox that while Hindu metaphysics centralises the feminine as the source of cosmic power, Hindu society has traditionally authorised the subjection of women. This downgrading of women is especially deplorable in view of the very great independence enjoyed by women in the earliest period of Hindu society, not to speak of the continuing idealisation – sadly, more in theory than in practice – of women throughout the history of Hinduism. At the same time, this study notes that Hindu women have consistently found in their faith resources for claiming selfhood both as religious and social subjects. At the very minimum, Hindu women have been able to create a niche of their own in their homes, where they perform religious rites often in their own way, while a great many have found space for worshipping through poetry, painting, dance, and music. Still more excitingly, in present-day social life Hindu women have gained the strength to claim decisive roles in shaping their own lives and the world at large. The chapters in this book will thus lead to understanding how women exist in Hindu society as religious subjects under social conditions that are deeply influenced by ideas derived – or claimed to be derived – from religious sources.

Before we venture into the discussion we would do well to keep in view a fundamental question: does it make sense to talk about women as a separate element of Hinduism? Or of any religion for that matter? Is a religion different for men and women? To the modern sensibility it is inconceivable that God (or the Supreme Being, if you prefer the term) is different for men and women or treats men and women differently. Were we to think so then we would be thinking of a religion actually as two separate belief systems, one for men, the other for women. Since we do not think so, we must proceed from the idea that there may be some difference in the way men and women think of God, feel God's existence, and seek God. This idea is perhaps best captured by the commonplace image of seekers of the same treasure travelling by different paths. That image dominates Hindu thought.

For Hindus plurality is not a surprising idea. Hinduism has no central doctrine, no single authority to lay down what Hindus should believe and how they should worship. That makes difference in belief and practice entirely defensible and feasible. It follows that men and women, as gendered categories, may well have different ways of believing in the Ultimate spirit and different ways of finding that spirit while adhering to the same spiritual impulse. Whether that spirit exists or is said to be merely a piece of self-delusion is not relevant here; the object of this study is to consider the ways in which belief in such a spirit expresses itself and works in the minds and hearts of men and women.

Bound as the human world is by the rules and conventions of social life, it is an everyday experience that spirituality finds its way through different modes of thought, expression, and action within a body of religious conduct. Such difference is very often defined by gender and bound by social practices, which explains why Hindu women's religious life is an amalgam of the worldly and the other-worldly, formed as much by spiritual impulses as by worldly necessities, whereby it has historically coalesced into a domain that is their own. To observe and understand the particulars of that domain and to chart the ways in which the Hindu religion shapes women's religious life is the goal of the present study.

Each of the chapters that follow begins with a brief introductory paragraph, and proceeds through the exposition of the chapter's topic supported by material quoted and cited from the source texts of the Hindu religion and related critical studies. Sanskrit texts, their translations, and critical studies referred to in the chapters are listed in the References section at the end of the book. Sanskrit texts cited here are standard editions in general unless noted otherwise; translated passages that appear without specific credit are mine. The purpose constantly pursued through the book is to encourage you, the reader, to develop and nurture your own understanding of the life of a woman as a Hindu. After going through the chapters you will, I hope, realise that there are endless opportunities for reflecting on and discussing the topics they deal with. Indeed, such reflections would be an essential part of the learning process, for the aim of these pages is not to load you with parcels of information and ready-made arguments or conclusions, but to build for you platforms from which you may launch your own enquiries. It is with that need in mind that I have listed broad topics for reflection, framed as questions, to keep the issue focused in your mind at the end of each chapter. They represent only a few of many possible issues and you will no doubt come up with many more. Although the discussion topics are presented as specific questions, please bear in mind that there is no single correct answer and you may find it useful to imagine each discussion as a debate within your own mind – unless you are fortunate enough to persuade somebody else to act as your foil. Your study and discussion will, I hope, be helped by a selective glossary of terms used in Hindu religious, philosophical, and sociological discourse, such as '*mokṣa*'.

All texts and critical works referred to in chapters are cited there, with full bibliographical information, as also in the References at the end of the book. To facilitate further enquiry and independent study, a briefly annotated list of books has been added at the end of the monograph. Note that compound Sanskrit terms, including titles of texts, have been separated into their elements, thus: *dharmaśāstra* appears as *dharma-śāstra, Devībhāgavatapurāṇa* as *Devī Bhāgavatapurāṇa,* and so on. When cited in published form, they appear as given on title-pages or journal citations.

A word of caution before we begin: Hindu religious culture is full of different views and narratives, many of them contradictory. There is no central, universally accepted narrative, let alone a unified doctrine. What we know is drawn from texts that vary quite widely in their views about gods, goddesses, and the world, and from worship practices, which vary of course even more widely. Dates too are often hard to pinpoint. Considering Hinduism's antiquity and the millennia of its evolution, this is not surprising but calls for disciplined study and reflection and, above all, for avoiding quick opinions. Given the great range of Hindu culture across philosophical ideas, religious rituals and conduct, myths and legends, social rules and practice, the study of Hindu thought and practice is often a hazardous journey through a minefield of contradictory views. But not to attempt that journey is to miss an adventure. I confess I would rather attempt leaps of judgement across that minefield than none at all, so long as those judgements are open to revision through sober reflection.

I
Divinity and Femininity

From its very beginning many thousands of years ago, Hindu religious thought has been deeply concerned with the idea of femininity. In this chapter we will look into the origins of that idea in Hindu philosophy and its development through time. Hindu religious beliefs and practices have pervaded the idea of womanhood, locating the feminine both in the material human world and in the realm of the spirit. How much force that tradition still exerts on Hindu social culture today with respect to women is an intriguing question and can lead to emotionally charged positions among Hindus and non-Hindus alike. The way that religious principles tend to turn into social and political rules and conventions will be part of the discussion developed throughout this book. So will the opportunities that exist within the Hindu religion for women to achieve self-determination both socially and spiritually. The present chapter will prepare the groundwork for that discussion.

Origins

As in other world cultures, philosophical and religious thought – the two usually converging – in Hindu society began with speculations about the origin of existence and its process, and with explanations of natural life. At its most adventurous,

Hindu philosophical thought admits that nobody really knows how and where it all began. A hymn in the *Ṛg Veda,* the earliest Hindu collection of religious thought, says, 'Existence, in the earliest age of gods, from Non-existence sprang' (*Ṛg Veda* 10.72.3), and a later one, the famous Nāsadīya hymn, asserts even more boldly:

1. Then was not non-existent nor existent: there was no realm of air, no sky beyond it. What covered it, and where? and what gave shelter? Was water there, unfathomed depth of water?
2. Death was not then, nor was there aught immortal: no sign was there, the day's and night's divider. That One Thing, breathless, breathed by its own nature: apart from it was nothing whatsoever.
3. Darkness there was: at first concealed in darkness this All was indiscriminated chaos. All that existed then was void and formless: by the great power of Warmth was born that Unit.
4. Thereafter rose Desire in the beginning, Desire, the primal seed and germ of Spirit. Sages who searched with their heart's thought discovered the existent's kinship in the non-existent.
5. Transversely was their severing line extended: what was above it then, and what below it? There were begetters, there were mighty forces, free action here and energy up yonder.
6. Who verily knows and who can here declare it, whence it was born and whence comes this creation? The gods are later than this world's production. Who knows then whence it first came into being?
7. He, the first origin of this creation, whether he formed it all or did not form it,

> Whose eye controls this world in highest heaven, he verily knows it, or perhaps he knows not.
>
> (*Ṛg Veda*, 10.129)[1]

Despite its confession of bafflement, this passage takes for granted the existence of an abstract Supreme Being who is self-originating and the source of all phenomena. Hindu thought attempted to grasp that abstract Being by picturing it in many forms as gods and goddesses. Imagined as divine beings in human shape and placed in a social order, Hindu gods and goddesses control everything that happens in the universe while they rule over human life. This belief in personified deities began to take hold of Hindu spiritual thought from its earliest phase, generally traced back to the fifteenth century BCE.[2] Gods and goddesses are immensely more powerful than human beings, but they are modelled on human beings and they exist in relation to humankind and other forms of earthly life.[3] They possess superhuman powers that they employ to regulate nature and support human life within a scheme of orderliness, mutual benefit, and justice.

In the earliest phase of Hindu spiritual thought, divinity in its full might resided mainly in male gods, who were

1 Translations from the *Ṛg Veda* in this and all following chapters are from *The Hymns of the Rigveda*, transl. Ralph T. H. Griffith [1889], ed. J. L. Shastri (Delhi: Motilal Banarsidass, 1973), unless otherwise noted. References to the Sanskrit text of the *Ṛg Veda* in this and all following chapters are from *Ṛg Veda Saṁhitā*, Maṇḍalas 1–10, ed. K. L. Joshi (Varanasi: Chaukhamba Orientalia, 2000) unless otherwise noted.

2 Gavin Flood, *An Introduction to Hinduism* (Cambridge: Cambridge University Press, 1996), 21. Like other early dates in India's civilisation, this is not beyond question and some scholars push the beginning of Hindu culture farther back.

3 Sukumari Bhattacharji, *The Indian Theogony* (Cambridge: Cambridge University Press, 1970); Alain Danielou, *Myths and Gods of India* (Rochester, VT: Inner Traditions International, c.1991).

worshipped as holders of power, and dispensers of both favours and punishment. While goddesses were part of the divine world, they performed only specific and usually narrow functions, mainly related to nurturing human life, ever-present but on the periphery of cosmic power. This vision of the divine world changed with new ideas developing some centuries later. In the classical period of the Hindu tradition, approximately from the fifth century CE, the idea of a single Great Goddess came to dominate Hindu thought as the energy that drives all creation.

That there is a gender division within the community of deities may seem startling, considering that they are not biological entities. But like other world cultures, Hinduism overlooks this inconsistency and treats divine beings as biological ones, treating every form of existence, whether open to direct human sense perception or not, as animated and gendered. Again, this is not uncommon in world culture but Hindu views on gender characteristics and roles are painstakingly elaborated and ceaselessly debated both in their theological positions and sociological implications. For practical purposes of capturing the indeterminate idea of an otherworldly life, Hindus, like others, have assigned biological presence to gods and goddesses. They have also placed gods and goddesses within a society that is their very own but again one that parallels human society.

Though they shared the same universe, Vedic gods and goddesses were not equal, for early Hindu thought held them within a hierarchy of power that included a hierarchy of gender as well. While the gods controlled cosmic forces and functions, such as the power of the wind, oceans/water, fire, thunder, and lightning, the goddesses were limited to prescribed tasks. Well into Vedic times when Hindu thought was crystallising into a distinct theology, goddesses were players in the support system of the universe rather than its controllers, carrying out a primarily nurturing role. From an early time, the gender division within the divine world determined the division of divine functions, with the broader, far-reaching control of creation resting upon male gods and the female deities carrying out particular tasks of keeping creation going. Another aspect of the gendering of deities is that goddesses were scarcely, if ever, independent actors but attached to gods in supporting roles. Any independence that some of them might have possessed initially eroded as the conception of the divine community firmed up through time. During the Vedic period, we find goddesses pushed to the periphery of power and influence. For sages and worshippers, goddesses diminished in importance in comparison to male deities such as Indra, Agni, Vāyu, or Soma, who were the principal gods of the time. Although we must not underestimate the importance of goddesses as philosophical notions or as objects of practical veneration, we do have to recognise their limitations. While the gods were controllers of the elemental constituents of the universe, the goddesses were nurturers, protectors, purifiers, energy givers, and mothers, as we may see in the profiles of Vedic goddesses, most prominent of whom were: Uṣas, Pṛthivī, Aditi, Sarasvatī, Vāc, and Śrī/Lakṣmī.[4]

Early Goddesses

Goddess Uṣas, or Dawn, is described in the Vedas as an auspicious and bright being who wakes up the world with her light and regulates time. A nurturer, she leads human understanding to *Ṛta*, or Cosmic Truth. Goddess Pṛthivī, or earth, is the consort of Dyaus, or Sky, and nurtures the material

4 For full accounts of Hindu deities, see Klaus K. Klostermaier, *Survey of Hinduism*, 2nd ed. (Albany: SUNY Press, 1994), and for female deities in particular, see Tracy Pintchman, *The Rise of the Goddess in the Hindu Tradition* (Albany, NY: SUNY Press, 1994).

world as its mother, supplying the needs of all human beings, birds, and animals. Goddess Aditi is important as the mother of the gods, free from their rule though not equal in authority, protector of *Ṛta*, and is later merged with Pṛthivī. A more complex figure is Goddess Sarasvatī, who first appeared as a nature spirit, a river, and thus a purifier who bestowed wealth, renewed and nurtured lives, and represented immortality. The epitome of purity, energy, eloquence, knowledge, music, and art, she was worshipped in Vedic times as the ruling spirit of sacrifices and was connected with other Vedic goddesses, such as Īḍā, Māhī, Bhāratī, and Hotrā. Sarasvatī is the one exception to the general rule of submission to male dominance, because from Vedic times down to the present, she has survived and has been venerated as an independent entity, with Hindu sacred lore showing her shaking off all claims upon her by even the creator god Brahmā, including one of incestuous desire on his part. A goddess associated with Sarasvatī is Vāc, who later became one with Sarasvatī. Vāc was controller of word and sound, inspirer and creator of three Vedas, protector of sacrifices and rituals, which depended on precision of word and sound to be potent.

One of the most important of these early female deities was Śrī, the giver of wealth, good fortune, and royal authority, who was later assimilated into Goddess Lakṣmī. The latter became not only one of the most fervently worshipped deities for Hindus as the source of wealth and well-being, but eventually came to occupy the very centre of all divine power and action as Viṣṇu's consort. Both theologically and socially Lakṣmī developed into one of the most influential goddesses of Hinduism, around whom entire systems of worship developed.

Among these early goddesses there were also others who were not so benevolent. Of negative aspect were Rātrī and Nrṛiti. Rātrī was the sister of Uṣas and exercised motherly care in facilitating sleep, rest, comfort, and safety but also induced hopelessness and barrenness. Nrṛiti was a distinctly threatening figure who commanded decay, greed, anger, cowardice, old age, and death, and was later identified as Alakṣmī, the spiteful opposite of Lakṣmī, the goddess of plenitude, much feared, and paid homage only to ensure her absence. In the conception of Nrṛti we may detect an instinctive fear of women's presumed potential for destruction, a fear later to be attached to Kālī, as Gavin Flood points out.[5] These disagreeable goddesses clearly represented what worshippers wished to keep at a distance and were not models for women, although they, especially Alakṣmī, could be cited to explain women's misfortunes in the form of barrenness or laziness; she also became the model of wicked women. As with benevolent goddesses, the human-divine correlation holds true even for otherworldly malice.

Peripheral Goddesses

The goddesses we have looked at so far are those mentioned in Vedic literature. But Hindu religiosity existed beyond the cultivated communities, which fostered philosophical speculations, and composition of hymns and complex sacrifices that went with their worship. The larger rural population that existed outside these communities had their own deities and it is likely that some of the Vedic deities, such as Rātrī, originated as village deities and later took more sophisticated shape in the imagination of the Vedic seers. But many deities had—and still have—only regional followings or even narrower village bases. Village gods and goddesses lived on in the popular consciousness and many have survived into present-day Hindu religious life, including urban life. Several village goddesses have continued to command devotion as spirits who can reward

5 Flood, *An Introduction to Hinduism*,179.

and protect, or punish and destroy. Some are benevolent and worshipped for the boons they may give, such as Ṣaṣṭhī, who grants prayers for the birth of children, or Bathukāmmā, who brings renewal to fields of crops and flowers. Some other goddesses have to be more carefully treated, such as Śītalā, Manasā, and Māriāmman, whom worshippers have to propitiate with *pūjā* to be protected from disease and similar misfortunes. Although their ritual worship is usually attended and arranged by women, they are not models for women. Represented often by rocks or trees – though images are also known – they have attracted more anthropological attention than philosophical efforts to relate them to the Hindu discourse on goddesses.

The Divine Feminine: the Great Goddess

Although the Vedic period was dominated by male divinities, the Vedic seers also sensed the presence of a divine feminine of all-pervasive power. Fleetingly glimpsed in the *ṚgVeda,* the earliest Hindu sacred book known, she is the divinity who 'holds together all existence' (*ṚgVeda,* hymn 10.125) but we learn nothing more about her. It took centuries for that female figure to grow in philosophical complexity, coming to dominate religious thought and worship from about the third century CE. That divine being came to be known as Mahādevī (the Great Goddess), or simply as Devī, to whom the Hindu seers attributed all the powers and characteristics of all goddesses and identified her as the cause of creation and the greatest of all divinities. This conception of a single goddess, who is the sum of all other goddesses, is so weighty that we will have to look at her at some length.

The concept of the divine feminine begins to expand vastly from about the third century CE. This was the era in which began the composition of the *purāṇas*, or the numerous encyclopedic chronicles of cultural memory that included philosophical reflections. To the authors of the different *purāṇas*, Devī appeared as the embodiment of *prakṛti* (nature), *śakti* (energy), and *māyā* (illusion), and even as *brahman*, the supreme creative will behind existence. She is the power that animates the gods. Composed between the fifth and seventh centuries CE, the *Devīmāhātmya* section of the *Mārkaṇḍeya Purāṇa* especially glorifies Devī as a warrior goddess who saves the world from evil. A later text, the *Devī Bhāgavatapurāṇa*, composed around the eleventh century CE, goes so far as to see her as 'the Mother of all the worlds who creates this universe' (*Devī Bhāgavatapurāṇa*, book 1, chapter 2, verse 8), creator of Brahmā, Viṣṇu, and Śiva, and the single authority who holds all gods and goddesses at her command.[6]

At the heart of this challenging concept of the goddess lies a perception of irresistible energy expressed through action both in the material world and in the unseen, imagined theatre of cosmic existence.[7] As the sum of that power, the goddess is she who activates all existence, holding together and protecting all existence in a state of material, moral, and spiritual harmony. Hinduism thus gained a female divinity of cosmic dominance. That divine feminine was considered to be the central creative energy or Śakti (the term for force, strength, and energy in Sanskrit) of the universe. Known in many forms, her supremacy was entrenched in Hindu scriptures by the fourth century CE, and worship of Her in the form of Durgā and Kālī became a cherished part of Hindu religious life. Such was her greatness that even Kṛṣṇa, believed to be Viṣṇu on earth, counsels Arjuna to pray to the Great Goddess before the

6 *Śrīmaddevībhāgavatam* [*Devī Bhāgavatapurāṇa*]. For a discussion of the text, see Pintchman, *The Rise of the Goddess in the Hindu Tradition*, 178–184.
7 Mandakranta Bose, 'Introduction', in *The Goddess*, ed. Mandakranta Bose. *Oxford History of Hinduism* series (Oxford: Oxford University Press, 2018).

great war of Kurukṣetra in the *Mahābhārata*. Arjuna exalts her in the persona of Kālī:

namaste siddhasenāni ārye mandāravāsinī |
kumāri kāli kapāli kapile kṛṣṇa piṅgale | |

I bow to you, O foremost of Siddhas, O Noble One who dwells in the forest of Mandāra, O Virgin, O Kāli! O wife of Kapāla! O you of a black and tawny hue.

bhadrakāli namastubhyam mahākāli namo'stu te |
caṇḍi caṇḍe namastubhyam tāriṇi varavarṇini | |

I bow to you. O Beneficent Kālī, I bow to you, O Mahākālī, O wrathful One. I bow to you. O Tārā the saviour, the great boon-bestowing one.

(*Mahābhārata, Bhīṣma Parva,* 23.4–5)[8]

The powers of Devī are invoked in greater detail in the *Devīmāhātmya*. She is the mainspring of everything conceivable:

tvayaitadhāryate viśvaṁ tvayaitat sṛjayate jagat |
tvayaitat pālyate devi tvamatsyante ca sarvadā | |
visṛṣṭau sṛṣṭirūpā tvaṁ sthitirūpā ca pālane |
tathā saṁhatirūpānte jagato asya jaganmaye | |
mahāvidyā mahāmāyā mahāmedhā mahāsmṛtiḥ |
mahāmohā ca bhavati mahādevī mahāsurī | |

8 The reference here is to the *Mahābhārata*, ed. Ramnarayan Shastri (Gorakhpur: Gita Press, 1964). Although this chapter is left out of the Bhandarkar Oriental Research Institute's 1966 critical edition of the *Mahābhārata*, Arjuna's prayer is a generally accepted part of the epic, as in the widely circulating Gita Press edition used for this citation, and included in the Kumbhakonam edition of the Southern recension of the epic, ed. T. R. Krishnacarya (Bombay: Nirnayasagar Press, 1906–1914).

> By you this universe is borne, by you this world is created. By you it is protected, O Devī, and you always consume it at the end. O you who are [always] of the form of the whole world, at the time of creation you are of the form of the creative force, at the time of sustentation you are of the form of the protective power, and at the time of the dissolution of the world, you are of the form of the destructive power. You are the supreme knowledge as well as the great nescience, the great intellect and contemplation as also the great delusion, the great *devī* as also the great *asurī*.
>
> (*Devīmāhātmya,* 1. 75–77)

Further attributes are listed a little later:

tvaṁ śrīs tvaṁ īsvarī tvaṁ hrīṁs tvaṁ buddhir bodhalakṣaṇā |
lajjā puṣṭis tathā tuṣṭis tathā tvaṁ śāntir kṣāntir eva ca | |

> You are the goddess of good fortune, the ruler, modesty, intelligence characterized by knowledge, bashfulness, nourishment, contentment, tranquility and forbearance.
>
> (*Devīmāhātmya,* 1. 79)[9]

This supreme deity is a figure of mystery that can be conceived in many ways, including humanised forms. She is power personified (*śaktirūpiṇī*), mother (*mātṛrūpiṇī*), wife (*sahadharminī*), and even daughter (*kanyārūpiṇī*). Power is of course her primary identity and animates all creation:

9 *Devīmāhātmya,* ed. and transl. by Swami Jagadiswarananda (Mylapore, Madras: Sri Ramakrishna Math, 1953), 17–18. All quotations from, and references to, the text are to this edition. Translations of this and other texts are mine unless otherwise stated.

yā devī sarvabhūteṣu śaktirūpeṇa saṁsthitā |
namastasyai namastasyai namastasyai namo namaḥ | |

To the Devī who abides in all living beings as power
I bow to her, I bow to her, I bow to her. I salute her!

(*Devīmāhātmya* 5.32)

But it is the role of mother that appeals most to the devotee, as a well-known prayer to Durgā shows:

yā devī sarvabhūteṣu mātṛrūpeṇa saṁsthitā |
namastasyai namastasyai namastasyai namo namaḥ | |

To the Devī who abides in all living beings as Mother, I bow to her, I bow to her, I bow to her. I salute [her]!

(*Devīmāhātmya* 5.71)

Not only is this a profound philosophical insight, it is also a statement of an inviolable link between goddess and humans, as only a mother–child link can be.

These views of Devī's limitless powers are both exciting and comforting in their promise of her readiness and ability to protect the universe. Besides the *Devīmāhātmya,* the most important text of scriptural authority in the history of Devī is *Devī Bhāgavatapurāṇa,* composed between the eleventh and twelfth centuries CE.[10] Here Devī is identified specifically as Goddess Durgā, who is the supreme deity, superior to Brahmā, Viṣṇu, and Śiva. She is the origin and creator of all existence, preserver and destroyer of everything, the source of all knowledge, and the only path to liberation. Envisioned as a deity of many aspects, Devī is imagined in this and other texts as nurturing all Creation, but also battling evil in the shape of terrifying demons. When Mahiṣa the buffalo demon

10 Pintchman, *The Rise of the Goddess in Hindu Tradition,* 128.

threatened to overwhelm the gods, they got together to focus all of their individual powers to bring into existence a goddess of irresistible might:

> *atulaṁ tatra tat tejaḥ sarvadevaśarīrajam |*
> *ekasthaṁ tad abhūn nārī vyāptalokatrayaṁ tviṣā | |*

> Then that unique light, produced from the bodies of all the devas [and] pervading the three worlds with its lustre, combined into one and became a female form.
>
> (*Devīmāhātmya*, 2.13)[11]

The abstract idea called Śakti was thus given a definite form. This is Goddess Durgā and it is by that name that Devī is most commonly signified, although her forms are many. The resplendently beautiful Durgā kills Mahiṣa in a fierce battle and saves creation, though only for the time being because evil is never in short supply, nor are crises. Such threats are met and resolved, again and again, by the divine feminine.

11 *Devīmāhātmya*, ed. and transl. by Swami Jagadiswarananda, 27.

Durgā as demon-slayer.

We must reiterate that the unity of all feminine divinities was, and remains, a common assumption and that unified divinity was designated as Mahādevī, the Great Goddess. The adjective '*mahā*' (great) has been applied also to Kālī and Lakṣmī by devotees to exalt them,[12] but no distinct cult of Mahādevi worship has evolved, perhaps because she is more of an idea than a distinct figure. When she is thought of as Durgā, she has a distinctive presence as a warrior figure backed by particular myths of such great appeal that it is Durgā who is commonly thought of as the Great Goddess, Devī.

Challenges to Devī keep coming. The threat from Mahiṣa repeats itself when two demonic siblings, Śumbha and Niśumbha, threaten the universe. As Durgā battles them, her fury becomes so great that it leaps out of her body to take form as Kālī, a goddess of terrible aspect, black, gaunt, devouring everything in sight with her fangs, and drinking blood with her lolling tongue. Even after Śumbha and Niśumbha have been destroyed, Kālī is summoned by Durgā to defeat the demon Raktabīja ('Blood-seed') whom she cannot put down because every drop of his blood that falls to the ground from his wounds germinates countless reproductions of him. His power keeps growing until Kālī drinks every drop of his blood before it reaches the ground. Other legends start with Śiva, one of the three principal gods of Hinduism, who calls on his wife Pārvatī, normally the gentlest of goddesses, to battle demons. When she undertakes the task, her beautiful form changes to the terrifying one of Kālī.

---

12 See David Kinsley, *Hindu Goddesses: Visions of the Divine Feminine in the Hindu Religious Tradition* (Berkeley: University of Los Angeles Press, 1988), chapter 9.

Kālī, aṣṭadhātu (metal alloy) figurine from West Bengal.

Kali trampling Shiva, V. Krishnamoorthy.

As she destroys her enemies, the intoxication of slaughter takes such strong hold of her that she cannot stop. All of creation faces the threat of extinction as she rampages through the universe until it is saved by Śiva, who places himself under her dancing feet to prevent their terrible drumming from tearing the universe to pieces.

The Mahāvidyās

Such transformative anger is a striking feature of the Hindu view of the divine feminine, because it acknowledges the feminine consciousness as a layered one rather than a single, unchangeable essence. It also acknowledges that just as benignity is associated with femininity, so is the capacity for boundary-crossing, destructive behaviour. To cite Pārvatī again as an example – bearing in mind that as a form of Durgā she is a form of Devī – let us turn to her previous incarnation as Śiva's first wife Satī, daughter of Dakṣa. When Dakṣa refuses to invite Śiva and Satī to his great *yajña*, the insult infuriates Satī and she decides to go anyway. Śiva refuses to let her go and in her anger at his refusal, she assumes ten dreadful forms known as Mahāvidyās (Great Revelations): Kālī, Tārā, Chinnamastā, Bhuvaneśvarī, Bagalā, Dhūmāvatī, Ṣoḍaśī (also known as Tripurasundarī), Kamalā, Mātaṅgī, and Bhairavī. They surround Śiva, forcing him to let Satī go. Of these, Ṣoḍaśī and Kamalā are beautiful and gentle, but the others are fierce, some being macabre in appearance, such as Chinnamastā, who is depicted as holding her self-decapitated head and drinking, with two companions, the blood spurting out of her neck. Satī herself takes a fearsome form, goes to her father's *yajña*, but rejected there, she immolates herself in the sacrificial fire. In his grief Śiva sends terrible spirits to destroy Dakṣa, his *yajña*, and all others present, he himself rushing through the world carrying Satī's corpse and scattering her limbs around as memorials. Satī thus emerges out of her normal role as a gentle, submissive wife to reveal the alternate element of violence intrinsic to the divine feminine as conceived in Hindu scriptures.

Mahāvidyās (Great Revelations).
[Mandala Publishing - Mahaveer Collection]

The Mātṛkās[13]

Far more alarming are the Mātṛkās, the 'Mothers', an ironic name if ever there was one, because this is a group of seven (in some accounts eight) dangerous goddesses who specialise in causing harm to children, making children ill, and even devouring them. Dating from approximately the first century CE, they and their doings are described in the *Vana Parva* of the *Mahābhārata*, where they are commanded by Indra to kill the baby Kārtikeya (*Vana Parva*, 215.16).[14] They do not carry out that task because their maternal instinct is aroused when they see him but they nevertheless remain dreaded threats to children in general. From about the fourth century CE, they appear in texts such as the *Devīmāhātmya* and *Devī Bhāgavatapurāṇa* as goddesses who battle demons as aides to Devī. Their fierce, destructive character has nonetheless kept them at arms length in Hindu religious life in general, and even though in later times they were ascribed some gentler traits, they are still dreaded figures and worshipped – if at all – out of fear.

Devī as Mother

The Mātṛkās constitute the dark side of Devī. But the two sides are constantly mixed in Hindu myths and beliefs. As we have noted above, the ten Mahāvidyās are expressions of Devī's wrath, some of them horrifying in appearance and action, such as Chinnamastā. Yet some of them are beautiful and benign, such as Soḍaṣī and Kamalā, which suggests that there is no fundamental alienation between the different forms

13 For full discussions of the Mātṛkās and Mahāvidyās, see Kinsley, *Hindu Goddesses*, chapters 10 and 11.

14 All references to the *Mahābhārata* in this and all following chapters are to the critical edition by V. S. Sukthankar (Poona: Bhandarkar Oriental Research Institute, 1933–1966), unless otherwise noted.

of Devī. It is no surprise that for worshippers it is her maternal aspect that draws intense devotion, centring on her benign form of Durgā, who embodies the life-affirming, nurturing function of the Great Goddess. This is the aspect that devotees wish particularly to hold in view. One of the largest religious celebrations of Hindus in India and abroad is Durgā Pūjā, the hugely popular autumn festival of Durgā in West Bengal and neighbouring states of eastern India. The legend that lends strong emotional appeal to the festival is that this is when she visits her natal home on earth with her children, Lakṣmī, Sarasvatī, Gaṇeśa, and Kārtikeya, on leave as it were from her husband Śiva's household, just as women on earth do.

Mother Durgā with her family.

An even more explicit emphasis on Durgā's motherly identity appears in the following image in a public Durgā Pūjā venue, with the goddess in the iconic domestic apparel

– a red-bordered white sārī – with a cute baby Gaṇeśa in her arms. The absence of weapons unambiguously signals her gentle presence as that of a mother in the average home. The emotional appeal of the idea of an all-powerful yet all-loving mother worshipped in the festival cannot be overstated.[15]

Clay sculpture, Kolkata.

What also cannot be overstated is the astonishing capacity of the Hindu theology of adoration for matching love and terror in the same divine body: the most moving example is Kālī. Even as she is worshipped in her most horrifying image, she is also adored as Mother, a beautiful and benevolent figure smiling upon the devotee. Even more moving is her conception as the devotee's daughter, a lovely, playful little girl. Kālī is in fact endowed with the most multiple personae among Hindu goddesses and commands intense personal attachment, especially in the influential tradition of Devī

15 The religious and social importance of the festival is reflected in UNESCO's December 2021 declaration of Kolkata's Durgā Pūjā as an Intangible Cultural Heritage of Humanity.

worship in Bengal. The intensity of emotional attachment and philosophical enquiry she commands has generated – besides scholarly work – entire genres of poetry and songs, especially in Bengal. The richness of the culture of Kālī is best observed in the songs of the eighteenth-century Bengali poet Ramprasad Sen in lyrics such as this:

You'll find Mother
In any house.

Do I dare say it in public?

She is Bhairavī with Shiva,
Durgā with Her children,
Sitā with Lakshmaṇa.

She's mother, daughter, wife, sister –
Every woman close to you.

What more can Rāmprasād say?
You work the rest out from these hints.[16]

She's playing in my heart.
Whatever I think, I think Her name.
I close my eyes and She's in there
Garlanded with human heads.

Common-sense, know-how – gone,
So they say I'm crazy. Let them.
All I ask, my crazy Mother,
Is that You stay put.[17]

---

16 Leonard Nathan and Clint Seeley, *Grace and Mercy in Her Wild Hair*, 2nd edition (Prescott, AZ: Hohm Press, 1999), 55. The irregular accent marks are those of the translators.

17 Nathan and Seeley, *Grace and Mercy in Her Wild Hair*, 59.

The emphasis in this strand of devotion is love for the goddess as a person, most often as a mother to be obeyed and served but also as a daughter to be tenderly cherished. Her infinite femininity is thus understood in terms of common human relationships.

Divine Benevolence

The idea of Devī takes us to the brighter end of the spectrum of divine feminine energy. In this part of the belief in the Great Goddess, we see her constructive power of enriching existence by means of wealth, authority, orderliness, and beauty. One form of the Goddess in which that power is embodied is Lakṣmī. First encountered in Vedic times as Śrī, who was the dispenser of prosperity, stability, royal authority, and beauty, she acquired a fuller profile as Śrī/Lakṣmī, then as Lakṣmī, who was the source of wealth and well-being. Her early history designates her as a prize to be earned by any god or even any demon worthy of her allegiance as his companion for his good deeds.[18] Recipients of her favour were Soma, Dharma, Indra (in some legends also Kubera, the god of treasures), and even the two virtuous demons Bali and Prahlāda. Lakṣmī was never imagined as being on her own and always attached herself to a male, not in the sense of a personal relationship but simply as a signifier of her companion's worthiness. That is why she left each when his worthiness declined, thereby gaining a reputation for fickleness.[19] This emphasis on deserving virtue being the rationale for her favours also explains why

18 Upendra Nath Dhal, *Goddess Laksmi: Origin and Development* (New Delhi: Oriental Publishers, 1978), 63–68; 88–96; Kinsley, *Hindu Goddesses*, 23–26.

19 For an account of Lakṣmī's various allegiances, see Kinsley, *Hindu Goddesses*, 23–26; the divinity and history of Lakṣmī is fully discussed by Mandakranta Bose, 'Śrī Lakṣmī: Goddess of Plenitude and Ideal of Womanhood', in *The Goddess*, ed. Mandakranta Bose, Oxford History of Hinduism series (Oxford: Oxford University Press, 2018), 78–97.

she eventually came to be permanently attached to Viṣṇu as her sixth and final consort from about 400 CE, because as a supreme being, he is free from the mutability of personal attributes and the good inherent in him can never wane. From the mobility of multiple relationships she has been brought into absolute immutability within a divine union. Not surprisingly, she receives homage from virtually every Hindu.

Lakṣmī is no warrior goddess but her gifts are the vital enabling ones of prosperity and stability. It is for these boons at her command that she is an aspect of the Great Goddess.

Like Lakṣmī, a goddess marked by her power to enrich life rather than destroy its enemies is Sarasvatī, who has similarly continued to command devotion since Vedic times as the ruling deity of knowledge, purity, the arts, and music. As a gentle goddess with only the arts of peace at her command, she may not seem to be on the same level as the Great Goddess, but we must bear in mind that she may also bring to her devotees the gift of sacred knowledge. That power may be the ultimate empowerment of human beings and the instrument of eradicating ignorance, from which evil may spring. It is for these reasons that there are hymns to Devī Sarasvatī that address her as Mahāsarasvatī.

Goddess Lakṣmī.

Goddess Sarasvatī.

As befits a purifying spirit, her classic representation is all in white, holding a *vīṇā* as the symbol of music.

Centring Womanhood

The vision of divinity centring on the feminine divine became both broader and sharper with the advent and growth of Tantric theology as represented in the Tantras, a body of texts from the sixth century CE onwards.[20] Especially important in the context of gender is the Tantric view that not only is the Goddess the power that creates, protects, and nurtures existence, the source of all Being, but that she is also inherent in every woman. A late text succinctly states:

tava svarūpā ramaṇī jagati ācchannavigrahā |

> Every woman, O Goddess, is your very form.
>
> (*Mahānirvāṇa Tantra,* 10. 80.1)

yā kācid aṅganā loke sā mātṛkulasambhavā |

> Every woman is born into the family of the Great Mother.
>
> (*Kularṇava Tantra,* 1. 64)

In the Tantric view every woman is part of Śakti even if in an unrealised state of consciousness.

This elevation of women in Tantra is of a higher order than the position taken in Devī cults in which the goddess is not literally equated with women, although at times they may be vehicles of her spirit. For instance, an important part of the worship ritual of Durgā is Kumārī Pūjā, which is the worship of prepubescent girls, usually very young children, in whom Devī is thought to be present – but just for the

20 Flood, *An Introduction to Hinduism,* 184–192.

duration of the ritual. Sometimes this is a long ritual in itself, at which a number of girls are worshipped together, a notable example being the worship of hundreds of such 'vehicles of the Goddess' at the Adyapith temple near Kolkata.

The little girls are sitting here in row after row, dressed up as goddesses in silk saris and crowns. The scale of this ritual is scarcely attempted at other locations but the ritual remains the same even with just one Kumārī, the virgin goddess. Nepal has an ancient tradition of electing prepubescent girls as ruling deities of certain temples who go through a far more complex and extended ritual observed during their tenure, coming to an end on reaching puberty.[21]

Girls sitting together waiting to be worshipped during Kumārī Pūjā festival in Adyapith near Kolkata.

21 See Brenda Beck, 'Becoming A Living Goddess', in *The Goddess*, ed. Mandakranta Bose, Oxford History of Hinduism series (Oxford: Oxford University Press, 2018), 201–227.

Kumārī Pūjā honours the temporary presence of the Goddess in women but only in prepubescent girls who are considered untainted by their sexual development. On the contrary, Tantra does not see any woman ever separated from Śakti, even though it does not deify mortal females. Given the spiritual importance of femininity, the devotee approaches the intangible idea of Śakti by focusing on her tangible manifestations as particular goddesses. In taking this position, Tantric theology developed along two branches, one focusing on goddesses who are gentle, loving, and beneficent, whose devotees must themselves be gentle, benevolent, and observant of social norms to receive her grace. This gentle Tantric tradition again has two divisions. One has for its reigning deity the beautiful and benevolent goddess Lalitā Tripurasundarī. In the other, Lakṣmī is the central divinity, either as the consort of Viṣṇu and the gateway to him or as the supreme deity herself, the ultimate consciousness behind all phenomena.

The other kind of Tantra venerates fierce, violence-prone goddesses who battle evil and can be approached only by rejecting worldly conventions of conduct and adopting taboo bodily practices. Turning away from the common world, this belief-system seeks Devī in her terrifying form of Kālī. Positioning themselves outside social norms and proceeding under the guidance of preceptors, believers adopt occult practices in which women play a vital role in their effort to release hidden energies in the human body to rise towards an unalloyed consciousness of divinity.

Whether one follows the gentle Tantrism of the Tripurasundarī cult or the asocial one of Kālī, one has to look to women for connecting with Devī. In Tantrism, not only are women essential to the process but they are also regarded as the most effective initiators into the secret processes, especially the mother of the seeker. Does this belief grant women any active capability in the world as Devī's representatives? In social life as it stands, such supremacy is doubtful but even a theoretical elevation of women does provide them with a base for self-esteem and self-assertion. On that basis, modern feminist thought has pointed out the resources that goddess worship has to offer in reorienting gender relationships and status.[22] It is a deeply empowering religious assurance for women to receive the Tantric assertion that Devī is the sum of all women, and that every woman is part of an unbounded femininity endowed with unbounded power.

The idea that Devī is present in every woman allows the possibility of actually sensing her in mortal women. Thereby a woman may well rise to goddess status, though that would have to be through her utter devotion and total surrender to a divine male. That is how two later female divinities entered the Hindu pantheon. They are Sītā and Rādhā, both of whom became recognised as goddesses because they submerged themselves in their chosen gods in human form.

In the case of Sītā, devotion means total wifely absorption in service to her husband, Rāma, who is Viṣṇu incarnate. The conviction that faithfulness and devotion to a husband are the highest virtues of a woman is an absolute value permanently etched in the Hindu consciousness in the figure of Sitā in the *Rāmāyaṇa*. Consider Sītā's action: a great princess about to become a reigning queen, Sītā renounces it all to follow her husband Rāma into exile for fourteen years. She remains faithful to him upon being abducted by the demon king Rāvaṇa, tempted as she is with his magnificence and threatened though she is with death, yet never losing her devotion to Rāma through her trials. Her loyalty is unshaken even after Rāma rescues her only to subject her to vile suspicions about her chastity not only

22 See Carol P. Christ's much reprinted landmark essay, 'Why Women Need the Goddess', *Heresies: The Great Goddess Issue* (1978): 8–13.

once but twice, exiling her while pregnant with his sons and finally sentencing her to an ordeal by fire. In traditional Hindu society and to a great extent even in modern Hindu society, this distressing story elicits sadness but sadness overcome by worshipful admiration for Sītā's devotion to her husband. It has also provided, to many observers of Hindu society, final proof of Hindu women's defining trait of submissiveness. To Hindus, however, Sītā's legend has elevated her to goddess status and her tribulations as divine self-sacrifice undertaken to establish order among humankind.

As a contradiction typical of the play of opposites in Hindu religious and ethical discourse stands another woman of hallowed legend, a late addition to the roster of classical goddesses. This is Rādhā, beloved of Kṛṣṇa but married to another man. A relationship that would be shameful in another woman and repugnant to the idea of marriage is extolled in this case because Kṛṣṇa is God. Although their love story has inspired countless romantic works of art, music, and poetry, the illicit nature of their relationship and its frequently explicit eroticism have caused considerable discomfort among many Hindus, not to speak of non-Hindus, because it is a violation of domestic morality that sets a very bad example indeed for women. Nevertheless, in the tradition of Vaiṣṇava *bhakti* founded on the need for absolute surrender to God represented as Kṛṣṇa, Rādhā's love qualifies her as the ultimate devotee while his limitless attraction for her raises her to the status as a goddess. Her divinity is not entirely unquestioned and she is worshipped mainly in company with Kṛṣṇa, or if by herself, then as an intercessor with him. The difference between these two deified women, Sītā and Rādhā, marks how Hindu society evaluates women. Sītā's love for Rāma falls within the expectation of society and is celebrated, while Rādhā's love defies all expectations of society. Sītā therefore remains popular and emulated; Rādhā is revered but kept at a distance. Notwithstanding her goddess status she is not a model for mortal women, for goddess or not, she is a threat to the sanctity of marriage. Her single-minded passion for Kṛṣṇa has inspired women rarely to emulate her, except for women who have dedicated themselves to Kṛṣṇa to the exclusion of all else and gained a reputation for holiness, the pre-eminent example being Mīrābāī. But it is precisely that world-renouncing devotion which is not encouraged in the average woman who is expected to carry out family roles above all else.[23]

Sītā and Rādhā are particularly important in understanding the place of women in the Hindu tradition because they represent complementary aspects of femininity in a chain of existence that links the most abstract divine feminine with socially defined mortal women. The deification of Sītā and Rādhā has been possible because there is, in Hinduism, a deep current of belief in divinity as an essential attribute of women. As we have noted before, in the highly influential Śakti tradition of Hindu thought, the Great Goddess is imagined to be present in every woman. Let us at the same time bear in mind that the Great Goddess is at once gentle and violent, creating on the one hand and destroying on the other, reinforcing the boundaries of life and breaking them down. This metaphysical insight of the opposition inherent in the idea of the goddess is precisely what the myths and

23 A wide-ranging discussion of Sītā and Rādhā appears in Heidi R. M. Pauwels, *Goddess as Role Model: Sītā and Rādhā in Scripture and on Screen* (Oxford: Oxford University Press, 2008). Also see Heidi R. M. Pauwels, 'Sītā: Enduring Example for Women', in *The Goddess*, ed. Mandakranta Bose, Oxford History of Hinduism series (Oxford: Oxford University Press, 2018) and Tracy Coleman, 'Rādhā: Lover and Beloved of Kṛṣṇa', in *The Goddess*, ed. Mandakranta Bose, Oxford History of Hinduism series (Oxford: Oxford University Press, 2018).

literature of adoration achieve. Not surprisingly, the weight of devotion falls on the gentle, nurturing aspect of Devī but does so against the background of her invincible power in battle.

It is particularly reassuring for both men and women that aid, succour, and eventually salvation are available from so great a power and one inherent in humanity. That belief results only infrequently in practical reverence, or even sympathetic consideration for women in the human world but it exists nevertheless and is reassuring – at least emotionally. In a practical sense that reassurance can be believable, given that within human reach exist women – each a part of Devī – to dispense help, no matter in how big or small a way. What follows from this position is at once empowering and exploitative for women. If Goddess Durgā is to be looked upon for supporting my life, may I not call upon mortal women for similar aid? This is the expectation that makes service to others the justification of women's lives and does so on the grounds of religious faith. It is not for nothing that a caring, prudent, and efficient housewife is so often addressed as Lakṣmī, the goddess of prosperity. For students of the Hindu religion, the move from theology to sociology is thus seamlessly executed. No surprise then that throughout its long history, the Hindu religion has shaped the life of women.

The Divine Feminine in Human Life

Summarising the discussion so far, we can say that femininity is central to Hinduism, that Hindus believe in the idea of a divine feminine broadly termed Devī, and that Devī is a philosophical unity manifest in many personifications distributed across archetypal roles as:

- protector/defender
- scourge of evil/destroyer

- nurturer/mother
- helpmeet/wife/daughter.

As you look over this list you can see how readily the last two categories can be transferred from the divine to the human realm, and how usefully, especially when the nurturing roles are made secure by the first two. This is not to deny or minimise how profound the conception of the goddess is as a philosophical abstraction, taken in itself and placed at the very core of existence as the motivating energy that 'holds together all existence'. It also signals to us the theological complexity of a metaphysical construction that at the same time underwrites action in the physical world. Human beings venerate power, even power terrifying in its intensity, when that power acts in human interest. That is where theological thinking merges with social and political impulses working in the human world. The advantages of that convergence appear clearly from the myths of the protector goddesses: the battles that Durgā and Kālī fight are cosmic but their benefits accrue to humanity.

The might of the Goddess can also provide women with personal confidence. Besides being a source of an almost infinite range of philosophical adventure, the conception of a feminine power ruling over all existence and experience holds the potential for women to claim self-determination as human repositories of Devī's energy. Since Devī controls everything, a woman may well see her own work in the world as her self-chosen exercise of power rather than labour forced upon her, especially as she may think that Devī's all-encompassing array of attributes is implicated in a woman's work. The variety of Devī's perceived functions is telling in its mix of serving the essential needs of human life, which may well resonate with a woman's understanding of what she does most of all: nurture of her family and protection of her children.

Socialising the Goddess

The Argument

In theory, the link between divinity and womanhood presumed in Hindu thought may be viewed (and extolled) as an empowering assertion. But when we shift the view from philosophical theory to worldly practice, we have to take that empowerment at best as selective. No woman (for that matter, no man) can be seen in real life to be exercising the degree of might that Durgā or Kālī wields, nor can the ferocity of a warrior goddess be welcome to a well-ordered society. If protective violence is taken off the table of what women are expected to do, then they are left with the tasks of nurturing life and maintaining its orderly unfolding. The transition from the cosmic arena to the social is thus made both unchallengeable and necessary. For women, dedicating oneself to a supporting role in society becomes a religious duty enjoined upon them by the innumerable accounts and representation of Devī's presence in the world. The hierarchy of powers and functions that characterises Devī's action fits well with the idea of stratified social functions of women.

Strategies

Elaborated through legend, iconography, and ritual, the goddess paradigm covers a wide range of identities that translate smoothly to ideal types by which women can be defined and their roles in life prescribed. Tracy Pintchman rightly urges us to examine how 'structures pertaining to the Goddess may help shape conceptions of the female gender, the treatment of women in Hindu society, and the roles that women are assigned'.[24] Because of their influence, goddesses are potent and ready models for idealising women, which facilitates the labelling of women in their social relations. The major goddesses are personifications of the virtues that Hindus wish to see in women. The most important of these wish-fulfilling models is Lakṣmī because she is the goddess of wealth and social stability as well as the consort of Lord Viṣṇu and thus capable of protecting the orderly prosperity of the world. No praise for a Hindu woman is higher than calling her Lakṣmī, whether she is a dutiful daughter or a newly married bride or a housewife of proven service to her family; it helps if she is also beautiful, as Lakṣmī is. A woman of learning, gifted in art or music, is admired as Sarasvatī and may be awarded that name as a title. That wealth and knowledge, the most desired of social goods, should be considered the province of female deities suggests that there is indeed space in Hinduism for revering womanhood. To underline the value of such benevolent figures, a contrast is offered in the exact opposite of the Lakṣmī model, in the malicious persona of Alakṣmī, who infects families with envy and brings about disputes, ill-fortune, and destitution. She is everything a woman must not be and thus an explanation of female mischief.

Lakṣmī on the other hand is just what the world wants: wealth, peace, order. What is more, as Viṣṇu's beloved consort she shares in his power to impose stability upon the world, bestow all the benefits that her devotees seek and intercede for them with him, and even prove to be a channel to Viṣṇu and his liberating grace. But in the medieval era her status outgrew even Viṣṇu's when she was equated with the abstraction termed Śakti and viewed as 'God's Śakti who is knowledge, bliss and activity . . . the subsistence of the absolutely existing God . . . His essential nature . . . the divine presence', as

24 Pintchman, *The Rise of the Goddess in the Hindu Tradition*, Introduction,18

Sanjukta Gupta sums up the tenets of the *Lakṣmī Tantra*, a text of the Viṣṇuite sect composed between the ninth and twelfth centuries.[25] Like the *Devīmāhātmya*, this text 'glorifies women in general as beings created in the cherished form of Lakṣmī, and it advocates their worship'.[26] For any woman to reach this level of adoration is unlikely but it may serve as an energising idea for women today in their efforts at gender validation in the social realpolitik.

Such casting of women in the goddess mould is reflected in the naming of girls in the hope of gaining for them an auspicious life. Lakṣmī, Śrī, Kamalā, Padmā, Sarasvatī, Mahāmāyā, Durgā, and Kālī have been popular names for girls for a long time, though not as much today. The hope attached to such names may even gain strength and centre on a particular woman in a crisis: during the 1971 India–Pakistan war over the emergence of a free Bangladesh, Prime Minister Indira Gandhi of India was not only feted as Mother Durgā in populist publications but also pictured as the goddess in calendar art.

On the other hand, casting a woman as Kālī is unheard of, though the name is sometimes given to girls; who would want a fierce, destructive – and more to the point, uncontrollable – female in the neighbourhood? Exceptions are those holy women who have stepped out of social roles and obligations in their devotion to Kālī. Unlike those who similarly dedicated themselves to the benign Kṛṣṇa, these women are held in both awe and fear as outsiders. But even in Kālī, Hindus have a ready model for critical occasions: Rani Rashmoni (1793–1861) was an immensely wealthy Hindu widow famous for her beauty, piousness, charity, and her very successful running feud with the British. On one occasion, when some drunken British soldiers or sailors attempted to force their way into

25 *Lakṣmī Tantra: A Pāñcarātra Text*, transl. with notes by Sanjukta Gupta (Leiden: J. Brill, 1972), xxiv–xxv.

26 *Lakṣmī Tantra*, transl. Gupta, xvi.

her palatial home in Kolkata, Rashmoni was reputed to have emerged from her quarters waving the cutlass of Kālī from the temple in the palace, thereby putting the godless foreigners to rout and earning reverence as Mother Kālī personified. True or not, what mattered was that everyone believed the tale, to the Rani's huge credit.

In traditional Hindu society, the highest respect one can pay a woman is to call her '*devī*'. Barely a step down is the practice of addressing a woman as 'mother'. This usage is of particular value to Hindus and of common currency in India, sometimes extending even to non-Hindus. Whether such terms of exaltation are true indicators of Indian women's actual position in their world is a different matter. On the surface of social interchange, these usages denote reverence, but looking deeper into their social function, one may be inclined to see this as a strategy to keep women bound within prescribed roles, facilitating their marginalisation, for a 'Devī' is by definition written out of common human interactions. Should we not ask where this ceremony of respect leaves a woman? Has it not written her out of common life, marginalised her socially by putting her on a pedestal? Can a Devī be part of a human family and of human society? A tragic example of that alienation is the fate of a young woman in Satyajit Ray's film *Devī* (1960), based on a Bengali short story of the same title by Prabhat Kumar Mukhopadhyay. She is led to believe that she is the Great Goddess in human form. Reality strikes when she finds that she has no power to give life to a dying child; she is stranded on the margin of life with her sanity gone and her faith replaced by despair at realising that she is neither a goddess nor part of a human family.

Heartbreaking as this demonstration may be of the pressure of religious belief on a woman, it should not be taken as women's inevitable experience within the Hindu fold. It would also be an exaggeration to say that requiring women to provide self-denying service to others plunges them into abject slavery or that such is the unvarying expectation of a patriarchal society from a woman. Ambiguity and contradiction mark

Sītā, considered an ideal wife in Hindu culture, on her wedding day.
[Mandala Publishing - B. G. Sharma Collection]

every area of Hindu constructions of womanhood as indeed they do everything else in Hindu thought. The widely varying definitions of womankind in Hindu religious culture through centuries include both denigration and subjugation on the one hand, and admiration and acceptance of autonomy on the other. For example, Sarasvatī's independence has not diminished her stature as a sacred being or as the deity to turn to for success as a student or artist. Among humankind, nonconformist women such as Mahādevī Ākkā or Mīrābāī are not reviled but venerated, even though Ākkā abandoned clothing and Mīrā abandoned her husband. There is indeed space in Hindu society to be claimed by women as their own, though it may often – indeed more often than not – have shrunk microscopically.

Continuing with that theme, I may point to the common experience that within the dynamics of family and personal relationships in Hindu society there is room for both self-assertion and self-determination. The biological authority of a mother, for instance, validates her rule over her children, at least for a while. The *Mahābhārata* provides the authority: *teṣāṁ pitā yathā svāmī tathā mātā na saṁśayaḥ* ('Just as the father is the master of his sons so is the mother; there is no doubt about this.' *Mahābhārata, Ādi Parva* 99.28). Even wives and daughters – who are fairly low on the scale of domestic influence – may wield some authority in contexts of moral conduct, given the vestiges of sacred power she retains as a legacy from *devī*. An ideal wife is expected to be submissive to her husband and senior members of the family (including senior females) but she may well urge right conduct and even argue for observance. Modernity obviously has enlarged women's social space but there are precedence-setting narratives also from the past. For instance, in the *Rāmāyaṇa*, Sītā insists on accompanying her husband Rāma into exile against his specific instructions to stay home (*Rāmāyaṇa*, Ayodhyakāṇḍa, *sarga* 27–30) with ethical arguments and he concedes the point.[27] Later in the epic, she cautions him against the lure of arms and counsels him to give up a warrior's violent occupation in favour of the gentle life of a forest-dwelling hermit (*Rāmāyaṇa*, Āraṇyakāṇḍa, *sarga* 9). Here again she is heard out with serious consideration. Nevertheless, women in general are expected to fit themselves to the profiles of feminine nature drawn on the traits admired in goddesses. Those traits – one cannot help suspecting – were wishful idealisations of what men wanted in women but moderated by the need to keep women, goddesses or not, under control. Because of that need, women's presumed share in the sacred power of *devī* has been easy to ignore. At the same time, the patriarchal compulsion to subjugate women has made it necessary to cast women as creatures of a lower intellectual and moral order, setting aside for practical social purposes the goddess–woman link.

But the link is there for the finding and, ironically, it is within Hindu religious orthodoxy that it can be found and invoked by taking such scriptural authorities as the *Devīmāhātmya* and *Devī Bhāgavatapurāṇa* literally. Conservative believers can be usefully asked why they revere the *Devī Bhāgavatapurāṇa* as holy, yet disregard its assertion that Devī resides in every woman, making every woman an object of reverence and consideration. Perhaps the key to unlocking women from restrictions purportedly sanctioned by the Hindu religion is to search for it within the principles of religion. That search would succeed best if those principles were not set aside in favour of a secular political approach but observed with respect – critical respect, certainly – for religious faith.

27 All references to the *Rāmāyaṇa* in this and all other chapters are to the critical edition of the *Vālmīki Rāmāyaṇa*, ed. P. L.Vaidya (Baroda: Oriental Institute, 1962), unless otherwise noted.

Discussion Topic: The Feminine Divine

- What might be the reasons for ancient Hindus to choose a female figure as the site of boundless power?
- What distinguishes the Vedic goddesses from the Great Goddess worshipped by Hindus?
- How would you reconcile the opposite traits of love and violence that characterise *Śakti*?
- If Durgā was created out of the combined powers of male gods, how can she be regarded as an independent, self-determined being?

II
Women and Sacred Knowledge

Since Hindu society has traditionally regarded knowledge, especially sacred knowledge, as the source of power and prestige, access to knowledge has been of crucial importance historically in determining an individual's worth. Women's social and religious position in Hindu society has, to a large extent, varied through time in relation to their access to knowledge, from the Vedic period's open opportunities, through the insurmountable obstacles of later times, till the widening of avenues to education from the nineteenth century onwards. But even through the long centuries of medieval and early modern times, when women were denied self-determination and held within the narrowest bounds of domesticity, there were many Hindu women revered for their intuitive religious insights, including some for their formidable erudition. What that learning consisted of and how it influenced Hindu religiosity will be of concern in this chapter, as will be the historical process through which women eventually gained freedom to pursue knowledge.

Unveiling the Unknown

One of the earliest of Hindu sacred books, the *Kenopaniṣad* (first millennium BCE), recounts how three of the most powerful of male deities, Agni, Vāyu, and Indra, failed to recognise a transcendent Presence who had appeared before them and how the answer that it was *brahman* was provided by Umā, daughter of Himavat (*Kenopaniṣad* 3.12, 4.1). That it was a woman who alone possessed the knowledge to unveil so profound a mystery is no surprise, for Hindu thought places the feminine at the core of existence as its active principle. Consistent with that belief is a presumption of women's proximity to the mystery of existence and thus to sacred knowledge. In the earliest period of Hindu belief, speech was imagined as the goddess Vāc, who commanded the power of comprehension:

> When, uttering words which no one comprehended,
> Vāc, Queen of Gods, the Gladdener, was seated,
> The heaven's four regions drew forth drink and vigour.
>
> (*ṚgVeda* 8.89.10)

In one of the most moving hymns of the *ṚgVeda*, composed by the female seer Āmbhṛṇī, at which we will take a closer look a little later, Vāc is the deity who represents truth and turns those whom she blesses into sages:

> I, verily, myself announce and utter the word that gods and men alike shall welcome.
> I make the man I love exceeding mighty, make him a sage, a Rsi, and a Brahman.
>
> (*ṚgVeda* 10.125.5)

Goddess Sarasvatī.
[Mandala Publishing - B. G. Sharma Collection]

David Kinsley explains: 'The importance of speech in Hinduism is both ancient and central. The entire creative process is held to be distilled in the syllable *om*, and the idea of creation proceeding from *śabdabrahman* (ultimate reality in the form of sound) is often mentioned in Hindu texts'.[1] This figure of supreme knowledge evolved into the goddess Sarasvatī, who is the deified figure of learning and enlightenment in Hinduism, by whose grace human beings may gain all secular and spiritual knowledge and mastery over poetry, music, and all the arts. The *Devī Bhāgavatapurāṇa* (1000–1200 CE) identifies her as one of the energy manifestations (*śakti*) of the Supreme Being and as the:

> Presiding Deity of knowledge, speech, intelligence, and learning. This third Śakti is named Sarasvatī. She is all the learning of this endless Universe and She resides as medhā (intelligence) in the hearts of all the human beings; She is the power in composing poetry; She is the memory and She is the great wit, light, splendour and inventive genius. She gives the power to understand the real meaning of the various difficult Siddhānta works; She explains and makes us understand the difficult passages and She is the remover of all doubts and difficulties. She acts when we write books, when we argue and judge, when we sing songs of music; She is the time or measure in music; She holds balance and union in vocal and instrumental music. She is the Goddess of speech; She is the Presiding Deity in the knowledge of various subjects; in argumentations and disputations.
>
> (*Devī Bhāgavatapurāṇa* 9.1.19 *ff*)

1 David Kinsley, *Hindu Goddesses: Visions of the Divine Feminine in the Hindu Religious Tradition* (Berkeley: University of Los Angeles Press, 1988), 59.

The theological significance of this description lies not only in exalting Sarasvatī as the goddess of speech and learning, but also in identifying her as one form of the unity that is the Divine Feminine located at the centre of the creative energy of existence. How appropriate, then, is sacred knowledge as the province of women!

It is necessary, however, to regard this seeming equation of women and knowledge with caution. In the matter of women as in virtually all matters of opinion in the Hindu tradition, nothing is univocal; there is always somebody to say 'On the other hand . . . '. The *ṚgVeda*, itself the repository of so many women's thoughts, contains some of the harshest opinions about women expressed in the foulest language imaginable. It is disheartening that this collection of some of the profoundest thoughts in human history should have initiated the millennia-long disparagement and oppression of women in Hindu society. This prejudice against women will be extensively reviewed in Chapter 3 of this study but some brief samples are worth citing here. Condemning women, the *ṚgVeda* says:

striyāḥ aśāyaṁ manaḥ | uto aha kratuṁ raghum

> The mind of women brooks no discipline. Her intellect has little weight.
>
> (*ṚgVeda* 8. 33.17)

Still more damning:

na vai straiṇānī sakhyāni santi sālāvṛkāṇām
hṛdayāṇyetā |

> With women there can be no friendship. Women's hearts are like those of hyenas.
>
> (*ṚgVeda* 10. 95.15)

How such contempt for women can run parallel to the unequivocal reverence in Hinduism for the divine feminine, or motherhood, is a question that is perhaps more appropriate for a study in social psychology than religious history.

The Beginnings

The question is the more pressing because views 'on the other hand' are neither feeble nor scanty. That women's learning was accorded the deepest respect in early Hindu thought is only too evident from Hindu legends and philosophical history. Bear in mind that the context of the present discussion is not knowledge in general but Hindu religious knowledge in particular, which comprises philosophical enquiries into the origin and nature of Being and Non-being, reality, the cosmos, the forces that energise the cosmos, where human beings are situated within the web of existence, and for what purpose. These are profound issues addressed ceaselessly by Hindu thinkers, men as well as women, past as well as present. Several formulations of Hindu sacred thought in the form of *sūktas* or hymns comprise the *ṚgVeda,* which is the earliest of Hindu texts – indeed the earliest extant text of theological speculation and statement in the world – and many of the hymns were composed by women seers numbering at least fourteen, possibly more, including Apālā, Ghoṣā, Lopāmudrā, Sikatā, and Viśvavarā.[2] I have referred above to one of the profoundest declarations in the *ṚgVeda* regarding the animating power of the universe composed by Vāc, known as Āmbhṛṇī because she was daughter to the sage Ambhṛṇa. The speaking voice is female, as indicated by the feminine form '*rāṣṭrī*' in the phrase "*ahaṁ rāṣṭrī*" ('I am the Queen') and thus

2 Mau Dasgupta, *Women Seers of the Ṛgveda* (New Delhi: D. K. Printworld, 2017), 1–35. Hymns by some of these poets appear elsewhere: Apālā (*Atharva Veda*.8.91); Viśvavarā (*Atharva Veda*.5.28).

the verse affirms the supremacy of the divine feminine in the scheme of existence. Declaring the identification of the self with the entire universe, Āmbhṛṇī concludes the 125th *sūkta* of the 10th *maṇḍala* with this climactic declaration:

> *ahameva vāta iva pravāmyārabhamāṇā bhuvanāni viśvā* |
> *paro diva para enā pṛthivyai tāvatī mahinā saṁbabhūva* | |

> I breathe a strong breath like the wind and tempest,
> the while I hold together all existence.
> Beyond this wide earth and beyond the heavens I have
> become so mighty in my grandeur.
> (Devī Sūkta, *ṚgVeda*, 10.125.8)

It is perhaps not fortuitous that this grand vision of an all-pervasive feminine power should come from a woman. This is only one of many female voices we hear in early Hindu philosophical discourse, to which many others then and later contributed memorably, taking part in learned assemblies and demonstrating their passion for knowledge.

One might of course demur with the claim that the author of this hymn was indeed Āmbhṛṇī and deprecate what may seem an over-estimation of women's place in the priestly milieu of the Vedic era.[3] But if the author was not a woman – Sāyanācārya thought it was – then the implication of the 'I' becomes especially interesting: does it not show an acknowledgement of the feminine power at the heart of creation? If the author was male, then does it not show a readiness to accord supremacy to a feminine power? What really matters is that the speaking voice is female, which leaves unaltered the idea of the paramountcy of the feminine in the cosmos.

---

3 Note that the fourteenth-century scholar Sāyana accepted Āmbhṛṇi's authorship; see *Ṛgveda Saṃhitā*, ed. P. Venkata Rao (Mysore: Śrī Sāradā Press, 1955), 689.

Access to Education: What did They Learn?

Admittedly, women of such intellectual and spiritual power as Āmbhṛṇī belonged to a small section of society – as did men of a similar persuasion – but early Hindu society clearly provided space for them and celebrated them. Considering that 'early' Hindu society goes back at least two millennia, we know little about the period beyond what is available in extant works that originated as oral texts. It would be fruitless to wonder whether women at large, or men for that matter, had access to what modern societies consider public education or even whether any such social institution at all existed in the general public sphere.[4] Learning may well have been a privilege enjoyed in the upper strata of Vedic society, even considered to be an essential activity but one that had to be provided for by personal initiative. A. S. Altekar asserts that the head of a family 'regarded the education of his children as a sacred duty. No distinction was made in this connection between boys and girls'.[5] It is impossible to assess how universal this equitable treatment was but it does seem that the education of girls was not constrained within domestic skills, but included the same kind of instruction as boys in mythology, liturgy, spiritual matters, folklore, occult practices, the fine arts, and even warfare, as Mau Dasgupta observes upon reviewing the hymns in the *ṚgVeda* attributed to women seers.[6] Through the first millennium CE women – those, that is, who received education – pursued the same types of knowledge as men, extending from

4 See Prabhati Mukherjee's discussion on the extent and duration of women's education in her study, *Hindu Women: Normative Models*, revised ed. (Hyderabad: Orient Longman, 1994), especially her last chapter.

5 A. S. Altekar, *Education in Ancient India*, 2nd ed. (Benares: Nand Kishore, 1944), 235.

6 Dasgupta, *Women Seers of the Ṛgveda*, 139.

abstruse metaphysical speculation about concepts of being and non-being, the processes of creation, and the powers that sustained creation, to rituals that could relate human beings with the unseen powers of existence. In addition, great stress was laid on language, grammar, music, and dance not only as tools of communication but also as spiritual sites of the energy that empowered communication within the material world and beyond. *Taittirīya Saṁhitā* (6.1.4–6) and *Śatapatha Brāhmaṇa* (3.2.4.3–6) refer to dance and music learned and performed by women, including performances in public. To support all this on the level of practical community life, there was instruction in personal conduct, duties, material sciences such as medicinal plants, and the politics of personal and communal interaction.

Using Knowledge

Again, these observations are drawn not from any school syllabus that has miraculously travelled down the dusty centuries. They are derived from extant works by women and from reports of what women scholars did and said. From the earliest text comes the evidence of a high poetic imagination and philosophical intuition in the hymn by Āmbhṛṇī I have already cited. But Āmbhṛṇī also shows her knowledge of conflict being a condition of the world: 'I bend the bow for Rudra that his arrow may strike and slay the hater of devotion/ I rouse and order battle for the people' (*ṚgVeda* 10.125). Other women poets deal with more practical matters. For example, considerable insight into marital relations is found in one of the *ṚgVeda* hymns (*maṇḍala* 1, *sūkta* 179) by the female seer Lopāmudrā, which is a dialogue between her and her husband Agastya, both of them ascetics and no longer young. There she argues for the resumption of their worldly conjugal life, having devoted much of their youth to ascetic discipline, and presses for a balance between ascetic rigour and mundane occupations. A different human situation appears in a hymn by Apālā (*ṚgVeda* 8.80), which is a dramatic cry by an unattractive young woman dejected in her loneliness for succour from Indra, ruler of the gods, to whom she offers *soma,* the nectar beloved by gods. This he accepts and rewards her by transforming her into a beautiful maiden. A very different kind of marital situation occurs in the tenth book of the *ṚgVeda* (hymn 145), attributed to a woman called Indrāṇī – who may or may not be Indra's consort – who invokes the aid of a potent herb 'sent by the gods' to create spells by which she may get rid of a rival wife. If we wonder whether this is religious, sacred knowledge or simply practical wisdom, let us remind ourselves that for early societies the distinction between the sacred and the secular was minimal. It was by connecting with the imaginatively conceived otherworld of divinities that Apālā or Indrāṇī could live their lives in the human world. Running the gamut of personal, social, and meditative life of early Hindu culture, these poems thus reflect the kinds of knowledge that women of Vedic times could acquire.

Much of this knowledge was of essential application in Vedic society's efforts to control human life within the unknown but imagined web of cosmic forces by means of rituals for communicating with the gods who ruled the conditions of life. These were central to life in Vedic times when the knowledge of their purpose, form, and performance was vital. The performers were typically men; whether in the earliest period of Hindu society women had the same authority as men to conduct sacrificial rites is not specifically known. It is difficult to believe that female composers of *ṚgVeda* hymns who display profound philosophical thought, high language skills, and knowledge of their world should have been mere onlookers at sacrificial rites. But whether they had the authority to initiate and lead the rituals is another matter. Stephanie Jamison has demonstrated that wives played a secondary role in Vedic sacrifices;[7] this, however, does not include independent and self-directed female seers. Women's participation in rituals is a vital issue that remains relevant to modern Hindu society and we shall come to it later in this study. What is germane to the present context of women's access to, and use of, sacred knowledge is that many women did have the training to be active in rituals.

Philosophical Discourse

Turning from religious practice to the realm of ideas, we find that early texts and traditional legends confirm that women belonged to the philosophical community of the ancient Hindu world as active members. This is not to claim that women were held as men's equals in their cultural, relational, or domestic roles. However, in their intellectual and cultural life there is no evidence of gender constraints, or of barriers to their self-expression. Some women were consorts or daughters of male sages, some regarded as sages in their own right, and some were revered teachers, whom Pāṇini, the fourth-century BCE grammarian, refers to by the terms *upadhyāyā, upādhyāyī* (Pāṇini, *Aṣṭādhyāyī, Kāśikā,* 3.3.21; 4.1.49) and *ācāryā (Aṣṭādhyāyī, Kāśikā,* 4.1.49). Especially worth noting are the legends of women participating in scholarly debates and engaging in abstruse controversy. Women of such deep learning were called *brahmavādinīs,* that is, expounders of the Vedas, their dedication to learning distinguishing them from *sadyovadhus* or women who led domestic lives. These learned women enjoyed the same respect as their male peers, and did so because they were learned.

7 Stephanie W. Jamison, *Sacrificed Wife/Sacrificer's Wife* (Oxford: Oxford University Press, 1996).

One woman seer immortalised in the *Bṛhadāraṇyaka Upaniṣad* (c.700 BCE) is the *brahmavādinī* Gārgī, whose increasingly probing questions at a philosophical debate about the nature of reality, existence, and the soul left Yājñavalkya, the leading sage of the time, with no recourse except to command her silence. Here is Gārgī's final question:

> *kasmin nu khalu brahmalokā otāś ca protāś ceti*

> "On what then are woven and rewoven the worlds of Brahman?"

And this is how Yājñavalkya answered her:

> *sa hobāca gārgi mātiprākśīḥ mā te mūrdhā vyapaptat*
> *anatipraśnyām vai devatām atipṛcchasi gārgi*
> *mātiprākṣīriti tato ha gārgī vācakanavy upararāma.*

Women listening to a spiritual discourse.

> "Gārgī," said he, "do not ask an improper question, in order that thy head may not drop down. Thou askest the deity who is not to be questioned. Do not question, O Gārgī." Thence Gārgī, the daughter of Vācaknu, became silent.
>
> (*Bṛhadāraṇyaka Upaniṣad* 3.6.1)[8]

Yājñavalkya admits that Gārgī has posed a question to which there is no answer, for the nature of the Ultimate is beyond comprehension, and warns her that her head would fall off (that is, she would lose her mental balance) should she not desist from pushing the boundaries of knowledge. The significance of the dispute lies not in who wins; the point is that it is a woman who takes the dispute to the farthest edge of human knowledge.

A similarly exciting exchange, but one in which a female sage reduces her male counterpart to silence, is reported as an ancient legend by Bhīṣma as he lies on his deathbed of arrows in the *Śānti Parva* of the *Mahābhārata*. In the '*Sulabhā-janaka-saṃvāda*' chapter of *Śānti Parva*, Sulabhā, a female mendicant sage, seeks the knowledge of *mokṣa* (ultimate liberation) from the royal sage Janaka, quite possibly testing his knowledge. Displeased by Sulabhā's evident *yogic* power, Janaka accuses her of an illicit invasion of his mind. He charges her with her lack of qualification to engage with him in debate because as a woman she is unfit to engage in disputation with a man, as a woman she cannot have risen above worldly ties, and – again as a woman – she cannot have mastered the dictates of her senses. To this attack Sulabhā responds with extensive explications of the unity of all forms of existence, the indivisibility of the Self, and the limitations of worldly life. Distinctions of gender and

8 *Bṛhadāraṇyaka Upaniṣad*, transl. E. Roer (Delhi: Bharatiya Kala Prakashan, 2000), 279–280.

individual personhood are delusional,[9] not to be entertained by those of a liberated consciousness. The sage-king is silenced; Bhīṣma concludes the story:

> *ityetāni sa vākyāni hetumantārthavanti ca |*
> *śrutvā nādhijagau rājā kiñcidanyataḥ param ||*

> Hearing these words fraught with excellent sense and reason, King Janaka could not reply to it.
> (*Mahābhārata, Śānti Parva,* 308:191)

Here is a perfect example of a female ascetic challenging the social norm of female subordination by employing abstruse arguments that women were not expected to command.

To return to Yājñavalkya: Gārgī was not the only woman who engaged him in abstruse discussion. One of his two wives was Maitreyī. Her life reached a critical point when Yājñavalkya decided to renounce all worldly ties after giving away all his possessions to her and her co-wife Kātyāyanī. Receiving his offer of a share in his riches, Maitreyī asked whether such goods would bring her immortality, that is, liberation from the material world. When Yājñavalkya said that it would not, she asked what use she might make of that which could not bring her immortality. Could Yājñavalkya instruct her in the knowledge of immortality? The story is told in the *Bṛhadāraṇyaka Upaniṣad* (2.4.1–4):

> "Maitreyī," said Yājñavalkya, "Behold, I am desirous of raising myself from the order [of householder]; therefore, let me divide [my property] amongst thee and Kātyāyanī there."
>
> Maitreyī said, "If, O Venerable, this whole world with all its wealth were mine, could I become

9 See Ruth Vanita, 'The Self is Not Gendered: Sulabha's Debate with King Janaka', *NSWA [National Women's Studies Association] Journal,* 15 (2003), 2.

> immortal thereby?" Yājñavalkya said, "Like the life of the wealthy thy life might become; by wealth, however, there is no hope of [obtaining] immortality."
>
> Maitreyī said, "Of what use would be wealth to me, if I did not become thereby immortal. Tell me, O Venerable, any [means of obtaining immortality] of which thou knowest."
>
> Yājñavalkya said, "Behold, [thou wast] dear to us before, [and now] thou sayest what is dear. Come, sit down; I will explain to thee [the means of obtaining immortality]; endeavour to comprehend my explanation."[10]

The dialogue that followed between Yājñavalkya and Maitreyī remains one of Hinduism's most cherished metaphysical expositions.

This thirst for knowledge marked many women in early Hindu society who dedicated their lives to contemplation, some renouncing worldly life but many others seeking knowledge within domesticity. Like their male counterparts, these women pursued esoteric learning rather than practical information, preferring philosophical wisdom to pragmatic competence.

Knowledge – A Worthy Pursuit for Women

Such philosophical affinities flourished within the intellectual elite community of early Hindu society to which these women belonged. Knowledge was cherished and its pursuit was not only open to women but also valued as a worthwhile goal for women. The *Bṛhadāraṇyaka Upaniṣad*

10 Transl. E. Roer, 235–236.

advises parents to perform a ritual to ensure the birth of a learned daughter:

> *atha ya icched duhitā me paṇḍitā jāyeta sarvam āyuriyāditi tilaudanam pācayitvā sarpiśmantam aśnīyātām īśvarau janayitavai.*

> Now, in case one wishes, 'That a learned [*paṇḍitā*] daughter be born to me! that she may attain the full length of life!'– they two [the husband and wife]

Hindu woman engaged in textual study.

> should have rice boiled with sesame and should eat it prepared with ghee. They two are likely to beget [her].
>
> (*Bṛhadāraṇyaka Upaniṣad*, 6.4.17)[11]

The desire for learned daughters that underlies this verse is a reflection of the prestige that women seers of the Vedic era enjoyed. Learning has always been greatly valued in Hindu society, scholars traditionally revered for their knowledge, and through the centuries that saw the origin and development of Vedic literature, women of learning received respect from their intellectual peers, kings and princes, and the public at large.

Doors Closing

That climate of respect did not altogether dissipate after the Vedic era and learned women continued to enhance the knowledge capital of Hindu society, earning renown and a place in cultural memory; but their entry into the world of learning became more and more difficult through later ages. Post-Vedic times saw an increasing constriction of women's access to education and of the social space in which women could pursue learning. In the early period of Hindu culture (roughly from around the second or third centuries BCE), a period through which the *dharma-śāstras* were composed as rulebooks to maintain the social and ethical integrity of society at large and individuals in particular as its members, women's lives became greatly restricted, as Chapter 3 of this study will consider in detail.[12] Not that there was an abrupt shutdown of women's pursuit of knowledge. Even with major shifts in the religious ideology and social culture of the post-Vedic era, when Buddhism began to assume increasing

11 Transl. Roer, 2000, 444.

12 Manu, Vasiṣṭha, Yājñavalkya, Gautama, Baudhāyana, and Nārada were the principal authors who wrote extensively on women's expected roles in society.

importance, there were women, such as Bhadrā Kuṇḍalakeśā and Nanduttarā, whose formidable scholarship and debating skills are mentioned in the sixth-century BCE account of Buddhist nuns called the *Therīgāthā* (canto 5). One might also note that no female scholar in Hindu society ever suffered the hideous fate of fifth-century CE Alexandria's renowned female scholar and teacher Hypatia, who was flayed alive by a mob for her influence over the city's elite.

Sacred Tasks and Women

Sadly, there is no question that the open intellectual and spiritual climate of Vedic times that nurtured women's pursuit of knowledge and contributions to it began to cloud over with gender prejudice. We have noted earlier that even the *ṚgVeda* exhibits deep disdain for women. Nevertheless, women's place in the fabric of religious knowledge and tasks was secure. That in Vedic times women were expected to perform religious tasks that required familiarity with religious customs and disciplined study is attested to in early sources, such as the *Gobhila Gṛhyasūtra*:

> *kāmaṁ gṛhye agnau patnī juhuyāt sāyaṁ prātar homau*
> *gṛhāḥ patnī gṛhya eṣo agnir bhavatīti* |
>
> The wife is the *gṛha* [home] and the fire is called *gṛhyāgni* [fire at home]. That is why the wife can perform both day and evening sacrifices if she wishes.
>
> (*Gobhila Gṛhyasūtra*, 1.3.15)[13]

In this dispensation Gobhila is taking for granted a level of esoteric knowledge on the part of such wives, and thus, the

13 *Gobhila Gṛhyasūtra* with Sanskrit commentary of Pt. S. Samashrami. Delhi: Choukhamba Sanskrit Pratisthan, 1992.

need for educating women. But the requirements for women are less stringent, for Gobhila also rules that far fewer *saṁskāras* (preparatory rites) are needed for a daughter than for a son; for instance, no *mantras* should be uttered at a daughter's *cūḍākaraṇa* whereas the full panoply of rites must be carried out at that of a son's.[14] The only vital *saṁskāra* for a woman is her participation at the fire sacrifice during her marriage ceremony (*Gobhila Gṛhyasūtra,* 2.9.21–24).

The great epics of India, the *Rāmāyaṇa* and the *Mahābhārata,* attest to similar expectations, as do some *dharma-śāstras*. This being so, it would seem that those who called for restricting women's participation in sacred rites in the post-Vedic era did so because they were thinking of women in the domestic sphere rather than of the rare individuals who dedicated themselves to a cultivated spirituality. Besides, women were not entirely shut out of sacred rituals. Jaimini (300–200 BCE) said:

> *svavatostu vacanādaikakāmyaṁ syāt*
>
> On the other hand, the husband and wife possessed of wealth are entitled to perform the one and the same sacrificial act.[15]
>
> (Jaimini, *Pūrvamimāmsā-sūtra* 6.1.17)

He goes on to say that women could perform rites, but only those rites that were specifically prescribed for them:

> *guṇasya tu vidhānatvāt patnyā dvitiya-śabdaḥ syāt*
>
> On the other hand, by reason of enjoining a quality, the dual shall be made up by the wife.[16]
>
> (Jaimini, *Pūrvamimāmsā sūtra* 6.1.23)

14 *Cūḍākaraṇa* is the ceremony of shaving off a child's birth hair, leaving only a tuft.

15 Jaimini. *Pūrvamimāṁsā,* ed. and transl. by Mohan Lal Sandal (Allahabad: Allahabad Panini Office, 1923).

16 Transl. Sandal, 1923.

But opinions did differ; in his commentary on Jaimini, Śabara (early Christian era) explained that women could not perform sacrifices because they were not taught the Vedas:

> *atulyā hi strī-pumsāḥ yajamānaḥ pumān vidvāṁśca*
> *patnī strī ca avidyā ca*

> Men and women cannot be compared as the man possessing education [should be] the sacrificer, the wife being a woman and uneducated.
>
> (Jaimini, *Aphorisms*)
> [Śabara on *Pūrvamimāmsā sūtra*] 6.1.24)

Evidently Śabara was not thinking of the women who authored Vedic hymns. Very likely Jaimini and Śabara had the average woman of their times in mind rather than the minority of women sages. As for those who lacked that degree of Vedic knowledge, they nevertheless had a role in the performance of rituals. Wives, for instance, were required to take an active part in sacrifices, such as the *soma-yajña,* and it was necessary for both husband and wife to perform sacrifices together. Noting that only a married man was qualified to offer sacrifices, Stephanie Jamison cites an array of early sacred texts to demonstrate that 'the presence and participation of his [the householder's] wife is required at all the solemn rituals', the wife's being 'a *structural role* in ritual with particular duties and activities that cannot ordinarily be performed by anyone else'.[17] Descriptions of such sacrificial rites as the horse-sacrifice held by kings specifically lay down the duties of his chief queen attended by the other queens in its performance, as we find in the *Śatapatha Brāhmaṇa* (Book 13, chapter 2, Brāhmaṇa 8, verses 3–4, pp. 322–323).

I have mentioned above that the epics *Rāmāyaṇa* and *Mahābhārata,* two of the most influential works ever to have

17 Jamison, *Sacrificed Wife/Sacrificer's Wife,* 30.

been produced in the Hindu cultural world, describe women's active participation in *yajña* (sacrificial rituals) as performers and initiators. Daśaratha's chief consort and Rāma's mother Kausalyā is a celebrant:

> *Kausalyāpi tadā devī rātrīṁ sthitvā samāhitā |*
> *prabhāte cākarot pūjāṁ viṣṇoḥ putrohitaiṣiṇī | |*
> *sā kṣaumavasanā hṛṣtā nityaṁ vrataparāyaṇā |*
> *agniṁ juhoti sma tadā mantravat kṛtamaṅgalā | |*

> Kauśalyā, then, having practiced austerities through the night, performed Viṣṇupūjā in the morning. Garbed in clean apparel, in good cheer and always observing her vows, performed the fire-sacrifice with the appropriate *mantras* for the benefits of the family.
> (*Vālmīki Rāmāyaṇa*, Ayodhyākāṇḍa *sarga* 17. 6–7)

Especially noteworthy is the authority the *Mahābhārata* accords a woman for her knowledge of religious rites. After King Vicitravīrya dies, it is to his mother Satyavatī that his elder half-brother Bhīṣma turns for advice regarding the funerary rites:

> *pretakāryāṇi sarvāṇi tasya samyag akārayat |*
> *rājño vicitravīryasya satyavatyā mate sthitāḥ | |*
> *ṛtvigbhiḥ sahito bhīṣmaḥ sarvaiś ca kurupuṅgavaiḥ |*

> Following Satyavatī's advice, Bhīṣma performed all of King Vicitravīrya's funerary rites, together with the priests and the entire Kuru clan.
> (*Mahābhārata*, *Ādi Parva*, 96.59)

Why were the priests bypassed in favour of Satyavatī? The reason appears a little later in the text:

vettha dharmaṁ satyavatī paraṁ cāparam eva ca |
yathā ca tava dharmajñe dharme praṇihitā matiḥ | |

Satyavatī, you know the *dharma* of both this world and the next. Your intellect is always immersed in *dharma*.

(*Mahābhārata, Ādi Parva*, 99.36)

She is indeed immersed in *dharma* as we observe her conduct: *samāśvāsya snuṣe te ca bhartṛ śokanipīḍite* (she consoles her daughters-in-law grieving for their husband).

A Continuous Tradition

While these instances of respect for women may sound reassuring, the reality is one of a growing denigration of women in post-Vedic times. But before reviewing that depressing history – to which Chapter 3 of this study is devoted – we must emphasise that in thinking about women's ventures in knowledge within Hindu culture we cannot limit ourselves to what many call the golden age of the Vedas. Then, as in later ages, women have continued to seek knowledge, sacred and secular, and to extend its limits. Through the long centuries of women's reduction to subjugation there continued to appear women famous for their intellect, such as Līlāvatī, daughter of the twelfth-century mathematician Bhāskarācārya and herself a gifted mathematician, made immortal in Bhāskarācārya's book named after her. Medieval Bengal knew the poet-astrologer Khanā, whose predictions about weather and crops still inform popular wisdom. Equally memorable and perhaps better known are the many women poets, some of them of high scholarly accomplishment, who appeared through the centuries – Kāraikkāl Āmmāiyār (fifth–seventh century), Āṇṭāl (ninth century), Mahādevī Ākkā (twelfth century), Lallā

Ded (fourteenth century), Mīrābāī (sixteenth century), and Bahinābāi (seventeenth century), to name only a few – and who have left poetry of such astonishing power that we will devote a later part of this study, Chapter 4, specially to study them by themselves as a distinct constellation.[18]

Admittedly, these women were exceptions. The opening years of the Common Era saw the increasing confinement of women to the domestic sphere and a systematic disparagement of their ability, whereby women came to be thought of as unfit for education, which was not only considered unnecessary for women but a perilous distraction from their family duties.[19] The reformulation of women's life in Hindu social culture invites immediate scrutiny as a matter of social inequity. A deeper and more troubling issue is that the denigration of women shows a fracture in the ideological fabric of the Hindu religion: how can a belief system that declares the feminine as the central, animating energy of existence also relegate the feminine to subservience in the human world? The gravity of the question compels us to consider it by itself in Chapter 3 of this study. But it would be useful here to correlate it with the matter of women's access to knowledge.

The erosion of women's freedom to pursue knowledge began with the advent of the *dharma-śāstras,* texts that legislated public and private conduct in both religious and worldly life with increasing strictness from about the seventh century BCE. The reduction of gender parity was indicated by the exclusion of women from the requirement for *saṁskāras,*

18 This short list excludes women poets of the *caṅkam* culture that flourished in South India from about the first to the third century BCE as their interests were not religious but secular.

19 None of the authoritative sources of Hindu social thought explicitly prohibited women from seeking education, but there is an implicit consensus that women's duty excludes devotion to learning; see Julia Leslie, *The Perfect Wife,* transl. of *Strīdharmapaddhati* by Tryambakayajvan (Delhi: Penguin Books, 1995 [1989]), 321–322.

or rites required to qualify an individual for a place within the Hindu social structure of rights and duties, including the vital rite of *upanayana* whereby a young person would be rendered fit to enter a life of spiritual and other learning. Yet it is a *dharma-śāstra* text that recalls women in Vedic times going through the *upanayana* ceremony:

> *purākalpe tu nārīṇāṁ mauñjībandhanam iṣyate*
> *adhyāpanaṁ ca vedānāṁ sāvitrīvacanaṁ tathā*

> In ancient times tying of the sacred thread used to be recommended for women, [as was the] study of the Vedas and the legend of Sāvitrī.
>
> (Hārīta and Yama quoted in Mitramiśra's *Vīramitrodaya,* Saṁskāra-prakāśa section, p. 402)

The lawgiver Manu lays down in detail the *saṁskāras,* including the chanting of Vedic verses, to prepare the three upper *varṇas,* or castes, for life but they are applicable only to men. The process, he says, is the same for girls except that Vedic verses must be left out as marriage rites are enough *saṁskāras* for a girl, for whom serving her husband is like living under the care of a guru (*The Laws of Manu,* 63–66)[20]. Presumably on the belief that the most appropriate social goal for a woman was marriage, no apprenticeship for any other role could be relevant, irrespective of the social stratum of her origin. Whether of high or low caste, a woman required no more than the *saṁskāra* set for marriage to fit into the fabric of Hindu society. Whether this injunction was universally followed is not known, for there is often a gap between what the rule-books say and what people actually do. There is, however, no evidence that the laws laid down by Manu and others were

20 *The Laws of Manu,* transl. Wendy Doniger and Brian K. Smith (London: Penguin Books, 1991), 24.

not followed, nor any record of women in the general run of social life receiving instruction in formal branches of learning such as philosophy, grammar, or mathematics till well into the nineteenth century. Again, lack of information is no proof of absence. Certainly there were women in locations of privilege, such as royal families, or the occasional priestly family, in which girls received education. But the organic relationship between women and knowledge that characterised Vedic society and partly survived through the classical era had decisively withered in India through medieval times and later, certainly from about the twelfth century till colonial times.

Alternative Paths

Let us bear in mind, though, that the lack of formal, socially approved modes of education does not mean that knowledge was extinct among women in those dark times. Especially when we are speaking of sacred knowledge, we have to bear in mind that knowledge, sacred knowledge in particular, is not always, nor necessarily, the product of deliberate and systematic mental cultivation. Some individuals are simply born with such knowledge, or they gain it through instinct or accident, or some epiphanic vision, of which all cultures offer examples. A person touched by some divine agency that implants knowledge within her or him is a common legend. Authors of sacred poetry in particular are reputed to be recipients of such grace. A great English poet who was unable to continue his writing because of his blindness welcomed his incapacitation even as he lamented that:

> cloud instead, and ever-during dark
> Surrounds me, from the cheerful ways of men
> Cut off, and for the book of knowledge fair
> Presented with a universal blank

> Of nature's works to me expunged and razed,
> And wisdom at one entrance quite shut out.
> *So much the rather thou celestial light*
> *Shine inward, and the mind through all her powers*
> *Irradiate,* there plant eyes, all mist from thence
> Purge and disperse, that I may see and tell
> Of things invisible to mortal sight.
>
> (John Milton, *Paradise Lost,*
> Book 3, lines 45–55 [my italics])

Here is an affirmation of knowledge received as a divine gift, a phenomenon recognised as a real condition of religious life in every religious culture. Side by side we may put those men and women, some of them poets, some of them inspiring teachers, who possess knowledge without having consciously sought it. Like other religious traditions, Hinduism has a rich history of countless such women revered for the knowledge that is not acquired but is simply integral to their being, especially in those streams of Hindu religiosity that valorise instinct and inspiration, sometimes above conscious efforts to explore spirituality.

A related but different notion is that women, by virtue of their sexual identity, are vessels of esoteric knowledge of the Supreme Being. If – and this is a big if – knowledge is understood as an instrument, a key to unlock mysteries, if women are sites of sacred knowledge, if sacred knowledge is intrinsic to womanhood, and if women command knowledge simply by virtue of being women, then may women not be gateways to the great Unknown? Tantra texts assert that:

Tava svarūpā ramaṇī jagatī ācchannavigrahā | . . .

> Every woman, O Goddess, is your form, your body
> concealed in the universe.
>
> (*Mahānirvāṇa Tantra,* 10.80,1)

nārī trailokyajananī, nārī trailokyarūpiṇī |
nārī tribhuvanadhārā nārī dehasvarūpiṇī ||

Woman is the creator of Universe; the universe is her form.
Woman is the foundation of the world; woman is the form.

(*Śaktisamāgama Tantra*, 2.13.43)

A short step from this declaration is the acceptance of women as the purest source of the transmission of sacred revelation. Women who cultivate their innate powers by esoteric yoga disciplines attain the status of *yoginis* and because of their inward knowledge can be the fittest gurus, as evident from the lists of preceptors of several sects, and from texts that mention men being initiated into tantric doctrine and practice by self-realised *yoginis*. Mahesvarānanda, the twelfth-century author of the *Mahārthamañjarī*, reports that his text was revealed to him in a dream by such a preceptor.[21] Another text, the *Kaulajñāna Nirṇaya* (tenth century), represents a tradition of knowledge orally transmitted by *yoginis*.[22] Tantra texts say that women have the authority to impart *dīkṣā* (initiation), and even that *dīkṣā* officiated by a woman is more efficacious than *dīkṣā* by a man.[23]

This is not to say that every woman has the recognised ability to play the role of a *guru*. But in the *Śākta* view, every woman does possess the potential to express the sacred knowledge that is inherent in her because she is an expression of the Goddess. The female ascetic is one who is self-realised.

21 *Mahārthamañjarī*, ed. Acharya Krishnanand Sagar (Varanasi: Krishnanand Sagar, 1985), 191.

22 *Kaulajñāna Nirṇaya*, ed. P. C. Bagchi (Calcutta: Calcutta Sanskrit Series, 3, 1934), 22.10.

23 *Śāktānanda Taraṅginī*, ed. Rāma Kumar Rai (Varanasi: Tantra Granthamala Series 19, 1993), 2.31a.

The majority of women are not, but could be, just because they are women. Here lies a crucial difference between female scholars from the Vedic age onwards and the *yoginis* of Tantra: for the former, knowledge was an acquisition, the fruit of deliberate cultivation; for the latter knowledge is innate, indivisible from their identity as women.

Whether knowledge is acquired or innate is not especially relevant to gender identities. What is relevant to this study is that Hinduism includes a highly influential philosophical system that asserts an essential bond between spiritual knowledge and womanhood. It is something of a paradox that in traditional Hindu society, including its long periods of women's disenfranchisement, when a woman achieved a reputation for learning and wisdom, she received respect even though she had broken out of her gender role, and even when she had received no formal education. In thinking of knowledge as it exists in and for women, we must recognise this variance from custom.

As Time Goes By

That our discussion so far has been focused on early Hinduism does not mean that women's quest for sacred knowledge ceased in later times. It is true that with the systematic denigration of women and the constriction of women's life from the end of the first millennium BCE onwards, women in general had little opportunity to pursue studies and to express their thoughts, always excepting those recognised within Hindu communities as ascetics, such as the twelfth-century poet-seer Ākkā Mahādevī whom I have mentioned earlier. It is among women such as Ākkā and Lallā that we can look for the survival of sacred knowledge. But whether they opened new frontiers of thought, as Maitreyī or Sulabhā did, is debatable even though the poems of women such as Āṇṭāl or Mīrābāī remain profound testaments to their understanding of their spiritual life. Note though that these women were nonconformists, publicly visible precisely because they repudiated social norms to dedicate themselves to their god. Countless women of saintly character appeared from early to late time – as they still do – throughout the Hindu world, bringing solace to men and women with their spirituality. Ma Saradamani of Dakshineshwar was one such whose spirituality was proclaimed by her husband Shri Ramakrishna Paramahamsadeva, the charismatic sage of modern times who saw in her the Great Mother in person. But there is no knowing whether she or women seers commanded sacred knowledge. There may have been women of great religious learning throughout the ages who never became known outside their immediate circle. It is true that Hindu women have always been keepers, practitioners, and teachers of religious duties rooted in sacred teachings but it is doubtful whether that should count for much more than uncritical rote learning. It was not until the nineteenth century that women began to be active in the public arena, but that wave of regeneration impelled women much more towards seeking materially useful and secular knowledge than sacred learning. Religion is not the pervasive force today as it was in Vedic times and even later. Women today have a vast array of options as students; secular studies bringing intellectual challenge and material benefit do tend to push the abstractions of religion off the bookshelf. Not that there are not many distinguished women academics who study the Hindu religion but we do not see them occupying centre stage in public life like the women seers of Vedic times. But the thought that should cheer us is that the way is open today for women to search for knowledge within the immense storehouse of the Hindu religion.

Discussion Topic: Women's Access to Knowledge

- What arguments could be advanced to support/deny women's fitness to pursue sacred knowledge?
- What has gender to do with the capacity or lack of capacity for receiving or cultivating sacred knowledge?
- Why are women's domestic roles *not* incompatible with their pursuit of sacred knowledge?
- Is the pursuit of sacred knowledge relevant to women's social and intellectual aspirations in the modern world?

III
Regulating Women's Lives: Scriptures and Injunctions

Initially marked by independence, women's life in pre-modern Hindu society became increasingly confined within rules for every aspect of life. These were set down by both priests and religious scholars, based on arbitrary notions of women's nature that led to the erosion of women's freedom; freedom was replaced by strict control of their activities within the home, away from public life. To find out how the ethic of women's subordination was legitimised, we will examine in this chapter the injunctions and opinions of Hindu books of conduct framed to regulate women's life and how far they prevailed in reality. We will further try to evaluate the ways in which the culture of women's dependency has fared in modern Hindu society, including diasporic Hindu communities.

A WEB OF RULES

One of the gloomiest aspects of history is the devaluation of women everywhere through all time well into our own. The situation in Hindu society, a society deeply permeated by its religious ideology, has been especially troubling since the end of its formative period, an era that had been marked by the intellectually and spiritually adventurous ethos of the Vedas. The values and attitudes of that ethos dominated that society till about 500 to 400 bce. Whether women were considered equal to men in the Vedic period cannot be claimed with any certainty – equality is in any case a modern value – but they certainly had access to learning and to the religious acts that brought the performer social standing. As we have seen in some detail in Chapter 2, in the Vedic age learning was in no way closed to women, many of whom contributed to philosophical knowledge and took an active part in Vedic society's intellectual and spiritual life. With the passing of the Vedic era, Hindu society became increasingly segmented into hierarchies of gender and caste, strict rules of conduct imposed on all but harsher for those at the lower ends of the social structure, their rights limited and often withheld by those at the top. Women fell into that category of the disempowered.

Women's position at that time, however, should not be etched in unrelieved black. True, the priests and philosophers who were arbiters of conduct laid down narrowly defined roles in common life for women and the rules that bound them to those roles. But there is no evidence that such roles were completely inflexible or that women were subjected to every single rule prescribed in the codes of conduct. Nor is it true that women were treated with disrespect or denied authority within the family or community. On the contrary, many learned men, authors of influential treatises on the governing laws of Hindu society, were vocal in their respect and admiration for women. What mattered, though, was that there were rules devised specially for controlling women on top of the many rules that governed Hindu society in general. Why rules particularly for women? As with other discriminatory conditions, these rules were ready instruments for those who wished to subordinate women to serve their own interests. We must also note that by the end of the Vedic era, Hindu society was beginning to tie itself up more and more in the web of rules for every aspect of life. This was true for men as well as for women, but the web was tighter in the case of women. Volumes of injunctions defining Hindu life held women in subjection from about the second century CE till the late nineteenth century. Some would say the reign of those expectations is not over yet.

How did this come about? How *could* this come about? The question gains urgency from our knowledge of early Hindu society's moral and practical inclusiveness, as demonstrated by such conventions as the flexibility of marriage practices and the equitability of inheritance laws. Many answers have been offered by religious scholars, philosophers, historians, and sociologists, but no one solution seems adequate. Falling back upon our own efforts, we might try to judge for ourselves, to which end we may go to the essential evidence available in the form of the rules and injunctions for governing women's lives, as found in early to late medieval Hindu religious, legal, and ethical texts. But here again we must question how widely these rules were applied and what women's life really was like in the past. Two lines of sight into that reality are open: women's own responses to their world, and women's particular activity in religion. The first we will consider in detail in Chapter 4, 'A Room of Their Own: Women's Writings', and the second in Chapter 5, 'Women at Worship'. But in preparation for the discussion there, the present chapter will focus on the rules framed to govern women within the dictates of *dharma*.

Dharma

At the outset it is useful to note that, in Hindu usage, the term *dharma* does not mean religion but right conduct according to certain principles and ways that hold life together in an orderly structure. But that is just where religious overtones can be heard, for true orderliness – as conceived by religious persons – can only exist within the divinely ordained scheme of existence, existence encompassing both spiritual and material conditions. It is in that context that *dharma* has both a religious and a social significance. That is also why the laws of social life can be seen to bear religious authority. An important aspect of the culture of the Hindus is their concern for orderly life, as evidenced by the extent of discussion and debate about how to run society and society's expectations from its members. Rules and regulations, codes for every part of social life were set down in abundance very early on, comprising a body of laws on *nīti*, that is, moral conduct, called *dharma-śāstras* (discourses on *dharma*) and *dharma-sūtras* (rules of *dharma*) that came to be accorded the authority of scriptures and still hold sway in Hindu society. The most influential writers on these principles of moral conduct and practical codes were Manu, Yājñavalkya, Gautama, Baudhāyana, Nārada, and Kauṭilya. Can we derive from them a *nītiśāstra*, that is, a body of moral and ethical laws written exclusively to guide women's private and public conduct? Indeed there is such a corpus, though not as a single, exclusive text. Of advice and injunctions, there is no shortage, as we shall see below. As for a single work exclusively directed to women, there is in fact one such text, but from a much later time, as we shall see further along in this chapter.

But before we look at injunctions directed at women, the conceptual context of ethical living needs to be noted, so let us pause for a moment to consider the meaning of *dharma* and *nīti*. In the Hindu tradition it is understood that *dharma* and *nīti* are the two fundamental concepts of conduct that hold all action together in perfect order and equilibrium. Any deviation from them means disorder and eventually chaos. *Dharma* encompasses more than one idea. It can mean duty, private and public, as well as religious activities that sustain the divine scheme of existence. *Dharma* is derived from the root *dhṛ*, which means 'to hold'. The *Mahābhārata* defines *dharma* in the *Karṇa Parva* as:

> *dhāraṇād dharmam ityāhur dharmo dhārayati prajāḥ |*
> *yaḥ syād dhāraṇasaṁyuktaḥ sa dharma iti niścayaḥ | |*

> It is said that the word *dharma* comes from *dhāraṇa*, sustaining, so *dharma* is what sustains living beings. *Dharma* is whatever helps to sustain living beings. This is certain.
>
> (*Mahābhārata*, 8.49.50)

The same view is reiterated in the *Śānti Parva* (12.110.11)

> *dhāraṇād dharmam ityāhur dharmeṇa vidhṛtāḥ prajāḥ |*
> *yat syād dhāraṇasaṁyuktam sa dharma iti niścayaḥ | |*

This is an ethical rather than a religious understanding of *dharma*. Similarly, in the context of the *dharma-śāstras*, *dharma* is not related to matters of divinity. Rather, it denotes a combination of several virtues, such as *kartavya*, that is, duties that must be performed, *sad-ācāra*, or good behaviour, and *nyāya-buddhi*, or the conscientious thinking of a dutiful human being. When these requirements are met by everybody, a healthy society comes into being. This is the message of all *dharma-śāstras*. Following these recommendations within the framework of *nīti* (moral laws) helps individuals to lead a perfect life. The word *nīti* comes from the root *nī* (to bring) and in this context, denotes the principles a person must follow to achieve moral advancement.

Dharma conveys more than one meaning: it is right action, duty, and in general all that upholds religious belief and purpose. If we think of it as duty, *dharma* can be of two types, general or *sādhāraṇa*, and special or *viśeṣa*. Sage Vasiṣṭha lays down the broad principle to be followed:

> *dharmaṁ carata mā adharmaṁ satyaṁ vadata mā anṛtam |*
> *dīrghaṁ paśyata mā hrasvaṁ paraṁ paśyata mā aparam | |*

> Practice action that is moral, not immoral; speak the truth, not untruth.
> Look far ahead, not close; aim to see the best, not the worst.
>
> (*Dharma-sūtra* (Vasiṣṭha), 30.1)[1]

To speak the truth and to act morally is the guiding principle of general conduct or *sādhāraṇa dharma*. It is applicable to all human beings and everyone should follow it. Put even more broadly, this is *mānava-dharma*, or right action for all human beings, the frame within which all must live. On the other hand, there are specific rules that apply to particular (*viśeṣa*) situations or types of people, and these fall under *viśeṣa-dharma*. An example of this type of rule is *varṇāśrama dharma*, or particular caste duty. It is into the category of *viśeṣa-dharma* that the duties and expectations from women fall, as enunciated by ancient lawgivers, consisting of injunctions covering a wide range of situations. These rules, written and unwritten, apply to women classified by age, station in life, and social status. Women are bound by this *viśeṣa-dharma* and their moral duty is to follow its provisions.

Defining Women

One may well ask at this point, why create a special category of rules for women? Are women beings thought of as a species different from men? There is no direct answer to this but the assumption of difference – and by prejudicial extension,

1 All references to *Dharma-sūtras* are from Patrick Olivelle, *Dharmasūtras: The Law Codes of Āpastamba, Gautama, Baudhāyana, and Vasiṣṭha*, ed. and transl. Patrick Olivelle (Delhi: Motilal Banarsidass, 2000) unless otherwise noted.

of inferiority – is implicit in the persistent examination and evaluation of women's nature in such detail that it comprises an entire discourse of gender by itself. This concern with the nature of womankind began as early as the *ṚgVeda*. Profound as it is in its philosophical speculations and declarations, the *ṚgVeda* descends to intemperate and inexplicable hostility when speaking of women as a sex:

> *striyāḥ aśāsyaṃ manaḥ | uto aha kratuṃ raghum |*

> The mind of woman[kind] brooks no discipline.
> Her intellect has little weight.
>
> (*ṚgVeda*, 8, 33.17)

Abuse descends farther to:

> *na vai straiṇāni sakhyāni santi sālāvṛkāṇām*
> *hṛdayāṇyetā |*

> With women there can be no friendship. Women's
> hearts are like those of hyenas.
>
> (*ṚgVeda*, 10, 95.15)

Nor is this the only Vedic text to voice similar disparagement:

> *anṛtam strī śudraḥ śvā kṛṣṇah śakunis . . .*

> A woman, a *śudra*, a dog and a crow are the
> embodiments of untruth, sin and darkness.
>
> (*Śatapatha Brāhmaṇa*, 14, 1.1.31)[2]

2 *Śatapatha Brāhmaṇa*, transl. Julius Eggeling (Volume 44 of *Sacred Books of the East*, edited by Max Müller. Oxford: Clarendon Press, 1900; reproduction, Delhi: Motilal Banarsidass, 1963), 446.

This litany of disparagement continues through early texts over centuries. In the opinion of the *Rāmāyaṇa* (c. seventh–third century BCE) women cannot be trusted:

> *svabhāvastv eṣa nārīṇām eṣu lokeṣu dṛśyate* |
> *vimuktadharmā capalās tīkṣṇā bhedakarāḥ strīyaḥ* | |

> Such is the nature of women as can be seen in the world. Women are [usually] careless about *dharma*, they are fickle-minded, sharp-[tongued] and they cause discord.
>
> (*Rāmāyaṇa, Araṇyakāṇḍa,* 45. 29–30)

The *Mahābhārata* (c. fourth century BCE) is even more scornful:

> *na strībhya kiñcid anyad vai pāpīyastaram asti vai* |
> *strīyo hi mūlam doṣāṇām tathā tvam api vettha ha* | |

> There is none viler than a woman. A woman is the root cause of all evil, you must know that.
>
> (*Mahābhārata, Anuśāsana Parva,* 38.12)

Another influential text, a compendium of moralistic and cautionary tales, is the *Pañcatantra* (c. second century BCE), which tells in the book titled 'Mitrabheda' story after story of women, all of them cruel, stupid, greedy, and promiscuous creatures who cause conflict among friends and cheat their husbands.

Women's Worth

Probing deeper into the reduction of women, we begin to wonder whether it does not assume women to be creatures fundamentally different from men. The close attention paid to defining women and to setting out their lines of life is a sign that gender differences were taken for granted as natural, essential, and thus unchangeable. These assumptions were applied to women's disadvantage, making up special rules that could contain women within social structures. Yet some uncertainty seems to go with this denigration of women. One of the most influential early texts that both praises and condemns women is the *Manu-smṛti* (the Laws of Manu, composed approximately some time between the second century BCE and the third century CE), attributed to the legendary Manu the Lawgiver, whose dicta still run true for many Hindus. Women, he says, must be revered and made happy:

> 3.55: Fathers, brothers, husbands and brothers-in-law who wish for great fortune should revere these women and adorn them.
>
> 3.56: The deities delight in places where women are revered, but where women are not revered, all rites are fruitless.
>
> 3.57: Where the women of the family are miserable, the family is soon destroyed, but it always thrives where the women are not miserable.
>
> 3.58: Homes that are cursed by women of the family who have not been treated with due reverence are completely destroyed, as if struck down by witchcraft.
>
> 3.59: Therefore, men who wish to prosper should always revere these women with ornaments, clothes, and food at celebrations and festivals.
>
> 3.60: There is unwavering good fortune in a family where the husband is always satisfied by the wife, and the wife by the husband.[3]

3 *The Laws of Manu*, transl. Wendy Doniger and Brian K. Smith (London: Penguin Books, 1991), 48–49.

These ideas have contributed substantially to Hindu attitudes to women, especially reverence for mothers, as indicated by common sayings such as '*mātṛ devo bhava*' (a mother is divine) and '*jananī janmabhumiśca svargādapi gariyasī*' (one's mother and motherland are nobler than heaven). Authority is in general readily acceded to mothers. Viewed in that context, it is astonishing that in the same text Manu issues the following wholesale condemnation of women:

2.213: It is the very nature of women to corrupt men on earth; for that reason, circumspect men do not get careless and wanton among wanton women.

9.2: Men must make their women dependent day and night, and keep under their own control those who are attached to sensory objects.

9.3: Her father guards her in childhood, her husband guards her in youth, and her sons guard her in old age. A woman is not fit for independence.

9.10: No man is able to guard women entirely by force, but they can be fully guarded by using these means:

9.11: He should keep her busy amassing and spending money, engaging in purification, attending to her duty, cooking food, and looking after the furniture.

9.12: Women are not guarded when they are confined in a house by men who can be trusted to do their jobs well; but women who guard themselves by themselves are well guarded.

9.13: Drinking, associating with bad people, being separated from their husbands, wandering about, sleeping, and living in other people's houses are the six things that corrupt women.

9.14: Good looks do not matter to them, nor do they care about youth; "A man!" they say, and enjoy sex with him, whether he is good-looking or ugly.

9.15: By running after men like whores, by their fickle minds, and by their natural lack of affection, these women are unfaithful to their husbands even when they are zealously guarded here.

9.16: Knowing that their very own nature is like this, as it was born at Creation by the Lord of Creatures, a man should make the utmost effort to guard them.

9.17: The bed and the seat, jewellery, lust, anger, crookedness, a malicious nature, and bad conduct are what Manu assigned to women.

9.18: There is no ritual with Vedic verses for women; this is a firmly established point of law. For women, who have no virile strength and no Vedic verses, are falsehood; this is well established.[4]

The only way to resolve these contradictory judgments is to assume that though the text is nominally the same *Manu-smṛti*, its authorship differs from part to part. But whoever penned the parts that vilify women clearly carried authority and expressed

4 *The Laws of Manu*, transl. Doniger and Smith, 38; 197–198.

notions that became integral to the gender discourse of the time and gained increasing dominance through the ages. So commonplace was this debasement of women that it spilled out of Hindu social ideology into Buddhist thought despite its leanings towards social equality. The first-century Buddhist author Aśvaghoṣa proclaimed in his *Saundarānanda*:

> 8.41: Just as a cow, if restrained from grazing in one object, goes straight to another, so a woman regardless of a former love, goes elsewhere to take her pleasure.
>
> 8.42: For women may mount their husbands' funeral pyre, they may follow them closely at risk of their lives, they may be subjected to no restraint, but they never bear love wholeheartedly.
>
> 8.43: Even those women who treat their husbands as gods and sometimes in one way or the other give them pleasure, from fickleness of mind please themselves a thousand times.
>
> (Aśvaghoṣa, *Saundarānanda*, pp. 45–46)

How a man who is admired as the finest poet in Sanskrit before Kālidāsa, and one who no doubt possessed both a keen intelligence and a refined sensibility, could spout such vile prejudice must remain one of the mysteries of the male psyche. This is all the more dispiriting because the inexplicable mixture of praise and blame we have encountered in the *Manu-smṛti* appears again and again through the *dharma-śāstras*, or treatises of lawful conduct both public and private, similarly clouded by contradictions. Although this degree of misogyny is rare, distrust of women is not. That women are not fit to be allowed self-determination is a common theme from the earliest authors of the *dharma-śāstras* such as Vasiṣṭha (5.1; 5.3), Baudhāyana (2.3.44–45), Gautama (18.1), Yājñavalkya (1.85), Viṣṇu (25.12; 13), and Nārada (13.30–31), to Kauṭilya in his highly influential socio-political treatise, the *Arthaśāstra* (third century BCE–second century CE). Kauṭilya recognises women as individuals by recognising women's rights to property and its disposition (3.2.14–16), yet shows the same distrust of women's independence in already having laid down the precondition that their choices are contingent upon her parents (3.2.10–11). He allows a widow to inherit her husband's property but she must return it to the donors with interest if she remarries (3.2.20, 23), in effect advising that women must remain subordinate to men. Such distrust can only have been derived from an unquestioned assumption that frailty of body and mind was integral and essential to womankind. What this assumption implies is that women must be kept under control because of their innate inferiority and even depravity.

As for Daughters . . .

The devaluation of women ran so deep in the Hindu discourse of gender that it extended even to childhood. Going beyond the preference – only too common in the world, Hindu or not – for sons over daughters, a section of the Hindu community – thankfully a shrinking section – has continued to hold the birth of a daughter to be a dire misfortune for the parents well into the twenty-first century. In the past there were anxious attempts to avoid the conception of a girl child, as we see in the *Atharva Veda*, a very early text, which provides a special *mantra* to avert the birth of a daughter and induce the conception of a son:

> The Lord of Creatures [gives] consent and active life (*sinivālī*) to shape the embryo. May He place a male here and the birth of a girl elsewhere.
>
> (*Atharva Veda,* 6.11.13)

Preference for the birth of a son over that of a daughter dominates Hindu thought, as we find in authoritative works from the beginning of the Hindu scriptural tradition. The *Aitareya Brāhmaṇa* says that 'a daughter is misery and a son is the light in the highest heaven' (3.33.1). The *Kṛṣṇa Yajurveda* similarly declares that 'the birth of a daughter spells misfortune for a father' (1.1.64). The rejection of daughters assumes so savage a form in the *Atharva Veda* that it recommends putting a girl child away altogether (6.11.3). Agreeing with this, the *Taittīriya Samhitā* says that daughters are to be subjected to '*parāsyanti*', which literally means 'alienated', which in effect implies that she ought to be abandoned in order to bring about death (6.5.10), although this may be to put too harsh a construction upon the opinion, as we shall see below.

Compassion

To our relief, such heartlessness is not the average Hindu stance on daughters. Even Manu, whom we have heard saying quite a few nasty things about women, commiserates with daughters, saying '*duhitā kṛpaṇaṁ param*' (*Manu-smṛti,* 4.185), that is, a daughter is the supreme object of pity, presumably because of the hard life she faces. Sāyaṇācārya, a fourteenth-century scholar of the Vedas, attempted to soften the *Taittīriya Samhitā's* judgment by interpreting the term '*parāsyanti*' as the act of transferring a daughter to another family by marriage ('*varakule parityajanti*'). Still more sympathetically, he says that since a daughter will be inevitably married off, causing her parents the pain of separation, she should be especially cared for as long as she is in her parents' home.

With equal tenderness, both the *Bṛhadāraṇyaka Upaniṣad* (6.4.9) and the *Nirukta* (2.4) attribute the begetting of a daughter not just to the body but also to the heart, which therefore requires that she be lovingly cared for. Compassion and practical wisdom leads the *Matsya Purāṇa* to remind us that 'no progeny can be born without a woman', that 'in the *Śāstras* at many places it has been said that a girl is equal to ten sons' (2.154.157), and that 'the birth of a daughter brings high merit' (2.154.414). Much later in time we see the same love for a daughter in Kālidāsa's *Abhijñānaśakuntalam* (c. fourth–fifth century), in which a particularly tender passage in Act 4, verse 6 expresses a father's sadness at his daughter's departure for her husband's home. A still later work, Bāṇabhaṭṭa's *Harṣacarita* (seventh century), has a passage that expresses the same sadness at losing a daughter when in Act 4 Rājyaśrī's mother laments her impending departure from home after her marriage.

An Inconsistent Tradition

Despite the words of sympathy we have just reviewed, the general attitude to daughters is one of devaluation aggravated by the extreme desire for sons. Aversion to daughters is hard to reconcile with the provision, in Vedic times, for women's education and the historical reality of Hindu women's intellectual and spiritual attainments. For example, the supposed anxiety of parents at the prospect of a daughter being born does not fit in with the *Bṛhadāraṇyaka Upaniṣad*'s advice to parents to perform a *yajña* to ensure the birth of a daughter who would be a '*paṇḍitā*', i.e., a savant (6.4.17). So many early writers advocate education for girls, their initiation in the sacred thread rituals, and their right and responsibility to participate in *yajñas*, that such provisions must be regarded as commonly accepted conditions of women's upbringing. But that liberal tradition gave way to the denigration of women and their demotion to virtually a lower form of life. Not only did women's status progressively sink but they also became captives within their narrowly defined, exclusively domestic tasks of serving their families, with husbands being their first priority. Performing those tasks defined women's life and in effect became their *dharma*.

Contradictions

It is a relief to find that many of the same Hindu authorities who issue strictures on women also place them high on the chain of being, not only on moral and emotional grounds, but on physical as well. For example, Baudhāyana (2.4.4) asserts that women are ever pure and free from the taints of the world because they purge impurities out of their bodies by means of their monthly period:

strīyāḥ pavitram atulam naitā duṣyanti karhicit |
māsi māsi rajo hy āsāṁ duritāny apakarṣati | |

> Women's purity is incomparable. They never become defiled, for every month their menstrual blood washes away their [impurities].
>
> (*Baudhāyana Dharmasūtram*, 2.4.4)

Vasiṣṭha holds the same opinion (5.5; 28.4). Going farther still, Baudhāyana asserts that,

somaḥ śaucaṃ dadau tāsāṃ gandharvaḥ śikṣitāṃ giram |
agniś ca sarvabhakṣatvaṃ tasmān niṣkalmaṣā striyaḥ | |

> Somadeva made women sacred and *gandharvas* gave them a melodious voice; Agni made them delightful to everyone; therefore they are free from sin.
>
> (*Baudhāyana Dharmasūtram*, 2.4.5)

Even Manu believes that a woman's impurity is washed away by her monthly menstruation (*Manu-smṛti*, 5.108). On occasion, the *Mahābhārata* takes Manu's line for praising women, as here:

> *mṛdutvaṁ ca tanutvaṁ ca viklavatvaṁ tathaiva ca* |
> *strīguṇā ṛṣibhiḥ proktā dharma-tattvārtha-darśibhiḥ* | |

> The sages who discuss the state of *dharma* say that gentleness, delicacy and timidity are the [proper] attributes of a woman.
>
> (*Mahābhārata, Anuśāsana Parva*, 12.13)

And again:

> *pūjanīyā mahābhāgāḥ pūṇyāś ca gṛhadīptayaḥ* |
> *striyaḥ śriyo gṛhasyoktās tasmād rakṣyā viśeṣataḥ* | |

> They are to be worshipped, they are pure, sacred and they are the lights of [our] homes. Women are the beauty of our homes. Therefore they are to be protected.
>
> (*Mahābhārata, Udyoga Parva*, 38.11)

Bearing in mind the weight of the *Mahābhārata*'s influence on Hindu personal and public conduct, let us see what it thinks of wives:

> *ardhaṁ bhāryā manuṣyasya bhāryā śreṣṭhatamaḥ sakhā* |
> *bhāryā mūlam trivargasya bhāryā mitraṁ mariṣyataḥ* | |

> A wife is half of a man, a wife is his best friend, and a wife is the base for fulfilling [his] *trivargas* [*dharma, artha,* and *kāma*].
>
> (*Mahābhārata, Ādi Parva*, 68.40)

Again,

> *nāsti bhāryāsamo bandhur nāsti bhāryāsamo gatiḥ |*
> *nāsti bhāryāsamo loke sahāyo dharma-sādhanaḥ ||*

> There is no other friend equal to [one's] wife, nor is there [anyone else] equal to her in [showing the ultimate path]. In this world, there is no one else comparable to [one's wife, for] helping in religious rites.
>
> (*Mahābhārata, Śānti Parva,* 142.10)

One may well ask how it was that these views were obscured by the unrelenting iteration of women's inferiority and their innate viciousness, which required them to be in thrall to their male relations. One may also doubt whether this scenario of utter dependency was a historical reality or a paternalistic piece of wish-fulfillment unlikely to function in practical domestic life. Perhaps this brand of misogynic ideology, however loud it sounds, had much less force in subjugating women than we estimate. But there is no doubt that women did live lives of dependency, increasingly harsh through time but still with the potential for release from the chains designed for women.

Women's Duty

Textual material from the ethical discourse on women's duty shows that the overall need to control women's life was taken for granted, given the common acceptance of women's inferiority. Following upon that, what rules of conduct would have been thought effective in fitting women into an inflexible, though well-ordered, social scheme? What duties should be required of women? The *Dharma-śāstras* discuss the duties of an individual under three headings: (a) *ācāra,* or rules and rituals,

(b) *vyāvahāra*, or the applications of rules and the procedures of rituals, and (c) *prāyaścitta*, or atonement/expiation. In addition to setting down women's duties in general, the chapter on *ācāra* also provides for particular situations for which special, mostly restrictive rules are laid down separately and in detail.

The need to control every aspect – indeed every minute – of female life came to be embodied in an extraordinarily detailed programme composed in the eighteenth century, a period in which Hindu society had become utterly inflexible in its anxiety to retain its identity. The work in question is the *Strīdharmapaddhati*, a Sanskrit treatise written by Tryambakayajvan, an orthodox Brahmin from Tanjavur in South India, which sets down the innumerable duties of a wife from early dawn till her husband retires at night. Tryambakayajvan proceeds from his belief that women are corrupt to the core and incapable of serious mental effort:

> *nanu svabhāvato duṣṭānāṁ strīṇāṁ*
> *nirūpitadharmaśravaṇe ca kathaṁ pravrtti*

> The problem is [*nanu*] how can there be any [real] inclination towards receiving religious inclination . . . on the part of women who are by nature corrupt?
> (*Tryambakayajvan*, 21r.3)[5]

Tryambakayajvan trots out the old indictment that women are impure because of their unavoidable condition of menstruation (33v.8–40r.3).[6] Even though many past authorities whom Tryambakayajvan quotes, such as Baudhāyana, Vasiṣṭha, and Yājñavalkya, assert that women are the purest of all human beings precisely because they are

5 Julia Leslie, *The Perfect Wife: The Orthodox Hindu Woman According to the Strīdharmapaddhati of Tryambakayajvan* (Delhi: Oxford University Press, 1995 [1989]), 246.

6 Leslie, *The Perfect Wife*, 283–288.

cleansed every month by menstruation, he takes exactly the opposite stand, repeating centuries-old assertions of women's fundamental *impurity*.[7]

Such being women's essential nature in Tryambakayajvan's view, they must be locked within a fixed and crowded roster of tasks. His sole concern is with the wife's total service to her husband, meeting his every need through the day. Her duties extend from house cleaning to cooking for her husband and his guests, ensuring his comfort, carrying out or anticipating his every command through the day, and to wind up her labours by serving him in bed at night – which she does not share afterwards. The perfect wife must get up before dawn to clean and pound grains for the day's meals, clean the house before the sun's rays touch the house, smear the floor and walls with cow dung,[8] prepare the implements necessary for worship rites,[9] offer prescribed salutations to elders, prostrate herself on the ground before her husband,[10] manage any money her husband may have given her for household expenses,[11] eat a meal only after her husband has had his, the meal being her husband's leftovers,[12] first having touched his feet.[13] The list is too long and tedious to go through here but to show how all-encompassing Tryambakayajvan's recommendations are, let me note that he even frames rules for the proper manner and location for her to relieve herself.[14]

---

7 For instance, *Pañcatantra*, ed. and transl. Shri Shyamacharan Pandeya (Delhi: Motilal Banarsidass, 1975), refers to women as the most impure, '*aśaucam*', in *Mitrabheda*, 207. See Julia Leslie, *Perfect Wife*, 283–88 for a detailed discussion of this issue.

8 Leslie, *The Perfect Wife*, 58–59.

9 Leslie, *The Perfect Wife*, 65.

10 Leslie, *The Perfect Wife*, 162.

11 Leslie, *The Perfect Wife*, 168–170.

12 Leslie, *The Perfect Wife*, 222–224.

13 Leslie, *The Perfect Wife*, 222.

14 Leslie, *The Perfect Wife*, 69.

This prescription of a wife's *dharma* itemised by every chore and every minute is a rarity in Hindu śāstric literature. But the general strategy is common enough for keeping women too busy to stray into mischief and that is the approach Tryambakayajvan follows to the extreme end. By his time the burden of wifely duty had already become very heavy indeed, and its rewards, always in terms of reputation and always to be gained in the next world, had increasingly come to be contingent upon absolute and unquestioning service to the husband. A course of unlimited, self-denying service is enjoined upon wives to the exclusion of all personal interest by ancient sages such as Manu, Bṛhaspati, Yājñavalkya, Vyāsa, Śaṅkha-likhita, Devala, Ṛṣyaśṛṅga, and Kātyāyana. Many such items of advice given, for instance, by Śaṅkha-likhita, Devala, Ṛṣyaśṛṅga, and Kātyāyana, were gathered in the (c.) fourteenth century compendium of moral guidelines titled *Smṛti-candrikā* (*Vyavahāra-kāṇḍa*) by Devana Bhaṭṭa, the burden of all being the duty of women to commit themselves to household tasks and to serve their husbands without question. This is the long tradition that Tryambakayajvan turns into a cast-iron scheme of life for wives; implicit here is the idea that this is the scheme that all women must follow because women's highest state in life is that of marriage.

More explicitly than any other ethicist, Tryambakayajvan requires wives to devote their lives to *'pati-śuśrūṣāṇām'* (service to the husband) without regard even to the saving of her own life (*'prāṇānam avigṇānayā'*). She must serve her husband even when it conflicts with other religious duties (*'itara-dharmopamardena'*), a requirement that in effect isolates her from the public world by alienating her from its rules and principles. In line with this abandonment of principles, the virtuous wife must abdicate her individuality so completely that she must accept her husband's every decision, even that of agreeing to selling herself (*'ātmavikraya'*[15]) to serve his interests. We may note that there is actually precedence for this eventuality in the *Mārkaṇḍeya Purāṇa* tale of King Hariścandra selling his queen Śaibyā to pay a debt of honour.[16]

There is little honour in treating a woman as disposable goods but this seems irrelevant to the ethos of total control that held Hindu women in an iron net of restrictive rules. Perhaps the worst effect of the centuries-old dominance of that ethos was that women themselves came to believe in its rightness and benefit. Had they not been told by authority figures that it was by submission that they would win? Was it not by total compliance that a wife would attain heaven? As an example of glorifying selfless service to others let me cite a couplet by Kamini Roy, an early twentieth-century Bengali woman poet:

> *āpanāre laye vivrata rahite āse nāi keha avanī pare.* |
> *sakaler tare sakale āmarā pratyeke āmarā parer tare.* | |

> None of us is born to think of ourselves alone. All
> of us are born to serve one another.

Though the author, a highly regarded and effective women's activist, addressed the lines to everybody, this verse from the 1920s continues to be anthologised in school textbooks but used mainly in girls' schools. She would have been pleased that notwithstanding the gender focus of school authorities, the couplet has become a rallying slogan for countless social service groups in West Bengal and Bangladesh.

But the notion of service to the family being women's duty is still taken for granted. What gave such authority to the rules laid out by venerable sages in the past? The question never

15 Leslie, *The Perfect Wife*, 305.

16 See the *Markaṇḍeya Purāṇa*, transl. F. Eden Pargiter (Calcutta: Asiatic Society, 1904) canto 8, 39–43.

arose in the past but had it been, then the answer would be obvious: first, women were not thought to have the capacity for independence, and second, their feeble moral character needed the strictest possible control. Rules for women were for their own good, and hard and harsh as they were, they were not to be questioned. These rules are varied and too many to be related here but to understand women's life under these conditions, it will be enough to examine three main areas of injunctions, namely, *satī* or the immolation of widows, women's *punarvivāha* or remarriage, and *niyoga* or levirate, which means the generation of a child by a husband's stand-in. If these practices sound horrifying, it is because they were.

But we must again emphasise that not every woman was subjected to these conditions without exception, nor would it be true that women's lives were spent in unrelieved slavery. Through the thousands of years of Hindu social history, women's creativity in poetry, music, and scholarship remained alive and women occupied a place of honour, though sometimes more in principle than in practice. Especially to be borne in mind is the honour that motherhood has always been accorded. The issue is not whether women, by and large, were slaves to men; women's predicament was that tradition denied them self-determination. By the end of the eighteenth century and the beginning of the colonial era, women had no freedom at all to resist even death by social fiat. Of this, the most grievous instance is the institution of *satī*.

Satī

A Hindu custom that gained great importance in the public eye, especially since the coming of the western powers to India, was that of *satī*, that is, the custom of the immolation of recently widowed women. The custom of women choosing (or being forced to choose) to die when their husbands did was known in many parts of the world long ago as it was in India. One of the best-known instances occurs in the *Mahābhārata,* in which Mādrī, one of the two queens of King Pāṇḍu, chooses to die on his funeral pyre. But it was neither a common practice, nor was it supported by early writers. On the contrary, Medhātithi (c. ninth century CE), the best-known commentator on the *Manu-smṛti,* specifically forbids it:

> *puṁvat strīṇām api pratiṣiddha ātmatyāgaḥ . . .*
> *ato'styeva patim anumaraṇe'pi striyāḥ pratiṣedhaḥ* | |

> Women are also forbidden to commit suicide just as men are . . . Therefore, a woman is forbidden to follow her husband into death.
>
> (*Manu-smṛti,* 5.155, ed. Ganganath Jha)

In laying down this judgment, Medhātithi was not alone, and many other writers on the *dharma-śāstras* sounded the same prohibition. The practice, however, did continue and became more common in medieval times. But the very idea is so repugnant to modern sensibility that it coloured, to a great extent, the European perception of India in general and was taken as a sign of the Hindu religion's depravity. It also spawned innumerable literary and artistic representations of the custom, a well-known example being the dramatic rescue of Aouda, a beautiful young princess (nothing less would do for nineteenth-century romantics), from the pyre in Jules Verne's 1873 novel *Around the World in Eighty Days.*[17]

Theoretically a voluntary self-sacrifice by a widow who deemed her life unbearable without her husband, female suicide was practiced in medieval times as a desperate response to imminent defeat in war, especially in Rajasthan, when the women

17 Thereafter, she is of course married to Mr. Phileas Fogg as propriety demanded.

of a fortress or city about to fall into the hands of enemies chose death over defilement at the hands of invaders. That, however, was regarded as a tragic escape from dishonour and not *satī* in the proper sense of the term, considering that the women who died did not die on the funeral pyres of their husbands. *Satī*, in the true sense of the word, did take place as early as Alexander's time (third century BCE) though extremely rarely, the numbers growing marginally from roughly the eleventh century, but it was never a well-known practice until about the eighteenth century. There are records of bereaved women voluntarily dying by entering the funeral pyre of their husbands; without dishonouring their memory it can still be said that in many instances, the practice of *satī* meant that unwilling wives were persuaded or forced to commit *satī*.[18] There never was any matching requirement for widowers to mount the burning pyres of their dead wives, just as there never was any bar to male polygamy. European visitors from the late eighteenth century onwards sometimes tried to intervene in the burning of widows but British authorities were wary about upsetting the sentiments of their Hindu subjects. Effective opposition was spearheaded in the early years of the nineteenth century by the social reformer Raja Rammohan Roy, whose horror at watching his brother's wife committing *satī* spurred him to mount an unrelenting campaign for its abolition. With his vast learning in Hindu scriptures, and wide social influence driving contemporary Hindu society and British authorities alike, the Bengal Sati Regulation was passed in December 1829. The criminalising of *satī* did not instantly eradicate this cruel practice, for it was advocated by its adherents as a religious duty, but it

18 See Mandakranta Bose, 'Satī, the Event and the Ideology', in *Faces of the Feminine in Ancient, Medieval and Modern India*, ed. Mandakranta Bose (New York: Oxford University Press, 2000), 21–32; and John Stratton Hawley ed., *Sati, the Blessing and the Curse* (Oxford and New York: Oxford University Press, 1994).

certainly saved a great number of women from its questionable glory. At the same time, it seems *satī* drew many women's admiration, willing participation, and connivance at leading other women to commit the act. Whether age-old orthodoxy can be stamped out by legislation alone remains debatable because most certainly there have been willing performers of *satī* in the past. More troubling are occurrences of *satī* performances in the late twentieth century. A much reported, discussed, reviled, and celebrated example is that of Roop Kanwar, an eighteen year old woman from Rajasthan who performed *satī* in 1987. Whether she did so voluntarily or under pressure from her community is a question that has been endlessly disputed. It caused an uproar across the world, huge protests in cities, academic debates, and publications. How or whether the shock of this tragedy affected modern Hindu sensibilities cannot be measured; what seems evident is the lasting power of age-old tradition.

Widow Remarriage

The other regulation for women that has caused similarly contentious and persistent debate throughout the history of Hindu society is *punarvivāha*, or remarriage. Only until fairly recent times was it viewed as a dishonourable act and allowed only under special conditions. In early texts of Hindu law, a woman who had remarried was called a *punarbhū*, and a child of such a union was a *paunarbhava*, and neither received more than marginal acceptance. Outright condemnation of *punarvivāha* came from the most influential of Hindu lawgivers, Manu, who strongly disapproved of it, underlining its undesirability by extolling wives who remain faithful to their dead husbands:

na tu nāmāpi gṛhṇīyāt patyau prete parasya tu | |
āsītā āmaraṇāt kṣāntā niyatā brahmacāriṇī |
yo dharma ekapatnīnāṁ kāṁkṣantī tam uttamam | |

. . . . . .

> *mṛte bhartarī sādhvī strī brahmacarye vyavasthitā |*
> *svargaṁ gacchati aputrā'pi yathā te brahmacāriṇaḥ | |*
>
> When her husband is dead . . . she should never even mention the name of another man.
>
> She should be long-suffering until death, self-restrained, and chaste, striving to [fulfill] the unsurpassed duty of women who have one husband.
>
> . . . . . .
>
> A virtuous wife who remains chaste when her husband has died goes to heaven just like those chaste men even if she has no sons.
>
> (*Manu-smṛti,* 5.155.2; 156; 158)[19]

Such urgings by so influential an authority, reiterated in chapters 8.226 and 9.47, were enough to condemn a woman's remarriage by implication and cast a stigma both upon her and her *paunarbhava* child.

Less hostile to the idea of remarriage were Baudhāyana, Vasiṣṭha, Yājñavalkya, Parāśara, and Nārada, who approved of such marriages though only under special circumstances. The key justification comes from Parāśara:

> *naṣṭe mṛte pravrajite patite klīve ca patite patau |*
> *pañcasu āpatsu nārīṇāṁ patiranyo vidhīyate | |*
>
> In case of disappearance or death or renunciation or impotence or lost caste-status of her husband: in these five predicaments a woman is allowed to take another husband.
>
> (*Parāśara-smṛti,* 4.30)

19 *The Laws of Manu,* transl. Doniger and Smith, 5. 157.2; 158; 160.

A similar view appears in other works of Hindu ethics, notably the *Baudhāyana Dharma-sūtra* (4.1.16), *Vasiṣṭha Dharma-sūtra* (17.20), *Yājñavalkya-smṛti* (1.67) *Nārada-smṛti* (45, 46, 97), and *Garuḍa Purāṇa* (107.8.29–30).[20]

Despite these provisions made for responding to practical necessities, it was Manu's opinion that shaped Hindu society's moral position, and widow remarriage never received social sanction till the nineteenth century. At that time, differences of opinion among past authorities were brought to bear upon the admissibility of such marriages and a prolonged, intense, and bitter struggle, for and against it, shook Hindu society. Scholars cited conflicting provisions for and against *punarvivāha* from ancient scriptures and from the little that was known of actual, provable social practice in the past. The fight to allow widow remarriage was led by Ishwarchandra Vidyasagar, a Sanskrit scholar and social reformer who brought his formidable scholarship to bear against opponents, some of them equally learned, to argue for the legitimacy of remarriage. Precedents from the *dharma-śāstras* were cited by either side. Those demanding the right of widows to marry bolstered their arguments based on authoritative texts with humanitarian appeals, while those arguing against remarriage cited sections of equally weighty texts and the sanctity of long-established practice that disallowed it. What made the denial of remarriage to widows especially painful to the supporters of remarriage was the number of very young girl children who were widowed, because there was no minimum age set in law to protect girl children from marriage. Vidyasagar's outrage at the suffering of Hindu widows was triggered when he saw the torment that a five year old girl was undergoing, fasting through

20 For a full discussion of *punarvivāha*, see Krishna Datta, 'A Controversy over a Verse on the Remarriage of Hindu Women', in *Faces of the Feminine in Ancient, Medieval and Modern India*, ed. Mandakranta Bose (New York: Oxford University Press, 2000), 8–20.

the entire day of *ekādaśī* (the eleventh day in each lunar phase), denied even a drop of water, as compulsory for Hindu widows. Moreover, the plight of Hindu widows showed up in very poor light indeed against the unquestioned sanction of polygamy, or *bahu-vivāha,* for men. After a long and heated struggle, the proponents of remarriage succeeded in persuading the ruling British government of India to legitimise the remarriage of Hindu widows by the Hindu Widows Remarriage Act of 1856, passed on 26 July 1856. This was a notable success for liberal modernists among Hindus. These debates over *satī* and widow remarriage show that, for the mindset that rejects women's *punarvivāha* and extols *satī,* the lives of men and women are validated very differently. From that point of view, a woman's life was seen to achieve its highest usefulness in marriage and the justification of her life evaporated when her marriage was terminated by her husband's death. It also became evident, from very early times, that even within marriage the essential value of a woman's life was that of ensuring the continuation of her husband's lineage by bearing sons. Thereby her allegiance to that lineage was justified and remarriage an unthinkable lapse from virtue, even to herself. This compliance of widows and their families with conservative custom was a hurdle to social change that proved too much even for Vidyasagar's resolute efforts. Nevertheless, the movement he and his supporters set in motion proved fruitful in time, given the powerful support of influential religious bodies such as the Brahmo Samaj of Bengal, the Arya Samaj of northern India, and the Prarthana Samaj of Mumbai.

Niyoga or Levirate

We have just noted above that a married woman's greatest achievement was deemed to be that of ensuring the continuation of her husband's lineage by bearing sons. It was to this end that a particularly obnoxious provision, termed *niyoga,* which is levirate or deputising, was made for a wife who lacked a son because her husband was impotent or because her husband had just died without fathering a son with her. In these very special situations, she might wish or be required by the husband's family to couple with a co-generational male of his family, ideally a younger brother, in the expectation of producing a son. A child thus born would be termed *kṣetraja,* a word that identifies the woman as the *kṣetra,* a field, to be ploughed by a man.

The irony here is that for such a woman, this narrowly purposeful and mechanically executed biological act, whether initiated by her or not, would justify her existence and bring her honour, even though the same act in any context other than that of preserving her husband's lineage would bring her shame. Perhaps the best-known example of *niyoga-vidhi,* the rule of *niyoga,* in early India comes from the *Mahābhārata* in the story of the sage Vyāsa, who is commissioned by the Kuru clan to father sons on Ambikā and Ambālikā, left widowed and childless by the death of King Vicitravīrya, as dictated by their mother-in-law Satyavatī for the preservation of the lineage. The situation repeated itself when Pāṇḍu, Vicitravīrya's brother and successor, instructed his junior queen Mādrī to obtain from his senior queen Kuntī a secret *mantra* to call up gods to father sons with Mādrī because Pāṇḍu could not do so, as he would die if he engaged in sexual union. As common in the *Mahābhārata*'s narrative design of echoing precedents, Kuntī herself had already employed the *mantra* to invoke four different gods for herself, the first when she was still unmarried and a virgin, and later to three others to bear sons. The first birth was concealed by her but the other three occurred with Pāṇḍu's consent, indeed at his urging, and thus constituted an application of the *niyoga-vidhi,* as it was for Mādrī.

It is likely that *niyoga* was a rarely used solution to childlessness and relevant more to the preservation of royal lines than of common folk. Manu was not in favour of *niyoga* and censured it as an unethical and bestial practice invented by uneducated Brahmins during King Vena's rule (*Manu-smṛti,* 9.64–68). His dislike was echoed by many *dharma-śāstra* writers but may have survived for a long time, although it is not the kind of practice that families or individuals are likely to broadcast in the public arena.

The constraints upon women placed by the custom of *satī* and prohibition of widow remarriage were directly related to yet another social custom that was far more extensive than *satī* and thus the cause of far more widespread suffering than either *satī* or compulsory, perpetual widowhood. This was the practice of *bahu-vivāha* or polygamy. A practice not uncommon around the world in cultures other than Hindu, polygamy had been known in the regions occupied by Hindus from the beginning of recorded history. In Vedic society, as in later ones, men were known to have had more than one wife, kings in particular as well as seers and common men. But the extent of the practice then, or in medieval times, was as nothing compared to its spread in the late eighteenth century, especially in Bengal, brought about by a chain of social requirements. In addition to the absolute compulsion to get their daughters married off to avoid the disgrace of having unmarried daughters, families also needed high-caste bridegrooms to gain prestige in order to retain certain social privileges. Well-born grooms being limited in number, families would solicit the marriage of their daughters even to much-married men. Often this required the search for suitable grooms to begin when a girl was still very young, hardly more than a child, and might end with finding only a much older man with multiple wives. The practice was particularly cruel in Bengal, where the grooms highest in demand were men from the uppermost stratum of the upper castes, known as *kulīns* who might have ten, twenty, or even more wives and made marriage a profitable enterprise as they lived off the families of their wives. The wives, of whom only one or two lived with their husband, spent their life in the home of their parents for the most part and received only occasional visits from their husband. The wives were mostly young girls, many of them prepubescent. Child marriage not only resulted in what amounted to child rape and shockingly, early motherhood but also, equally tragically, to early widowhood. It was not until the Child Marriage Restraint Act was passed in 1929, setting the minimum age for marriage at fourteen, that provision was made for protecting girl children.

Polygamy, or *bahu-vivāha,* thus exposed women to a double jeopardy: the husband's death might lead to calls for his wives to perform *satī,* or to live the harsh life of a widow, given the prohibition of remarriage. In reality, it is highly unlikely that multiple *satī* deaths resulted from the death of a single man. But a widow's life was little better than death. Manu did not approve of polygamy and advocated *eka-patnītva,* or monogamy for men, and ruled that a man could take another wife only after his present wife died and was properly cremated (*Manu-smṛti,* 5.166). A widowed man was advised to follow this rule before marrying again, which was necessary to fulfill social obligations and to perform everyday religious rites, for which he would need his wife by his side. Following Manu, Medhātithi, the most respected commentator on the *Manu-smṛti,* similarly denounced polygamy. In theory at least, monogamy has been generally admired, though more as a sign of the virtue of abstention than of concern for women. A case in point is the reputation of Rāma, *maryādā-puruṣottama* or icon of manly virtue, as a paragon of *eka-patnī-vrata* (commitment to one wife) since he never married any woman other than

Sītā. But that did not stop him from inflicting pain and shame upon her. Nevertheless, he does stand out as an exception in a society that expected kings and other men of wealth and power to have more than one wife. Polygamy became almost an epidemic in Hindu society in the nineteenth century, in contrast to the relative rarity of *satī*, and continued into the twentieth until it was banned in 1956 by the Hindu Marriage Act of 1955. As in many communities elsewhere in the world, it persists among Hindus as an underground practice. But at least legislation has set aside the legal and religious sanctions behind the victimisation of women in former times, resulting in a more open and free life for women.

Women's Wealth

An important cause of women's subordination was their economic exploitation. The amount of housework women, young and old, were required to do was of substantial economic benefit to the family. It is immaterial whether this was in the minds of the authorities who prescribed women's confinement within the home and bound to domestic tasks of family; what matters is that restrictions and prescriptions generated free labour, surely a substantial economic benefit and one willingly contributed because its providers were driven by a sense of moral obligation as taught by custom.

Even if women were conscious of their unrewarded labour and resented it, what option did they have? Confined within the home, they had no economic power to gain independence even if independence was on their horizon at all, given the weight of tradition that pressed them into willing compliance. The only wealth women might get would be from inheritance and gifts. Women's inheritance drew constant controversy and created pressures on women who did inherit property to turn it over to males in the family. Not every authority supported

A woman adorned with jewelry.

a woman's inheritance of her father's or husband's property, Baudhāyana being one (*Baudhāyana Dharma-śūtra,* 2.3.46). But other authorities declared in favour of daughters and wives, such as Āpastamba (2.14.4; 2.29.3–4), Gautama (28.21; 24–6), and Yājñavalkya (2.115; 2.123; 124; 2124; 2135). Bṛhaspati appeals to people's sense of justice to protest the denial of a daughter's inheritance rights:

> *aṅgāt aṅgāt sambhavati putravat duhitā nṛṇām |*
> *tasmāt pitṛdhanaṁ tv anyaḥ kathamgṛhṇita mānavaḥ | |*
>
> A daughter is born from [the same] human bodies as a son. Why then should the father's wealth be taken by another person?
>
> (*Bṛhaspati-smṛti* 25.56)

Much later in history Kauṭilya supports women's right of inheritance in the *Artha-śāstra* (3.5.9; 3.5.21). The one kind of wealth to which women had a right came to them when they got married and received gifts of economic value, mainly in the form of jewellery or – less commonly – property. This was known as *strī-dhana,* that is, a wife's treasure, which a woman received upon her marriage from her family according to the *sāstras* and custom, as we learn from the recommendations of powerful authorities such as Manu (9.118,194), Yājñavalkya (2.143–144), Nārada (13.7, 8), and Kauṭilya (3.2.14–41).[21] That this was not just a theoretical right, but an actual one, is seen in references to it in Sanskrit plays, such as *Mṛcchakaṭikam* (Act 3, prose passage after verse 26) and *Cārudattam* (Act 3, prose passage after verse 17). It is doubtful how widespread this benefit was because the woman's family had to be wealthy enough to endow her with any substantial amount of wealth.

---

21 For an exhaustive study of *strī-dhana,* see Subratā Sen, *The Institution of Strīdhana in the Dharmaśāstra* (Calcutta: Sanskrit College,1995).

But in theory, if not always in practice, *strī-dhana* could provide a woman with an opportunity to exert some control over her life. It could also carry some risk. First, overbearing husbands or male relatives could force a woman to part with what was legally hers. Second, a far graver problem arose with the spread of *satī* because persuading a wealthy widow to commit *satī* would be an easy, if heartless, way to gain her property. The reason why *satī* was more prevalent in Bengal than elsewhere in India was that Bengali Hindus followed the *dāya-bhāga* code of law that allowed widows to inherit the property of their husbands, which could make them targets of unscrupulous family members.

SUPPORT

But there again we need to be cautious and not treat these risks as inescapable conditions of every woman's life. *Satī,* for instance, was by no means universal. There was also weighty advice from revered authorities in favour of using reason and good sense, rather than blindly following tradition. Manu, himself a tradition-setter, reminds us that changing times,

Widows practicing lives of devotion in Vrindavan, India, purchase fruit from a local vendor.

especially the long, successive periods known as *yugas,* and their changing needs, must dictate changes in a society's laws and even in the understanding of *dharma*:

> *anye kṛtayuge dharmās tretāyām dvāpare pare |*
> *anye kaliyuge nṛṇām yugahāsānurūpataḥ | |*

> [The religious duties of people] are different in *kṛta-yuga* from *treta-yuga* and [similarly] are different in *dvāpara-yuga* and in *kali-yuga,* proportionately following the ages.

(*Manu-smṛti,* 1.85)

Nārada's argument is very clear when he says that,

> *dharmaśāstravirodhe tu yuktiyukto vidhiḥ smṛtaḥ |*
> *vyavahāro hi valavān dharmas tena avahīyate | |*

> When *dharma* and the *sāstras* clash, a logical discussion is appropriate. [In such cases] custom is of greater force and *dharma* [here: *śāstra*] is overruled.

(*Nārada-smṛiti,* 1.40)

Bṛhaspati's advice is:

> *kevalaṁ śāstram āśritya na kartavyo vinirṇayaḥ |*
> *yuktihīne vicāre tu dharmahāniḥ prajāyate | |*

> One should not act by following *śāstric* injunctions alone. Acting without deliberation only destroys *dharma.*

(*Bṛhaspati-smṛti,* Vyāvahārakāṇḍya, 114)

No advice could be more applicable to the treatment of women caught in the elaborate rules of many of the *dharma-*

śāstras. As we have noted earlier in this chapter, Bṛhaspati and other lawmakers, such as Nārada, offer sensible advice about widow remarriage and inheritance. The sage Gautama warned that Vedic scholars were indeed learned in *dharma* but even they sometimes digressed from its path, causing injustice and misery. For example, the legendary hero Paraśurāma was forced into the crime of killing his mother unjustly suspected of infidelity by his father, the great sage Jamadagni. Clearly, rules and laws must be modified by sober reflection, as must custom and precedent. The fact that this counsel was seldom heeded in the past does not make it invalid, and in modern times relief to women has been urged by questioning the sanctity of traditional *dharma* by leaders of thought like Raja Rammohan Roy and Ishwarchandra Vidyasagar. The guiding principle in determining what is *dharma* was laid down by no less an icon of Hinduism than Lord Kṛṣṇa, whose assertion in *Karṇa Parva* of the *Mahābhārata* we have noted earlier in this chapter:

> *dhāraṇād dharmam ity āhur dharmo dhārayati prajāḥ* |
> *yaḥ syād dhāraṇa-saṁyuktaḥ sa dharmaḥ iti niścayaḥ* | |

> It is said that the word *dharma* comes from *dhāraṇa*,
> sustaining, so *dharma* is what sustains living beings.
> *Dharma* is whatever helps to sustain living beings.
> This is certain.
>
> (*Mahābhārata*, 8.49.50)

Humanity Restored

Ultimately, though, it is not logic and scholarship that bring about change so much as the human instinct of sympathy for victims, the sense of justice intrinsic to humanity, and above all, plain human tenderness. That in reality was how the liberation of Hindu women from centuries of rule-bound suffering came about. Although there is no reason to think that all women, or the majority of women, were enslaved in the past – even the recent past – by strictures against womankind in the name of religion, morality tells us that even one victim is one too many. Why this injustice came to be institutionalised remains a puzzle. How could this have been authorised by a religious culture that placed femininity at the very core of the universe as its creative energy? Since gods and goddesses do not actually intervene in human life, it was by human design that the life of Hindu women came to be damaged, the instinctive patriarchy of Hindu society constructing an ideology to ensure women's subservience. That ideology worked by open repression indeed, but it also succeeded by creating a rhetoric of virtue that made women's disempowerment palatable and even desirable to women. You may well ask, what has religion to do with this?

This is the broad question that reformers of Hinduism began to ask with mounting urgency from the beginning of the nineteenth century and then acted upon the disquiet it caused. Much of the movement towards re-evaluation came from women who, with their experience of female subjugation made explicitly recognisable by modern education and access to public platforms, began to insist on being heard. The founding of girls' schools and women's journals, for instance, in major urban centres such as Calcutta and Bombay among others, made women's status a matter of close attention. The reform of Hindu religious practice and organisation similarly challenged tradition, even as it returned to the essential principles of Hinduism shorn of ritualism and obscurantism. Religious movements by the Brahmo Samaj in Bengal, the Arya Samaj in northern India, the Swaminarayan Sampradaya in Gujarat, and other faith communities brought not only changes in spiritual belief and practice but also deep social changes, including changes aimed at women's release from age-old, dubious religious strictures.

The Inner Power

From our survey of a society claimed to be driven by religion, it may seem that women's liberation must occur by the attrition of Hindu ideas. The exact contrary is the truth. A unique feature of Hinduism is that, at its conceptual core, there exists a woman-centred ideology, while in much of its practice it is heavily reliant on women's mediation between the worshipper and the spirit worshipped. Hindus agree that the creative action of existence is performed by the feminine divine and much of Hindu thought sees that divinity in every woman:

tava svarūpā ramaṇī jagati ācchannavigrahā |

> Every woman, O Goddess, is your very form.
>
> (*Mahānirvāṇa-tantra,* 10.80.1)

On the practical side of Hindu religious life, women have been facilitators of worship practices since Vedic times and despite Brahminical injunctions regarding pollution (e.g., touching holy objects during menstrual periods, participation by widows), worship tasks, such as the washing of ritual vessels, preparing sacred food offerings, decorating the sites of rituals, and so on, are largely performed by women, affirming their rights in a very physical sense. But in addition to these obvious signs of women's religious functions, their spiritual validation is visibly and continually affirmed by one of the most powerful currents of the Hindu religion in the form of Vaiṣṇava belief and practice. For Vaiṣṇavas, nothing can be more efficacious in aspiring to reach God than female love,

Kṛṣṇa and his consort Rādhā.
[Mandala Publishing - B. G. Sharma Collection]

conceived in every imaginable form, from distant longing to erotic desire. This last form of the human quest has not only turned Kṛṣṇa's consort, Rādhā, into a goddess herself but has led some Vaiṣṇava men – leaders of communities, no less – to assume a female persona, judging womanhood to be the dearest to God. How can the devaluation of women withstand the sweep of the instinct of divine love? Nor is this instinct a mere throwback to the past. Whether one is conscious of overt Vaiṣṇava practices or not, one simply cannot remain unaffected by its cultural legacy which dominates in both form and content the music, poetry, and imagery of Hindu beliefs and derived from them, imbuing modern life with the essentiality of women in human life.

Modernity

It is thus from resources within Hindu religious philosophies that women's regeneration as self-determined individuals has been activated as much as from Hindu society's contact with other cultures. The secular counterpart to this development is education, which has drawn as much upon the storehouse of India's multi-faith cultural past as upon exposure to external cultural and political forces. The correlation between women's education and their participation in the cultural, political, and religious life of the Hindus is not accidental; women's advancement was, and still is, higher at urban centres of education than in remote villages. This is being proved increasingly today as we witness the correlation between the rapid spread of women's education in rural areas and their leadership in social action. This is not to say that women in Hindu communities in India and abroad are abandoning their faith or their religious observances as they receive education and embrace modernity. Rather, their lives have come to be enlivened by an easy acceptance of traditional religious faith without surrendering to its former irrelevancies.

Discussion Topic: Women's Life in the Social World

- From what you have learned about the veneration of the Great Goddess in Hindu thought, how would you argue against constraints on women's freedom in traditional Hindu society?

- A question posed in this chapter is: why were rules of conduct drawn up to be applied specially to women. What would be your answer?

- A number of authors of the Hindu *dharma-sūtras* expressed reverence for women; on what grounds?

- What might be the reasons (biological, historical, sociological, security-related) for defining women as weak and incapable of independence?

- Despite widespread denigration of women in Hindu society till modern times, women noted for their religious devotion have always been held in high regard. What does this say about the place of religion in Hindu social culture?

- Is it possible to argue for the legitimacy of *satī*? On what religious or social grounds?

IV
A Room of Their Own: Women's Writings

Enquiry and declaration of belief are at the heart of Hindu religious life, to which women's contribution through Hinduism's long history has been both complex and rich. Beginning in the Vedic age, women have expressed in poetry and song their philosophical perceptions and their quest for the divine, covering a wide range of religious positions. In doing so, women have often flouted oppressive social rules regulating women's lives, thereby enriching Hindu spirituality in general, while asserting the independence of faith, and defining women's sense of their particular, gendered spirituality.

The Heritage

Women's writings in India began many hundreds of years ago with hymns composed by women seers of the Vedic civilisation. At the centre of that civilisation were philosophers given to reflections on the origin and nature of existence, the meaning of reality, and the phenomena of life. In setting up that foundation of religious thought and feeling, women were as engaged as men in giving voice to visions of the unknown powers behind existence. That voice, orally transmitted for centuries, expressed itself through poetry in the form of hymns to gods, goddesses, and personified elements of nature, for it is poetry that can bring within grasp, and bring together, abstract thought and emotional perception. In the Vedic age, poetry was philosophy and women were philosopher-poets. Women of the time could choose a scholarly occupation over domestic life, though they could, and sometimes did, combine the two. Notably learned women were called *brahmavādinīs* – 'those who speak of *brahman*' (the ultimate idea behind everything) – because they were adept in esoteric knowledge and engaged in exploring spiritual and abstruse matters. Some of these women were poets who put their thoughts and views on life in the form of hymns to the unseen and imagined powers of the universe.

The Vedic hymns have survived as the core wealth of the Hindu religion. Hymns by the women poets range from grand spiritual visions to worldly experience set against perceptions of the human–divine connection. One of the most famous of the hymns in the *ṚgVeda* is called the Devī Sūkta (hymn 10.125), composed by a woman in adoration to Devī, or the Great Goddess. Attributed to Vāk or Āmbhṛṇī, daughter of the sage Ambhṛṇa, as we have noted in Chapter 2, this hymn is a bold declaration of Devī's supremacy in the universe, in which the feminine divine that energises and controls the universe is imagined as asserting her powers:

1. I travel with the Rudras and the Vasus, with the Ādityas and All-Gods I wander. I hold aloft both Varuṇa and Mitra, Indra and Agni, and the Pair of Aśvins.
2. I cherish and sustain high-swelling Soma, and Tvaṣṭar I support, Pūṣan, and Bhaga. I load with wealth the zealous sacrificer who pours the juice and offers his oblation.
3. I am the Queen, the gatherer-up of treasures, most thoughtful, first of those who merit worship.

Thus Gods have stablished me in many places with many homes to enter and abide in.

4. Through me alone all eat the food that feeds them,—each man who sees, breathes, hears the word outspoken They know it not, but yet they dwell beside me. Hear, one and all, the truth as I declare it.
5. I, verily, myself announce and utter the word that Gods and men alike shall welcome. I make the man I love exceeding mighty, make him a sage, a Ṛṣi, and a Brahman.
6. I bend the bow for Rudra that his arrow may strike and slay the hater of devotion. I rouse and order battle for the people, and I have penetrated Earth and Heaven.
7. On the world's summit I bring forth the Father: my home is in the waters, in the ocean. Thence I extend o'er all existing creatures, and touch even yonder heaven with my forehead.
8. I breathe a strong breath like the wind and tempest, the while I hold together all existence. Beyond this wide earth and beyond the heavens I have become so mighty in my grandeur.

(*Ṛgveda,* 10.125)[1]

It is not only philosophical statements that distinguish the female voice in the *ṚgVeda* but also expressions of personal crises, such as the plea of the woman ascetic Lopāmudrā to her husband Agastya, also an ascetic, to turn to a fulfilling conjugal life (hymn 1.179). The inclusion of these women's work in this body of sacred literature speaks of the regard that women of ability enjoyed in Vedic society, a recognition that was to disappear later in Hindu social culture. Through the

1 *The Hymns of the Rigveda,* transl. Ralph T. H. Griffith [1889], edited by J. L. Shastri (Delhi: Motilal Banarsidass, 1973).

centuries of Vedic culture though, women took an active part in the intellectual life of their community, notably in religious discussions. The legends of Gārgī and Maitreyī (see Chapter 2) testify to women's participation but if there were literary or philosophical works by them, they have not come down to later ages. From about the beginning of roughly the fourth century CE, women's intellectual presence began to fade because of their ever-increasing confinement within the home to serve their husband and family.

Yet this institutionalised discouragement did not extinguish women's reflections on their life, their emotional experience, or their spiritual needs. In a social system that denied women self-determination and engagement in intellectual work, a small minority found in poetry opportunities for claiming selfhood, at least in some locations of Hindu society. The bulk of these writings was in regional languages, not in Sanskrit, which was the vehicle of works seriously taken by the scholarly establishment of the time. But women writing poetry, some of them on secular themes and some on their religious perceptions, struck a chord deep enough in the public consciousness to have survived the ages, gaining in volume through medieval times. Hindu women's religious poetry and songs from those early days remain a rich heritage not only in the languages in which they wrote but also, increasingly, in translations. The religious instinct is faint, though not extinct, in modern women writers' work, which tends to be mainly secular.

As mentioned above, despite the constriction of self-expression for women in post-Vedic times, women's creativity did not disappear from the Hindu cultural world, although many of the surviving examples are from secular, not religious, literature. The cultural life of the region now called Tamil Nadu was of a very high level indeed at the turn of the first millennium, from about the first century BCE to the third century CE, known as the Sangam era. Numbering about 2000, these secular poems in the Tamil language are either expressions of romantic and erotic love, or of heroic celebration, and these are the interests that mark the 150 or so poems by women poets. We know from several sources that women of early times pursued literary work, one source being a fourteenth-century anthology by Śārṅgadhara, who refers to four women poets by name, praising their learning and poetic ability. The best known of them is Vijjā, also known as Vijjaka or Vidyā, who lived in the eighth or ninth century CE. Remarkable in being written in Sanskrit in an age when women's access to education seems to have been limited, Vijjā's poems on love, nature, and feminine beauty were so highly appreciated in her own time, and later, that many of them were frequently cited by other poets and included in early Sanskrit anthologies. She is also thought to have composed a play called *Kaumudī Mahotsava* in prose with 33 verses included, all of it again on a secular theme. Neither her poetry nor that of any other women writers from the first till the ninth century so far discovered is religious. But their contemporary reputation and survival attest to women's recognition in the public sphere as contributors to public culture. It also shows the continuity of women's writing as a tradition, suggesting that women's presence in creative work may have shrunk but had not disappeared. It is against that reassuring historical reality that we may place the resumption of women's devotional writing.

Regeneration

Although women's religious self-expression seemed to wither after the Vedic age, it is evident that the tradition of female creativity in word and thought survived, because from the sixth century BCE onwards poetry by women begins to reappear, although initially not by Hindu women but by Buddhist nuns. Their poems show them to be women from ordinary walks of life, not of scholarly pedigree, which makes these poems particularly intense expressions of the sense of freedom from social constraints that religion brought them, constraints that applied to women across society, no matter of what religious identity. It is likely that these women poets turned to their Buddhist faith precisely because it offered them the liberation, social as well as spiritual, inherent in the Buddha's message. The first poem here, by a nun named Mutta, shows the sheer joy of release from the restrictions of contemporary society and her thirst for peace, tranquility, and the freedom to seek spiritual solace:

> O free indeed! O gloriously free,
> Am I in freedom from three crooked things:
> From quern,[2] from mortar, from my crookback'd lord.
> Ay, but I am freed from rebirth and from death,
> And all that dragged me back is hurled away.[3]

The freedom she celebrates is as much from obstacles to her spiritual journey as from the 'crooked things', that is, the corruption of humankind's natural, God-given life. A similar yearning for liberation informs a poem by another Buddhist nun called Sumanā:

> Hast thou not seen sorrow and ill in all
> The springs of life? Come thou not back to birth!
> Cast out the passionate desire again to Be
> So shall thou go thy ways calm and serene![4]

2 A stone mill for grinding corn.

3 *Psalms of the Early Buddhists: I. Psalms of the Sisters,* translated by Caroline A. F. Rhys Davids (London: Pali Text Society, 1909), Canto 1, no. 11.

4 *Psalms of the Early Buddhists: I. Psalms of the Sisters,* translated by Caroline A. F. Rhys Davids (London: Pali Text Society, 1909), Canto 1, no.14.

Both poets find worldly life unbearable and find in poetry a way to define their intense hope of escaping to the spiritual life. The distinctive feature of the poetry of the Buddhist nuns, generically called *Therīgāthā,* that is, poetry by *therīs,* or nuns, is this relief at escaping the bonds of domesticity into the tranquility of Buddhist monastic life.

Buddhism offered a spiritual shelter to countless people who found the rule-bound life and excessive ritualism of Hindu society irksome, and that society's increasing regimentation unbearable. As society became more settled towards the end of the Vedic period, around the third–fourth century BCE, its leaders attempted to hold on to its stability by insisting that both personal and public life needed to be ordered, controlled, and stratified. Treatises on conduct and law, known as *dharma-śāstra*s, began to be composed with the intention of codifying the conduct of people. Rules and restrictions on how to live a good and honest life, including the duties required from each caste and their privileges, were laid down in the minutest detail. Distinctions between high and low caste became more and more rigid, with the idea of pollution determining contact between social classes. The Brahminical establishment claimed religious and moral supremacy and their hereditary access to knowledge, one jealously guarded by them, that had allowed Brahmins to lay down injunctions determining private and public conduct as well as relationships. Kings as *kṣatriyas* had the power to rule and the duty to protect society, while the caste of *vaiśyas,* or the merchant class, looked after its wealth. *Śūdras,* who belonged to the lowest caste, were required to serve the three upper castes. As for women of all castes, their lives became more and more confined to looking after their homes and families, their first priority being of service to husbands, fathers, and other dominant males, even though upper caste women had an easier life in material terms. Strictly organised as Hindu society was, with its countless rules and restrictions justified by religious precedence and enforced by tradition, it was ready for change. Change did come for those who followed the Buddha's path. For them it was an escape from a dry, authoritarian system, though the institutional discipline of Buddhism did not make them exactly free individuals. It was an escape to a fresh regime nevertheless.

A New Wave

Escape, however, was not the mainspring of women's poetry as it evolved through the Hindu cultural milieu. As we come down the centuries we discover a yearning for spirituality similar to that in the *Therīgāthā* but with a very great difference: it is not escape from a harsh world that motivates the poetry of Hindu women from medieval times on; quite the opposite: it is the expectation of union with the deity they adore. Even though they sometimes speak of the heavy yoke of social constraints they have to bear, their emphasis is on the hope of finding god as a personal friend and lover. If the poet shows any distress at all, it is the lover's sweet pain at separation from a god with whom she knows her union is certain. This conviction lends to these poems both philosophical depth and emotional intensity. The combination of insight and feeling in these poems becomes the signature mark of women's religious poetry.

Freedom through Surrender

The most powerful impetus in pre-modern times, both to women's religious life and their poetry, as indeed to Hindu social culture in general, came at the beginning of the early Common Era when a new wave of Hindu religious thought swept across India. This was a mode of approaching one's deity founded on the total surrender of one's self, intellectual and emotional, to the deity worshipped. Termed *bhakti,* this absolute immersion of the self in the Godhead was a revolution in the religious as well as social life of Hindus, for it gave rise not only to highly sophisticated theologies pertaining to major deities such as Viṣṇu, Lakṣmī, Śiva, and Kālī but also to an ever-expanding culture of art, music, and literature. *Bhakti* also led – perhaps most noticeably – to social changes in personal and public life. The roots of *bhakti* lie very deep indeed in Hinduism's history. Some historians have detected elements of *bhakti* even in the *ṚgVeda* and more distinctly, in the Upaniṣads, in their theoretical underpinnings.[5] For everyone who ever wanted to find God, *bhakti* opened the way to do so with love (*prema*), devotion (*bhakti*), and total surrender (*prapatti*) to whichever God s/he sought. Its exponents argued that reaching the transcendent and Supreme Being cannot be exclusive to those who tread the path of knowledge. As Rāmānuja, a great eleventh-century *Śrī Vaiṣṇava* philosopher said, if one has *bhakti* or devotion with *prapatti,* that is, total surrender to God, he/she will find the way to reach God. His message was that if a person totally surrenders to God with devotion, his or her knowledge will automatically be the right one, which will lead her/him to proper action. The ethos of *bhakti* had at its centre the conviction of God's love for humanity and equality before God, which put the traditionally disempowered on the same level of social legitimacy as the privileged. Until the recognition of *bhakti* as a burgeoning movement sometime around the sixth to seventh century CE, the increasingly restrictive rules governing the lives of women and *śūdras,* the lowest of the four Hindu castes, had turned them into an underclass, with doors to both education and religion closed to them as independent participants. Women

5 Klaus K. Klostermaier, *A Survey of Hinduism,* 2nd ed. (Albany: SUNY Press, 1994), 222–223.

were forced to depend on men for family and social functions, *śūdras* on the upper castes for common, everyday tasks, while both women and *śūdras* had to pursue their religious life under the direction and permission of Brahmin priests and teachers as interceders. Even so, they could never gain parity. It was this vast underclass to whom *bhakti* brought the possibility of spiritual autonomy. Erasing division on the basis of gender and caste, *bhakti* foregrounded gentleness and love for all, interpreting strength as giving rather than taking, enjoining peace rather than violence.

On the Path of Bhakti

As noted above, the theology of *bhakti* had been initiated many centuries back in the Vedic era. Much more directly and forcefully the *Bhāgavad-Gītā,* composed sometime between the fifth and second centuries BCE, urges devotees to adopt *bhakti* as the preferred path to God. But as a phenomenon of public culture, the *bhakti* movement began in South India from about the fifth century CE, under the influence of two important Hindu sects called the Ālvārs and the Nāyannārs, the first being worshippers of Viṣṇu and the second of Śiva, and their ideas spread very quickly, carried by itinerant poets and singers. Between the sixth and ninth centuries *bhakti* became the most powerful and popular religious movement of Hinduism that surged through India, with particular force in Bengal and eastern India. Though *bhakti* was, and remains, theologically complex, what drew countless adherents to its fold was (and still is) its uncomplicated central tenet that surrender to a personalised deity is the surest path to the deity. A very important addition to that belief is that just by itself, surrender brings spiritual ecstasy. Add that a life in *bhakti* is open to all, and you have the key to understanding the power of *bhakti* as a movement that is at once religious and social. Its impact was assured by the leadership of some of the most charismatic figures of the Hindu community, such as Rāmānuja (eleventh–twelfth century) and Śrī Caitanya (fifteenth–sixteenth century), who gathered vast followings and left an abiding legacy of Hindu religiosity. It has also influenced, through the centuries, every branch of Hindu culture and conduct, from poetry to cinema, dress code to poster art. The most potent reason for the spread and survival of *bhakti* was that it embraced all, with no regard for caste, gender, or social standing set by education, financial status, family pedigree, and public position. Knocking down all barriers to a life in religion, *bhakti* made everybody equal before God. Held in that empowering embrace, women could act and speak as independent individuals and many did, some of them by disregarding all social conventions of relationships, speech, and dress, some by poetic or musical self-expression. In that climate of liberated and authenticated selfhood, women's quest for *finding* God went beyond philosophical debate to emotional assertions of *claiming God as a lover*. That is a state of consciousness for which poetry and music are the best tools of expression, and that is the tool we find women wielding within the world of *bhakti*.

The Poets and Their Poetry

One of the earliest poets of that world was Kārāikkāl Āmmāiyār, a Tamil poet who lived in Kārāikkāl in South India, sometime between the fifth and the seventh century CE. Even in her own time she came to be recognised as one of the sixty principal devotees of Śiva, known as the *Nāyannārs*. All her surviving poems articulate her yearning for Śiva and her efforts to transcend the barriers of worldly affairs. Recognising the limitations of the flesh, including her own beauty, she wished to gain an unobstructed view of the reality of the Lord divested of ceremony. A passionate devotee of Śiva, she reached beyond the vision of ordinary mortals limited to material forms and saw the truth beyond mere appearance. Material existence and social life are distracting illusions; finding herself estranged from her husband, she begs of her Lord:

> So I pray to Thee that the flesh of my body, which has been sustaining beauty for his sake, may now be removed from my physical frame and I may be granted the form of the ghosts which dance round Thee with devotion.[6]

Believing that Śiva's unkempt looks had to be penetrated by the power of the devotee's love for him to reveal his majestic beauty, she said:

> They who are incapable of understanding His real nature make fun of Him. They see only His fine form besmeared with ashes and bedecked with a garland of bones like a ghost.[7]

Looking beyond the immediate experience of the world, which she understood to be illusory, she perceived the beauty of her lord Śiva beneath his beggarly exterior. As a way to seek union with him, she thought of herself as Kālī, who is an intrinsic part of Śiva, seeing behind her threatening form divine beauty and grace. Kārāikkāl Āmmāiyār thought her own identification with Kālī would ensure for her Śiva's love.

A poet with a much greater body of work to her name who lived around the seventh or eighth century CE was Āṇṭāl, a major voice in early medieval Tamil culture. Regarded as one of twelve *ālvārs* or models of Viṣṇu *bhakti*, she is now worshipped

6 S. Pillai, 'Karaikkal Ammaiyar', in *Women Saints of East and West: Śrī Sāradā Devī (the Holy Mother) Birth Centenary Memorial* (London: Ramakrishna Vedanta Centre, 1955), 18–19.
7 Pillai, 'Karaikkal Ammaiyar', 21.

as a consort of Kṛṣṇa in the great temple at Srirangam temple.[8] Beginning a life of total devotion to Kṛṣṇa as a very young girl, Āṇṭāl remained unmarried because she considered herself a bride of Kṛṣṇa. In some of her poems she portrays herself as a maiden eager for union with Kṛṣṇa. In others she imagines herself as his bride and recalls, in erotic imagery, the joy of her mystical union with him. These two forms of her devotion fall into two distinct groups of short poems that make up consecutive parts of a total scheme of devotion over a two-month period. The first part, called *Tiruppāvai,* represents the early phase of her spiritual journey that matches a Tamil tradition of the *pāvai* vow observed in the month of Mārkali (mid-December to mid-January). The vow is made by young girls to ensure their happy marriage, for which they prepare themselves by self-purification. They invite their desired one by making idealised clay images and singing songs of invitation and praise. This format lends itself well to Āṇṭāl's yearning for her Lord, especially as the ritual ends in celebrating the arrival of the beloved – which in her case means a mystical experience of the Lord's presence. In Āṇṭāl's *Tiruppāvai* poems we encounter just this sense of self-preparation and joy, as these examples show:

> The month of Mārkali's full moon is here
> This auspicious morning.
> O maidens bejeweled!
> Come out,
> Those who wish to bathe in this water clear.
> O sweet maidens
> Of blessed cowherd clan!
>
> Nanda's son,
> Cruel as a sharp spear,

8 Vidya Dehejia, *Āṇṭāl and Her Path of Love* (Albany: SUNY Press, 1990), 2.

Young lion,
Child of Yaśodā of loving eyes,
With his dark body and
Visage like the Sun and the Moon,
Rosy-orbed One!
Will fulfill our desire.

Nārāyana himself has offered us his drums,
To sing his praise
And gain the world's applause.[9]

The second group of Āṇṭāl's poems is the *Nācciyār Tirumoli* set, which imitates a worship vow just like the first part. The celebration it purportedly recreates is a follow-up of the *Tiruppāvai* ritual vow. It takes place in the month of Tai (mid-January to mid-February) immediately after the month of Mārkali, which is dedicated to the *Tiruppāvai Tirumoli.* Tai is a period of prayer and worship that expresses the devotee's anguish at the uneasy feeling that the Lord, whose presence had been felt at the end of *Tiruppāvai,* is no longer close. As Āṇṭāl recalls the joys of her union with her Lord, the pain of separation becomes the harder for her to bear. This sway between remembered joy and present pain she understands and expresses in the human idiom of love and physical desire. Speaking as a bride separated from her spouse, she embodies her love in highly sexual imagery that humanises God and marks the speaker's spiritual approximation of the divine as a concrete experience rather than as an abstraction. Further examples show how the spiritual and the material meet in Āṇṭāl's imagination:

---

9 P. S. Sundaram, *Poems of Andal* (Bombay: Ananthacharya Indological Research Institute, 1987), *Tiruppāvai,* verse 1, p. 2.

O Manmatha, I invoke you!
With sugarcane and pressed rice
Cooked in palm-sugar.
I worship you
With sacred hymns in your praise.

Bless me,
So that Trivikrama,
Who spanned the world three times,
May caress with his sacred hands
My breasts and my waist
With love,
Granting me fame on earth
And glory eternal![10]

O cool clouds
From the conch-filled ocean
The lotus-eyed Venkata churned,
Lay at His feet
My humble plea –
Tell him:
Enter me
Only for a day,
Wipe away the saffron
On my breasts.
I will then live.[11]

The tradition of *bhakti* developing in the poetry of the women we have noted so far surged forward in both poetic subtlety and complex mysticism with Ākkā Mahādevī (1130–1160) who came from Karnataka. In her works, written in Kannada, we see not only a fervent spirituality but also an

10 Sundaram, *Poems of Andal, Nācciyar Tirumoli*, hymn 1, verse 7, p. 41.
11 Sundaram, *Poems of Andal, Nācciyar Tirumoli*, hymn 8, verse 7, p. 104.

assertion of female selfhood rooted in her devotion to Śiva, which made her free from the roles that traditional society ordained for women. A follower of the Śaivite Vīraśaiva sect, she was initiated into Śiva worship at the age of ten and she took that event as the moment of her real birth. She betrothed herself to Śiva and rejected all other claims upon her attention, even though many human lovers pursued her with urgent suits. She was finally married to Kauśika, a king who had fallen in love with her, but Ākkā never accepted that marriage as real, for, apart from being merely human, the king was an unbeliever and therefore ill-qualified to be a righteous husband. When Kauśika attempted to force her into submission, she left him in disavowal of her marriage as a gesture not only of defiance to his power, but also of social norms. So strong was her conviction of being beyond the rule of the human world that she wandered the land naked, with her body covered in nothing but her tresses, walking towards Kalyāṇa, a centre of Vīraśaiva saints, where she was not accepted till after she extensively debated noted saints, such as Āllāma. When Āllāma asked, 'Why take off clothes, as if by that gesture you could peel off illusions? And yet robe yourself in tresses of hair? If so free and pure in heart, why replace a sari with a covering of tresses?' Ākkā answered, 'Till the fruit is ripe inside/the skin will not fall off'.[12] At the end of this ordeal by disputation, she was accepted in the company of the sages. What this exchange shows is a remarkable mix of Ākkā's courage of conviction, her power of philosophical perception, and her command over metaphoric invention.

Her induction into the company of sages gave her the independence from social restrictions she needed, allowing her to wander about in search of Śiva, whom she is thought to have found on Śrīśaila, the Holy Mountain. The poems she composed throughout her quest capture her yearning for the

12 A. K. Ramanujan, *Speaking of Śiva* (London: Penguin, 1973), 112.

Lord in the idiom of traditional love poetry, using the three main forms of love recognised in formal literature. The first, love forbidden, is expressed thus:

> I have Māyā for mother-in-law;
> the world for father-in-law;
> three brothers-in-law, like tigers;
>
> and the husband's thoughts
> are full of laughing women:
> no god, this man.
>
> And I cannot cross the sister-in-law.
>
> But I will
> give this wench the slip
> and go cuckold my husband with Hara, my lord.
>
> My mind is my maid:
> by her kindness, I join
> my Lord,
> my utterly beautiful Lord
> from the mountain-peaks
> my lord as white as jasmine,
> and I will make Him
> my good husband.[13]

The second form of love poetry, about love in separation, is adopted in the following passage:

> If he has to go to the battlefield
> I can understand and be quiet.
> But when he is here on my palm
> And within my heart,

13 Ramanujan, *Speaking of Śiva*, verse 328, p. 141.

How can I bear it,
If he does not speak to me?
If the memory of love
Does not make Cenna Mallikārjuna love me,
How will I bear it?[14]

This cry of anguish at separation is followed by the third kind of love poetry, about love in union:

Behold love's wonderful ways!
When you shoot your arrow
Take care to plant it well
So that the feather does not show
When you hug a body, bones crack and crumble,
Join but the joint must not show –
How wonderful then is the love of Cenna Mallikārjuna![15]

Applying the traditional imagery of Indian love poetry to the experience of spiritual longing and consummation, Ākkā metaphorises the phases of human love as steps in a mystical approach to the divine, drawing her images from nature, birds, and beasts. As in secular love poetry, Ākkā's divine lover is an aesthetic construction, her very own Cennamallikārjuna or Lord White as Jasmine. By the time this extraordinary woman died in her twenties, she had given voice to the widest imaginable range of the human yearning for the divine in humanly understandable rhetoric in countless poems. Their brilliance, evident even in the small selection below, deserves close attention:

Like a silkworm that secretes her dwelling,
Wrapping herself tightly

14 Armando Menezes and S. M. Angadi, transl., *Vacanas of Akka Mahadevi* (Dharwar: Shri Manohar Appasaheb Adke, 1973), verse 60, p. 18.
15 Menezes and Angadi, *Vacanas of Akka Mahadevi*, verse 43, p. 14.

With her body's thread and dies,
I am dying, pining for my heart's desire.
Help me, O Lord, cut all my greed,
Show me the way to you,
Cenna Mallikārjuna![16]

You can confiscate the riches in hand,
But how can you take away the body's glory?

You can strip off clothes from the body
But how can you take away nothingness
That wraps around the body?

For one who adorns herself
With the morning light of
Lord Cenna Mallikārjuna,
Shedding all shame,
Where is the need for cover and veil?[17]

Why must I be a puppet
Of this world? A cask of illusion?
A worldly mansion peopled by passions,
Leaking at its foundation?
With your finger you may
Feel and squeeze the fig
But can you eat it?

. . . . .

O Cenna Mallikārjuna, take me
With my faults and all.[18]

---

16 Menezes and Angadi, *Vacanas of Akka Mahadevi*, verse171, p. 68.

17 Menezes and Angadi, *Vacanas of Akka Mahadevi*, verse 146, p. 62.

18 Menezes and Angadi, *Vacanas of Akka Mahadevi*, verse 139, p. 60.

> I love the beautiful One,
> The formless One.
>
> He has no death nor decay
> The beautiful, the fearless, the dauntless One,
> Beyond birth is He . . .
>
> Cenna Mallikārjuna is my Lord –
> Take these mortal husbands
> And feed them to the fire in the kitchen.[19]

Deeply feminine in attitude and voice, these poems stand as testaments to the power of women's liberation from social bonds that the spiritual assurance of *bhakti* brought.

We have seen that from the earliest times, it was in poetry that Hindu seers and devotees had voiced their sense of the divine, as indeed we find in other religions, Christianity being an obvious example. For Hindus, by the middle ages the use of poetry had become central to religious life, not only as a celebration of faith but equally as a personal instrument for unveiling the divine presence. Poets like Kabīr and Sūrdās enriched literature as much as religious faith, especially by their insistence on the authenticity of a personal relationship with the object of one's devotion, rather than through priests or institutional interceders. Of no less importance as contributors to this tradition of elevated poetry are the women whose works we have looked at. One more to be added is a *Śaiva* poet, as Mahādevī Ākkā was, but from a later time, a different place, a different language, and a different philosophical school. This was the Kashmiri poet Lāllā Yogeśvarī (1320–1392), also known as Lāl Ded. At the age of 24, her sufferings at the hands of her husband and in-laws drove her to leave her family and choose the life of a renunciate, into which she was initiated by a Kashmiri Śaivaite guru. A learned woman,

19 Menezes and Angadi, *Vacanas of Akka Mahadevi*, verse 51, p. 16.

she combined intellectual devotionalism with the esotericism of tāntric yoga, and this philosophical orientation led her to employ the technical language of monistic *vedānta* with that of tāntric philosophy, resulting in poetry of a layered sensibility. Like Mahādevī Ākkā, Lāllā became a mendicant, similarly dispensing with her clothes and attaining *mokṣa* (spiritual liberation) early in the course of her long life. A *nirguṇa bhakta,* that is, the devotee of an abstraction rather than a personified divinity, she distinguished herself as a philosopher by seeking union, not with a personal deity, but with an abstract principle or Being, with which she claimed her oneness. Because of this philosophical position, her poetry deals more with abstractions than with emotional experience. Her sense of Śiva as an idea, rather than a bodily presence, invests all her poetry with the excitement of philosophical thought rather than that of personal relationship, as these examples illustrate:

> Let Him bear the name of Śiva, or of Keśava,
> or of the Jina, or of the Lotus-born Lord, –
> whatever name he may bear, –
> May he take from me, sick woman that I am,
> the disease of the world,
> Whether He be he, or he, or he, or he.[20]

> He who hath deemed another and himself as the same,
> He who hath deemed the day (of joy) and the night (of sorrow) to be alike,
> He whose mind hath become free from duality,
> He, and he alone, hath seen the Lord of the Chiefest of gods.[21]

---

20 *Lāllā-Vākyāni,* edited by George Grierson and Lionel D. Barnett (London: Royal Asiatic Society, 1920), verse 2, p. 30.
21 *Lāllā-Vākyāni,* ed. Grierson and Barnett, verse 29, p. 27.

> Look upon thy mind alone as the ocean of existence.
> If thou restrain it not, but let it loose, from its rage will issue angry words, like wounds caused by fire.
> If you weigh them in the scales of truth, their weight is naught.[22]

> Lord, I have not known myself
> Or other than myself.
> Continually have I mortified this vile body.
> That Thou art I, that I am Thou, that these are joined in one
> I knew not.
> It is doubt to say, 'Who am I?' and 'Who are Thou?'[23]

This is poetry of the most profound philosophical perception. The intensity here is not emotional, not the ecstasy that Āṇṭāl or Ākkā feel just at the thought of union with the Divine Beloved. Lāllā's joy is cerebral, gained by penetrating the veil of illusory difference between herself and her Lord to discover the philosophical truth of oneness with 'whatever name he may bear'. Lāllā offers a confident philosophical assurance that adds a new dimension to women's devotional poetry.

Personal ecstasy, however, remains the dominant tone in that tradition of poetry. Perhaps the best-known representative of that tradition is Mīrābāī, a princess from Rajasthan who encountered relentless persecution from her husband for her absolute absorption in the contemplation of Kṛṣṇa. Her life is in itself a poetic narrative of high romance. Legend has her married to the crown prince of Mewar, but for her it was a

22 *Lāllā-Vākyāni*, ed. Grierson and Barnett, verse 12, p. 45.
23 *Lāllā-Vākyāni*, ed. Grierson and Barnett, verse 5, p. 29.

marriage only in name, for she thought of herself as married to Kṛṣṇa, whom she addressed as Giridhārī Nāgara. Mīrā refused to pay obeisance to her mother-in-law and even to the dynastic deity, which drew upon her head endless torment. For instance, her sisters-in-law tried to stop her from meeting *sādhus* as an activity improper to her birth and her married status. When her husband failed to turn her from her allegiance to Giridhārī Nāgara, his notion of honour drove him to try to kill her on two occasions. But according to legend, each time Kṛṣṇa's grace miraculously saved her. Mīrā spent most of her adult life in worship and devotion, eventually leaving Mewar and travelling east as a pilgrim to places sanctified by Kṛṣṇa's presence. It is not known for certain when and how she died but numerous legends about her tell how, when she was being forced back to her husband's domain, she entered Kṛṣṇa's temple and never reappeared, for she had been taken to his bosom by Kṛṣṇa himself.

Mīrā's poetical works consist of songs addressed to Giridhārī and these songs comprise, with those of Kabīr, Tulasīdās and Sūrdās, almost the entire body of Hindusthani (the music of northern India) devotional music. Since Mīrā thought of Kṛṣṇa as a *saguṇa* being, an embodied divinity, her imagination endowed him with personal form and character, much of it playful. In her songs she sees herself in a relationship with Kṛṣṇa as a real person, whose presence is always actual, immediate, and intimate, a familiar being whom she places in every kind of loving relationship of domesticity, imagining herself variously as his bride, friend, and mother. In place of the passionate fervour of Āṇṭāl or philosophical brilliance of Lāllā, here we have a gentle though all-consuming love that seeks only the submersion of the self in the divine, which she understands as the essence of love. This absorption in love is perhaps the reason why Mīrā's songs continue to move

A statue of Mīrābāī at Chittorgarh Fort in Rajasthan, India.

scholars and common people alike, filling them with a promise of God's accessibility, as these examples will show:

> I am dyed in love for the Dark One, Rāṇā, dyed in love for the Dark One,
> Clapping to the beat of drums, I dance before the sages.
> My mother said I was mad to be in love, for Śyām's love is fleeting.
> I drank the cup of poison the Rāṇā sent me, asking no questions.
> Mīrā's Lord is the handsome Giridhārī whose love holds true through the ages.[24]

> The Bhil woman brought the good, sweet plums, tasting each first.
> The devout woman said, 'She has not a grain of beauty,
> This low-caste, low-born woman in unsightly rags.'
> Rāma took the soiled fruits, knowing they were marks of love,
> For he knows nor high nor low, only that she has the taste for love.
> What Veda has she studied? Yet in a flash she mounted a chariot
> Bound for a swing in heaven put up by Hari just for her.
> Your servant Mīrā is like all who have such love.
> My Lord, Saviour of the fallen, take unto you the cowherd girl of Gokula.[25]

---

24 Bhagwandas Tiwari, ed., *Mīrā kī Prāmānik Padāvalī* (Allahabad: Sahitya Bhavan, 1974), verse 48, p. 201.

25 Krishna Deo Sharma, ed., *Mīrābaī Padāvalī* (Delhi: Regal Book Depot, 1972), verse 185, p. 343.

Let us go to that unreachable land that death fears to see,
To that lake brimming with love, on which swans play,
And the company of sages and saints brings wisdom,
The mind alight as it cleaves to the Dark One,
Wearing ankle bells of pure thought, all dance in contentment
And decked in golden bracelets practice the sixteen arts of delight,
In love with the Dark Lord, turning away from all others.[26]

THE HERITAGE

Even on a quick reading of the poems quoted here it becomes clear that their authors were not only superb writers but also original thinkers, both philosophically and socially. Their deep spirituality apart, their assertion of independence from all dictates of society marks them out as revolutionary personalities. Whether there were others like them is impossible to tell. The real extent of written work by women in India has not been mapped, although the anthology of women's writing in India by Susie Tharu and K. Lalita is a pioneering effort of very great value.[27] But nobody has collected – nor is it feasible to do so – the poems, stories, and essays by women written for their private circles, such as in my own family. Nevertheless, what is available in the public domain is impressive enough, for the poets discussed above created a rich tradition of spirituality that is distinctive in its

26 Sharma, *Mīrābaī Padāvalī*, verse 192, p. 350.

27 Susie Tharu and K. Lalita, eds. *Women Writing in India, 600 BC to the Present. Vol. I, 600 BC to the Early Twentieth Century* (New York: Feminist Press, 1991).

femininity of style and feeling. To their company we may add others who are less widely read, such as Jānābāi and Bahinābāi from Maharashtra,[28] Ātukuri Mollā from Andhra, Gaṇgāsatī and Ratanbāī from Gujarat, Rāmi and Candrāvatī from Bengal.

In their and other women's poetry we find an ever-widening variety of experience, perception, and poetic strategy as we travel down the ages, their work often coloured by their response to the restraints upon women's lives and their pain. Good examples are poems by the early Marathi poet Jānābāi (1298–1350) and by a much later one, Bahinābāi (1628–1700), who also wrote in Marathi using the *abhang* form of lyric. Jānābāi comforts herself by recalling the common state of the world:

> Let me not be sad because I am born a woman
> In the world; many saints suffer in this way[29]

Not much of Jānābāi's poetry is extant but the little that we have shows her range of thought and her passion for Kṛṣṇa. Here is an example of her absorption in the thought of the divine:

> What I eat is divine
> What I drink is divine
> My bed is also divine
> The divine is here, and it is there
> There is nothing empty of divine
> Jani says – Vithabai has filled
> everything from the inside out.[30]

---

28 This Bahinābāi is not to be confused with the later poet Bahinābāi Chaudhari (1880–1951).

29 Tharu and Lalitha, *Women Writing in India*, 82.

30 Rajeshwari V. Pandharipande, 'Janabai: A Woman Saint of India', in Sharma, ed., *Women Saints in World Religions* (Albany: SUNY Press, 2000), 161.

In her passionate attachment to Kṛṣṇa, she casts off all consideration of what society might say:

> Cast off all shame,
> and sell yourself
> in the marketplace;
> then alone
> can you hope
> to reach the Lord.
> Cymbals in hand,
> a veena upon my shoulder,
> I go about;
> who dares to stop me
> The pallav of my sari
> falls away (A scandal!);
> yet will I enter
> the crowded marketplace
> without a thought.
> Jani says, My Lord,
> I have become a slut
> to reach Your home.[31]

This intensity of love places Jānābāi in the company of poets such as Āṇṭāl, Ākkā, and Mīrā, marking so absolute a surrender to the Beloved a characteristic of women's poetry in the idiom of *bhakti* and the poets themselves as social rebels.

Bahinābāi, however, strikes a different set of notes, some critical of society and some utterly submissive to convention. She reacts to strictures on women sharply:

> (1) The Vedas cry aloud, the Purāṇas shout that no good comes of a woman. (2) Now I in the natural way have a woman's body. What means

31 Tharu and Lalitha, *Women Writing in India*, 83.

> then have I to acquire the supreme spiritual riches [*paramārtha*]? (3) The characteristics (of a woman) are foolishness, selfishness, seductiveness, and deception. All connection with a woman is disastrous. (Such is their opinion.) (4) Says Bahiṇā, 'If a woman's body brings disaster, what chance is there for her to acquire in this life the supreme spiritual riches?'[32]

In despair she cries out:

> 64 (1) I wonder what sin I committed in a former birth as a human that in this birth I should be so separated from God [*Purushottama*]? (2) I am born with a human body, but in the form of a woman. It is evident that the innumerable sins (from my former birth) I have committed, have now come to their fruitage. (3) (As a woman) I have no right to the reading of the *Vedas*. The Brahmans have made a secret of the *Gāyatrī mantra.* (4) I am told that I must not pronounce the sacred '*Om*'. I must not listen to the philosophical ideas. (5) I must not speak to anyone about them. My husband was Jamadagni (if I did those things). (6) Says Bahinī, 'My soul is very downcast. God has no compassion on me.'[33]

Surprisingly, for a woman who feels so strongly about the institutionalised injustice against women, in another poem she sets aside her protest against the denigration of women to proclaim her acceptance of the traditional role of a wife, declaring her devotion to her husband who is her god:

---

32 Justin E. Abbott, *Bahiṇābāi* (Poona: Scottish Mission Industries, 1929), *Abhaṅga* 63, p. 39.

33 Abbott, *Bahiṇābāi*, 39.

> (5) If my heart wanders from my husband, then my abode will be hell. (6) If a day should pass without seeing my husband, that in itself will be a great heap of sins. (7) Says Bahiṇā, 'His commands are my law. My Svāmi is himself the Eternal Brahma.'[34]

Although this statement arises from the conventions of patriarchy, it nevertheless valorises itself in a religious context when it equates husband and *brahman*. If this is social orthodoxy, it still justifies itself by drawing upon a fundamental source of faith, faith in *brahman* as the Eternal Good.

Though less familiar than these poets, many other women poets can be named, such as – to name a very few – Gaṅgāsatī from Gujarat (twelfth–fourteenth century), Ratanbāi also from Gujarat (twelfth–fourteenth century), and Rāmi from Bengal (fifteenth century). They were talented poets of great faith, well known in the regions of their birth but not all over India.[35] Gaṅgāsatī was fortunate to be married to a man of faith and they spent their lives joined in worship. When her husband decided to end his life by entering into *samādhi*, or meditative trance, she wanted to join him but was advised by him to stay behind and teach their daughter-in-law Pānābāi to follow the right path. How well she performed that duty shows in the following lines:

> Devote yourself to God, O Pānābāi!
> Be faithful to your words;
> Here's a word of advice from Gaṅgāsatī
> Submit yourself wholly to the true Guru –
> The Meru mountain may be swayed, but not the mind of Harijan.[36]

34 Abbott, *Bahiṇābāi*, *Abhaṇga* 37, p. 26.

35 See Tharu and Lalita, *Women Writing in India*, 82–90.

36 Tharu and Lalita, *Women Writing in India*, 89. The term 'Harijan' is used here to denote a devotee of God in the form of Hari, i.e., Kṛṣṇa. It is not to be taken here in the sense of low-caste people, as used by Mahatma Gandhi.

Another medieval poet from Gujarat was Ratanbāi, most of whose work is lost, but people of Gujarat are familiar with those that still exist. A woman of low caste who was abandoned then reclaimed by her husband, Ratanbāi led a life of hardship but sought the solace of worship. Similarly of low-caste origin, herself a washer-woman, Rāmi from Bengal was in love with the famous *bhakti* poet Caṇḍīdāsa and spent her life in serving him. The earliest known Bengali woman poet in the devotional idiom, she also wrote love poems to Caṇḍīdāsa, discovered only after her death.[37]

Speaking of the World

Especially in these comparatively minor women poets, we find a sense of their hard life made bearable by the comforts of faith. It is useful to set side by side Jānābāi and Bahiṇābāi, one from the thirteenth century, the other from the seventeenth, to make the point that a gap of several hundreds of years did not dull women's sense of the injustice the world meted out to women, a condition of being women that they attempted to overcome by writing about their faith – even about its weakness. They and other women poets were only too aware of the heavy hand of society on women, though they may not have cared what society thought, having secured their personal freedom by turning society's strictures irrelevant. But if we were to shift some of these poems from a religious to a secular framework, they might well be taken to articulate resistance to the gender typology that characterises one trend of Hindu thought. This is not to claim that these poems should be taken as gestures of conscious defiance; but it cannot be denied that they are keenly aware of a social system tilted against women. This awareness underlies some of women's poetry in the religious vein.

37 Tharu and Lalitha, *Women Writing in India*, 84–87.

One such poet who bridged the religious and the secular was Ātukuri Mollā, an early sixteenth-century woman of the *lingayat* potter caste, born to parents who were devotees of Śrīkaṇṭha Malleśvara. Mollā – the name stands for jasmine – accepted a challenge from Brahmins and composed, in five days, a Telugu version of the *Rāmāyaṇa* in 138 stanzas spread over six chapters. Secure in her devotion, she asserts her faith both in her lord and her poetic ability in these lines:

> Untrained though,
> In composing poems and epics
> In mastering lexicons and rules
> I do write poems
> By the grace of the famous Lord
> Sri Kantha Mallesa.[38]

In these lines Mollā declares her faith at the same time as she claims her place in the community of letters. When she legitimates herself by invoking 'the famous Lord', she is not expressing the same kind of spiritual passion as we have found in the poetry of Āṇṭāl, Ākkā, and Mīrā. Rather, she is adopting the rhetoric of religion to set up her personal authority against the strictures of her would-be social masters. The poetic exchange here is not so much between deity and devotee as between the author and an overbearing society.

Like Mollā, another woman poet, also the composer of a *Rāmāyaṇa*, founded her work on the injustice that the world visits upon women. Candrāvatī, a poet from sixteenth-century Bengal, suffered a devastating betrayal by a man and sought solace in recounting the sacred lives of Rāma and Sītā.[39]

38 Tharu and Lalitha, *Women Writing in India*, 97.

39 Her life story, 'Candrāvatī', by Nayanchand Ghosh is included in *Maimansiṁha Gītikā*, ed. Sukhamay Mukhopadhyay (Calcutta: Bharati Book Stall, 1970).

But instead of a religious celebration, her *Rāmāyaṇa* turned into a dirge for women. Sītā is the victim of the most ungodlike jealousy, suspicion, and anger of Rāma, while Rāvaṇa's queen Mandodarī suffers from his predatory sexuality, and this seems to be women's lot in a world supposed to be protected and regulated by a just god. Candrāvatī points no accusing finger at Rāma whose divinity she accepts; she blames none but her own fate:

> What shall I say about my fate, what story shall I narrate? The Lord of fate created me a sufferer from birth.[40]

It should not be hard to see that by shifting the responsibility for Sītā's suffering from Rāma to some distant 'Lord of Fate', Candrāvatī makes Rāma's betrayal (surely an echo of the betrayal she herself had suffered) all the more evident. Her poem works within the conventions of a sacred legend but that legend is systematically undercut by the experience that the world's protector god not only leaves women unprotected but actively causes their misery.

Modern Times

The liberation that *bhakti* brought to the Hindu world has remained a permanent strength of Hinduism. But the potential for spiritual liberation is perhaps more an undercurrent than an overt ideology. Besides, the practice of *bhakti* in itself has gone through institutionalisation and varieties of ritualism, requiring surrender not only to the deity worshipped but also

---

40 *Prācīna Pūrvavaṅga Gītikā*, ed. Kshitish Moulik (Calcutta: Firma K. L. Mukhopadhyaya, 1970), p. 307, my translation. For a translation of Candrāvatī's *Rāmāyaṇa*, see Mandakranta Bose and Sarika Priyadarshini Bose, *A Woman's Rāmāyaṇa: Candrāvatī's Bengali Epic* (London and New York: Routledge, 2013).

to sectarian discipline. Nevertheless, it is probably fair to say that strict as the discipline of a sect might be, it is willingly accepted by its adherents, although there may be exceptions. The spiritual pull of *bhakti*, however, has retained its force because of the solace it promises, whether one actually embraces it fully or not. One may see the power of *bhakti* in the popularity of *bhakti* music such as Mīrā's *bhajans*, of images of deities as well as of traditional symbols of *bhakti* such as Rādhā-Kṛṣṇa icons, and portraits of Tulsidas, to cite only some of its many cultural signifiers.

The assurances of *bhakti*, however, have not obscured the sense of worldly life in Hindu women's writings, especially as we travel down the ages. On the contrary, in the poetry of Āṇṭāl, Ākkā, Jānābāi, Candrāvatī, and many more, the obstacles women face in their social life and religious observances are only too keenly marked. In addition, it is important to note that belief systems other than *bhakti* remain part of Hinduism's spiritual capital, as indeed they have through the ages. A variety of intellectually rigorous, sometimes sceptical enquiries into the nature of the divine have shaped Hindu religiosity. For instance, it is apparent that Mīrā's total absorption in her devotion to a literally envisaged Giridhārī Nāgara is as authentic as Lāllā's metaphysical perception of the unpersonified Infinite. In legitimising this culture of difference, the contribution of women has been of immense value.

Sadly and surprisingly, this particular cultural capital of Hinduism, the imaginative religiosity of women, seems to have stopped growing after medieval times. As we have seen, till the late medieval era, women poets found themselves elevated above all worldly concerns by their belief in a chosen deity, which was so all-consuming that it expressed itself as a passionate love. There may be historical causes of the weakening of that fervor, one perhaps being the increasing political instability of India with the unraveling of Hindu political power and the scattering, or even absence, of influential religious leaders. Another reason for women's absence from the religious scene was undoubtedly their increasing incarceration within the home and discouragement of their independent self-expression. It is not accidental that in the Tharu-Lalita anthology of women's writing in India, there is a gap of a full century between the last late medieval poet Bahiṇābāi (1628–1700) and the first modern one, Tarigonda Vengamamba (c. 1800–1866). And Tarigonda herself seems to be a lone representative of the tradition of worship we have been considering. She did indeed write in the idiom of Āṇṭāl and Ākkā, as these lines show:

> And so again, fool that I am,
> I believe the charming rogue
> And suffocate him with my kisses.
> And as I lie in love-drugged sleep,
> He leaves me, as is his wont,
> For another bed.
> Tell me, my dear, where Tarigonda's Lord is now.[41]

But even here, though we must grant the poet some authenticity of feeling, we encounter imitation rather than originality. Hereafter little, if any, religious instinct appears in women's writing as an animating power.

It is not that we find current magazines or publications entirely lacking in religious poetry by women. But religious literature today merely reiterates hand-me-down religious sentiments, rephrases traditional prayers, and conveys nothing noticeably original in thought or feeling. A personally derived spirituality is hard to discover. What we find in great quantity, in fact increasingly so, is critical and scholarly writing on

41 Tharu and Lalitha, *Women Writing in India*, 125.

the Hindu religion and comparative religion of a very great variety by a great number of women, not many of whom are themselves Hindu. In terms of scholarship that identity is irrelevant but what does matter is that scholarship has not brought women's creative vision of the Godhead back to imaginative and emotional life. This may well be a temporary suspension of spiritual creativity; predictions of the death of God have been many and so far have proved to be premature. So have declarations of the irrelevance of spiritual individuals in a materialistic world. Perhaps even as we read these lines somewhere in the world a Mīrā or an Ākkā is tuning her *vīṇā*.

Discussion Topic: Women's Writings

- What – if any – are the distinctive marks of 'women's voice' in Hindu religious literature?

- Most religious writings by women belong to the *bhakti* frame of spirituality and embody the ideal of surrender. Can you explain why?

- What elements can you find in women's religious poetry that has the potential to elevate women's status in Hindu society?

- Many poems by Hindu women poets are subversive in respect of prescribed social relationships and rules (e.g., Āṇṭāl, Ākkā, Mīrā) and yet command both love and respect. What do you think this tells us about the potential for personal freedom in Hindu religious ideology?

- What would be your reason to think of Hindu women's poetry as a key to Hindu spirituality?

V
Women at Worship

The home has been the primary location of personal worship for Hindus, especially for Hindu women, for a long time. Responsible for the well-being of their families, women turn to gods and goddesses to obtain blessings and boons for their husbands, children, and others. They perform not only the traditionally prescribed worship rituals in general, but also home ceremonies designed to please particular deities in expectation of specific boons. Differing in many ways from the dominant worship tradition established by Vedic and Brahminical religious practices, these rituals are part of home-worship regimes as a living part of Hindu religious life. This area of Hindu religiosity, its informal part so to speak, is very much in women's hands, and although males are by no means excluded from devotional tasks, the main performers are almost always women. How these rituals are performed and how they affirm women's sense of their connection to the sacred will be the subject of this chapter.

Religious Observances

The public ceremonies of the Hindu religion in modern times are big affairs, complicated, colourful, and crowded, often stretched over several days and held at considerable cost. Hindu worship has not always been so. In Vedic times, worship centred on the fire-sacrifice, performed by sages as an integral part of their worship. They also conducted large, public, and highly complicated ceremonies, such as those held to invoke divine power for affirming and legitimising a ruler's authority. At these ceremonies the male principal and his consort were guided by sages through the complex details of the rites. For householders, carrying out fire sacrifices at home was an essential duty of married couples, who thereby sanctified their home. These were daily events carried out at home, where the principal worshipper was the husband but the wife was viewed as his indispensable partner. For high caste families, the *ṚgVeda's* ruling was that husband and wife must jointly offer sacrifices, a duty that was central to religious life (*ṚgVeda* 8.31.5), even though the wife's role was limited to some preparatory tasks and to her presence at parts of the ritual.[1]

An example from Vedic times is that of the *soma-yajña*, of which enough details are available for modern-day Brahmins to practice it. A twelve-day-long performance of the fire ritual termed *Agnicayana* at Panjal village in Kerala was filmed in 1975 by the scholar Frits Staal and his colleagues. The documentary is available under the title 'Altar of Fire'.[2] Though it was feared that it would be the last such performance, it has since been revived. In the recent past other scholars have recorded sacrifices that have been performed in Brahmin communities through at least the past seventy years, including South India and Benares. As a student of Sanskrit College, Calcutta, I was privileged to witness a *soma-yajña* there in the late 1950s, performed by priests brought in from Madras (now called Chennai) who conducted the sacrifice, following all the detailed rules and procedures of the ritual. The wife of the main priest sat beside him. Wives are silent partners in

---

1 See Frederic M. Smith, 'Indra's Curse, Varuṇa's Noose, and the Suppression of the Woman in the Vedic *Śrauta* Ritual', in *Roles and Rituals for Hindu Women*, ed. Julia Leslie (Delhi: Motilal Banarsidass, 1992), 17–46.
2 May be accessed at https:||store.der.org/altar-of-fire-p143.aspx

sacrifices but their presence is vital. They serve as assistants, setting out material, cooking sanctified food, serving priests, and cleaning the sacrificial space, but are excluded from the actual rite of sacrifice.

There is an exception though in one area of traditional Hindu worship, which evolved in post-Vedic times with the advent of the Śākta theology of *Tantra*. In the tāntric rites we find not only that women have direct participatory agency but in fact have a role equal to, and often superior than, that of men. Women participate fully in the tāntric rituals that they practice, often as principals, including the ritual of *dīkṣā* or religious initiation. Citing tāntric texts, Madhu Khanna tells us that 'initiation by one's mother is considered to be the best form of transmission'. She considers that Tāntrism 'is a rare instance of gender inclusive *dharma*' and that 'the Śākta attitude toward women appears to be relatively more consistent and in harmony with lofty abstractions of the image of the feminine principle who is both divine and mortal, transcendent and immanent, ideal and real simultaneously'.[3] This, however, is a highly specialised and unusual area of the Hindu religion and by no means representative of women's religious life in general. Female practitioners of *tantra* do exist but are so few as to be virtually invisible in common society. The general situation that developed within Hinduism after Vedic times was one of women's exclusion from sacred duties except in supporting roles. In recent times some women have acted as official priests in marriage and other ceremonies but that is still not general practice either in India or in the Hindu diaspora. The niche in which women have steadily remained in control of religious observance since the earliest time is the home. To understand how women's religious life unfolds, we must know their roles in worship ceremonies as initiators, planners,

3 Madhu Khanna, 'The Goddess-Woman Equation in Śākta Tantras', in *Faces of the Feminine in Ancient, Medieval and Modern India*, ed. Mandakranta Bose (New York: Oxford University Press, 2000), 120–121.

and performers. What then is the nature and extent of their participation in their faith?

Belief and Action

Discussions about Hinduism tend to stammer when it comes to the topic of women's participation. How is it that in a system of belief that locates, at its centre, the idea of an energy identified as the divine feminine, women are accorded little authority in religious observance? On a closer look, however, this broad view can be refocused. It is much too common to regard Hinduism as a programme of philosophical contemplation embodied in esoteric rites, both of which need to be expounded by scholars and specially trained priests, traditionally male. Viewed in this light, worshippers are bystanders with no direct engagement with the objects of their devotion. But in reality, religious belief among Hindus overflows institutional channels and believers may approach

Women performing Chhath Puja
on the bank of River Ganges in Varanasi, India.

gods and goddesses on their own by means of whatever they happen to know of ritual processes or even without any, simply as a matter of direct prayer. As a matter of fact, common worshippers do know a fair amount of religious protocol even if they have to call upon priests to perform the complex, often occult material and mental procedures inherited from a past when everybody is presumed to have had full knowledge of them. Looking back, it appears that at some point in post-Vedic times, formal worship became a far more specialised affair under the professional management of Brahmins trained in rituals and learned in theology. But home worship on a daily basis, or even on special occasions, has been performed for a long time by non-professional though informed men and women in Hindu families, much of the responsibility falling upon women. Tryambakayajvan (see Chapter 3) instructs wives to get the home ready in the morning for the daily fire-sacrifice and declares, *'homa tūbhayoḥ sannidhānaṁ mukham'* ('The important thing is that both [husband and wife] should be present for the *homa* offering'. *Strīdharmapaddhati* 8v. 10 in Leslie, 1995, p. 131). Julia Leslie shows how this right of a woman was 'gradually whittled away' through later times (Leslie, 1995, p. 108). What survived was women's responsibility as indispensable aides to the preparation of rituals. Confirmation comes from present-day reality and from the past in living memory.

Running parallel to women's supporting role in formal worship is the tradition of women's instinctive devotion as expressed in women's poetry and music, reinforced by the piety and fame of women such as Mahādevī Ākkā, Lāllā Yogeśvarī, and Mīrā, among many others we have encountered in Chapter 4 ('Women's Writings'). The full history of Hindu women's religious life is yet to be written but the vigour of women's faith has animated formal literature and folk culture equally through past centuries. These sources, and current experience, suggest that much of Hindu common worship practice is under female management because such worship is mostly located within the Hindu home, which is the domain of women. This is the reality we need to keep in sight when we talk about the religious life of Hindus.

In talking about that life we keep getting back to the centrality of feminine energy, an idea that continues to excite metaphysical speculation and shape entire schools of worship. That it has not endowed women with active authority in the everyday world of Hindus, rather than token regard, remains a dismal fact of Hindu social history. But the power of the idea of divinity being indivisible from femininity is so lasting that even through two millennia of systematic devaluation, Hindu women have held on to their sense of closeness to divinity in intuitive, emotional, and intellectual ways. In previous chapters on women's sacred knowledge and women's self-expression in poetry and songs, we have looked at Hindu women's achievements in engaging with the idea of the divine in the idiom of sophisticated reflection. That is only half the story. Here we will look into more down-to-earth, popular acts of worship that are common to women's everyday life within families and immediate communities. There is no identifiable point in time when that tradition may be said to have begun but we can at least see that it is in the area of home worship that women have created a sacred space for themselves.

Worship Redefined

Within that space exists a varied range of devotional acts, some as simple as offering food and water to the deity, lighting a lamp and burning incense, and prostrating oneself before the deity in reverence and in expectation – of blessings at the least and particular boons at the most. This makes up

Hindu religious life at its very basic. Obviously, that is not all of Hindu practice, nor are religious occasions confined to private homes. As I have noted earlier, there are many very great sacred festivals with public participation tied to special days in the Hindu calendar that are consecrated to particular deities. Much in the public eye are such festivals as Durgā Pūjā, offered to Goddess Durgā on a set range of days in the autumn, and Dīpāvalī, on the first night of the new moon beginning four weeks after the beginning of Durgā Pūjā, when Goddess Lakṣmī is worshipped in much of India but Goddess Kālī in Bengal, other parts of eastern India, and Nepal. But prominent as these festivals are, Hindu religious observance has a much wider base in the home across the year rather than limited to a few days. For observant Hindus, worship is a regular religious duty called *nitya* (daily) *pūjā* as well as worship undertaken to serve specific purposes known as *naimittika* (from '*nimitta*' or purpose) *pūjā*. The term *nitya pūjā* is not restricted to particular daily rituals but means a general,

Women performing a religious festival together.

regular routine of worship followed every day and week, while *naimittika pūjās* are performed for special purposes or occasions. Home worship in the form of *nitya pūjā* is women's business in the main, although men do participate. Every Hindu woman, normally a mature lady, no matter of what caste or class or education, has the authority at home to perform the regular daily or periodic *pūjā* in the form she has learnt from family precedents or perhaps social connections. It is only on special occasions of worship, involving elaborate rituals requiring formal training and invocations to the deity from Sanskrit texts, that she would call a priest. But even so, she carries out the supporting tasks.

Nitya Pūjā

The daily religious observances in a Hindu home are simple and can be of short or long duration, depending on the devotee's wish and habits. The standard practice is that the senior lady of the family, such as the mother or the grandmother, begins the day with a short prayer, often silent, as she lights a lamp and incense sticks. Quite often a young daughter-in-law may be asked to do this daily ritual. The day ends with a conch being blown three times to announce the end of the day and the arrival of *sandhyā* (evening), while a lamp is lighted in front of a *tulasī* plant (if available) and incense burnt in the household shrine. Girl children often assist their mothers in the evening rituals and often they sing devotional songs with their mother. In urban areas, these rituals are no longer as commonly practiced as they were a few decades ago, but they are still observed fairly regularly in small towns or villages. Somewhat more elaborate – though not much more – are the *nitya pūjā*, which are set forms of religious observance on a daily or weekly basis. They are performed within the family's physical space by women of the family, not of course by excluding men, some of whom may be devout enough to sit by and recite hymns or pray or perform some such task as cleaning the floor. But the conduct of the *pūjā* is women's business. Spacious homes usually have a room reserved for the deity, with formal seats for deities built like small thrones, and shelves, boxes, and utensils for storing sacred objects and other supplies required for the daily *pūjā* and for special occasions. Homes that are not so spacious usually have a shelf in one corner of a suitable room, on which are placed the deity and all the objects needed for the *pūjā*. The general pattern of the *pūjā* is a careful cleaning of the *pūjā* space, including the seat of the image or idol of the deity, lighting a lamp, burning incense, placing fresh flowers, *tulasī* leaves, and some simple food offering in front of the deity's seat, the whole arrangement sprinkled with holy Ganges water. Sitting in front of the deity's throne, the celebrant waves the lamp and the incense burner in front of the deity, and perhaps a fan. She prostrates herself in front of the deity and prays, then recites, reads, or sings one or more verses in adoration of the deity, though the daily *pūjā* is complete even without the last part. Extending it is the devotee's choice and women have been known to make each step quite elaborate, adding tasks such as waking up the deity in the morning, bathing the idol, dressing the deity, and putting the deity to sleep in the evening. The reading or chanting can be short or long, the food offering can be substantial and varied, and in general there could be more of everything, including the time the devotee spends. She is in charge of all this. It is only on special occasions of worship, involving elaborate rituals requiring formal training and invocations to the deity from Sanskrit texts, that she would call a priest, helping him with the supporting tasks. Women in charge of these duties are thoroughly knowledgeable about the rites, and priests depend on their detailed knowledge of the procedures.

Vratas

A class of ceremony that falls within both *nitya* and *naimittika* types of *pūjā* is known as *vrata,* which is especially within the province of women's worship. A *vrata* is the worshipper's commitment to offer *pūjā* to a particular deity, on a day reserved for that deity according to the lunar calendar used for religious purposes by Hindus,[4] and its practice follows a routine that includes sacred objects and rules particular to that deity. Worshippers find out the dates set by the lunar calendar from priests, temples, or *pañjikās* (religious almanacs), internet sites, and sometimes from newspapers if a *vrata* is especially important. *Vratas* are not compulsory and can be undertaken for a limited period, although in some families women do observe them regularly. It is not uncommon to find them observing more than one weekly *vrata*. A *vrata* may be a regular periodic undertaking, such as the *ekādaśī vrata,* observed every eleventh day of each phase of the moon. Or a *vrata* may be performed to express devotion to a particular deity with a particular goal in mind, such as a *vrata* performed to seek Goddess Ṣaṣṭhī's blessing for the protection and well-being of children. Some *vratas* of this purposeful kind are backed by binding vows that include penalties if they are not carried out. These are similar

4 Four types of calendars are used in traditional Hindu astrological calculations: first, the *Saura* system, which sets month divisions by the sun's movement (365 days); second, the *Cāndra* system, which follows the movement of the moon and is used for religious rituals; the third, the *Nākṣatra* system, which follows the movements of the stars for astronomical calculations; and finally, the *Sāvana*, reserved for calculating dates for funeral rites, in which calendar months are counted from the day of a person's death, and it is according to that start day that the astrologer prescribes rites appropriate to each *varṇa* or caste. The performance of rites according to this complicated calendrical system is explained by the sixteenth-century scholar Raghunandana Bhattacharya in his *Malamāsa-tattvam,* which is part of his *Aṣṭāviṁśatitattvam, vaṅgābda* 1347 [1940], 260–301.

to rituals mentioned in some early scriptures as *kāmya yajña,* that is, rituals aiming at obtaining a particular boon, such as the *putrakāmeṣṭi yajña,* which the devotee vows to perform in the hope of securing the birth of a child. In general, though, *vratas* are undertaken out of a broad sense of sacred duty, not because of a contractual commitment.

A *vrata* begins with a ritual bath, and the performer fasts before and during its course until its end. It requires an audience of family and close friends, and most *vratas* end with the reading of a legend that describes that deity's action in the world. A menstruating woman fasts but does not perform the rituals. A *vrata* can be performed by either a man or a woman, and some indeed do have worshippers of both sexes, although the practice varies from one region of India to another and from one cultural group to another. For example, going back to the *ekādaśī vrata,* we find that it is performed in northern India by both men and women, while in Bengal and other parts of Eastern India, it is performed primarily by Hindu widows

A Hindu woman offering prayers during her vrata.

and very few men, never by unmarried or married women. Many *vratas* are held for deities of local origin, such as Ṣaṣṭhī in Bengal, although major deities like Lakṣmī, Gaṇeṣa, and Śiva have *vratas* dedicated to them. Whether the composition of *vratas* and their inclusion in the religious calendar have come through women's initiative is hard to tell but women are certainly the most frequent performers of *vratas*. Quite possibly they are simplified versions of formal worship adapted to specific goals of obtaining favours from a deity or averting hazards. Their distinctive mark is the reading or recitation of a legend that glorifies the deity and emphasises, on the one hand, the disasters that visit the family on failing to offer *pūjā* to the deity, and on the other hand matched by the reversal of the deity's wrath on the resumption of devotion resulting in endless benefits. The narratives are drawn from the *purāṇas,* which are cyclopaedic chronicles of myths and legends, and sometimes the same *vrata* may have several legends explaining its origin and purpose; the much-practiced *vrata* of Dhanteras is an example, centred alternatively on Dhanvantarī (the heavenly physician) or Lakṣmī or Kuvera (both of them being sources of wealth).

The worship procedures are modelled on Brahminical rituals that the performers may have observed priests conducting at temples or formal home devotions, and they may have received help from sympathetic priests in constructing the rites and the narratives. Certain ritual objects, materials, and processes are often products of personal or folk conjectures about what the deity might like. The course of performing *vratas* is very much the same as that for mainstream Brahminical rituals and includes very similar auspicious objects, signs, mystic diagrams, and materials. Keeping close to Brahminical practice, women recite short prayers mostly in Sanskrit, which they read from collections of *stotras*, or prayers, available at local bookstores under such titles as *Stava-kavacamālā* or *Stava-kusumamālā*. These volumes are kept in home shrines as sacred objects in their own right. Some of these prayers may have also come down through their mothers. Women further legitimise their worship by following standard Brahminical regimes of self-purification through bathing, fasting, putting on garments made of unpolluted material, such as silk and wool, cleaning the *pūjā* location, sprinkling sacred Ganges water on it, and decorating the space with flowers and leaves considered to be auspicious. Many women also decorate the floor with designs painted in rice paste or powdered grain; these are a feature of worship that we will consider later.

Ideally, a *vrata* is not a solitary act of devotion but performed before an audience. Following A. K. Ramanujan's discussion of India's cultural history in *Speaking of Śiva*, we can see how a new stream of Hindu religious life has been created in religious observance by replicating classical rituals and reconstituting them as a 'little' tradition, which contains a variety of regional and local devotional practice.[5] Not directly dominated by any central authority, individual feeling and understanding have fostered the free growth of religious forms and practices. *Vratas* reflect the imaginative potency of the Hindu religious instinct that clings to the traditional devotional spirit, even as it moulds it into new forms of practice. Much of the energy that feeds this new tradition comes from women.

As I have said above, *vratas* are undertaken by a woman to ensure the welfare of her husband, children, and family in general. The objects of her prayers may be health, wealth, security, relief from some misfortune, success in examinations, and similar worldly benefits rather than spiritual advancement. Observance of these vows continues to this day and in recent times new *vratas* have been added to the list of existing *vratas*

5 A. K. Ramanujan, *Speaking of Śiva* (London: Penguin, 1973), 22–23.

that many women observe diligently. As mentioned earlier, the dates for *vratas,* as indeed for all religious events, are set for each year according to astrological calculations, varying slightly within a traditionally prescribed range. Women take charge of the ritual procedures, materials, and conduct. Instructions for carrying out *vratas* are not always written out but orally transmitted from generation to generation by mothers, grandmothers, and mothers-in-law in a family to daughters and daughters-in-law. Sometimes special rules are made up, which often vary from family to family. An example is the practice of pouring holy water on the *śivaliṅgam* while engaged in the *śivarātri vrata*: one family may require only four libations through the day while in another family it may be an hourly act. A vital part of many *vratas* is the verse narrative with which they end, functioning as a climactic declaration of faith and hope. These narratives are known as *vrata-kathās* but also as *pāñcālīs* in Bengal, and widely available in local bookstores. The language of the narrative is not Sanskrit, as in the *stotras,* but the language of the region, such as Oriya, Hindi, Marathi, Gujrati, Bengali, Tamil, and so on, their style being a mix of formal and conversational words and sentence structures, occasionally old-fashioned.

Two issues are at once impressed upon the performers of the *vrata* as well as upon the audience: first, the *vrata* is not just a devotional act but also a proselytising one of instructional value; second, the tale suggests male carelessness in matters of faith and devotion, precisely matched with the contrasting demonstration of female devotional propriety. Nothing could more forcefully identify the women of a family as the keeper of the family's *dharma* and its core strength. In the performance of *vratas,* women have the support of their menfolk, who believe that the women's religious conduct will bring the family material well-being and blessings from the gods. Just as women are thereby socialised into accepting their highest purpose in life as service to the family, so is the family taught the value of women as the primary agents of its well-being. Whether the women who undertake *vratas* are themselves conscious of these implications of their devotional acts can neither be claimed nor rejected, but their commitment to performing them is in itself a claim to a devotional space of their own.

Vratas: A Selection

Tied as they are to the basic human instinct for seeking the divine and for securing the worldly needs of home and family, *vratas* have proliferated vastly over time. Long lists and yearly dates for each are available on several websites, such as this:

https://www.drikpanchang.com/vrats/hindu-vrat-list.html

Many others are similarly listed in print form in almanacs in most Indian languages. Since it is not possible to describe or even list all the *vratas* that Hindus practice, we will content ourselves with a short selection of major *vratas* from some of India's regional traditions.[6] Some of them also have simpler counterparts in the daily worship routines of family life, and we may think of these *vratas* as elaborations of the customary *pūjā* offered to the deity concerned, indicating the importance of that deity.

Two Major Observances: Vratas for Lakṣmī and Śiva

As the ruling deity of wealth and fortune, Goddess Lakṣmī is worshipped by virtually every Hindu as part of daily and

6 For a critical overview, see Monika Saxena, '*Vratas*, rituals and the Purāṇic social hierarchy', in *Women and the Purāṇic Tradition in India* (Abingdon, Oxon. and New York, NY: Routledge, 2019).

weekly domestic worship, the weekly ritual conducted by many families – with especial regularity in Bengal and other parts of Eastern India – in the *vrata* mode every Thursday evening. This *vrata* is entirely conducted by women of the family, usually the mother or mother-in-law or a daughter-in-law, requiring no Brahmin priest, and takes place at the home shrine or corner of the home where most households have a statuette or icon of the goddess, sometimes painted on a convex clay plate.

In front of the figure or painting is placed a sacred metal pot with auspicious marks painted on it in *sindoor* (vermillion) and filled with Ganges water, which is set on a bed of unhusked rice. A five-leaf spray of mango is placed on the mouth of the pot, with a fruit placed on top. Cowries are placed around the pot to represent wealth, flowers daubed with sandalwood paste are laid in front, a lamp is lighted, incense burnt, and dishes containing fruits, sweets, and a *pān* (betel leaf) with a whole areca nut are placed in front of the sacred pot. The officiant blows a conch three times to announce the beginning of the *pūjā* but no bells are rung, nor gongs beaten, because harsh noise is said to displease Goddess Lakṣmī. The officiant then begins the ritual proper by reciting a Sanskrit prayer, with women of the household sitting around her with flower offerings in their hands listening to her. She then offers a simple *ārati* by waving the lamp, the incense, and a fan in front of the image. All those present there then offer the flowers in their hands and bow to the goddess, praying for whatever boons they may seek.

In Bengali homes the officiant then reads Lakṣmī's *pāñcālī* or *kathā*, the celebratory narrative that urges devotion to the goddess, declaring her benevolence when pleased and her wrath when neglected. It tells the audience how important it is to perform the Lakṣmī *vrata* every Thursday in the format laid down in the story – which the attendees have just witnessed.

The story is interesting enough in itself to be summarised here, especially as it is of a pattern common to many *vratas*, as we shall see shortly. After it is read out, the officiant again blows the conch three times to announce the end of the *pūjā*. The food offered to the goddess and considered to have been partaken by her power of consuming it in spirit becomes her *prasāda*, her sacramental gift, which is distributed to all those present. This is especially important to worshippers who are particularly devout and have been fasting during the day before offering *pūjā* in the evening, for they break their fast with this *prasāda*. At the end of the ritual, male members of the household join to bow before the image and to receive blessings and to take *prasāda* with the family members. It is quite usual to see a married woman performing this vow through her entire life.

Lakṣmīsarā, showing Goddess Lakṣmī flanked by fan-bearers with her owl at her feet.

The narrative demonstrating the need for the *vrata* runs thus: a man of means neglects his devotions to the deity (here, Lakṣmī, other deities in similar *kathās*) and as a result he loses all his wealth, he and his sons or sons-in-law are thrown into prison on some false charge, the women of his family have to beg for their food, and so on until some kindly Brahmin or visitor – possibly the deity in disguise – advises them, usually the women, to hold a worship ritual of the form prescribed for that deity's *vrata*, which exactly mirrors the *vrata* of which the narrative is the climax. The result, the *vratakathā* declares, is the instant restoration of the family's fortune and in fact, great additions to it. That, the tale emphasises, is how the deity's power and benevolence are affirmed in the world.

This *vrata* is linked to the wider practice of Lakṣmī worship. In Bengali homes, the annual plan for the *vrata* includes the festival known as *Lakṣmīpūjā*, held on the special full-moon day known as *kojāgarī pūrnīmā*, which falls in October after the annual *Durgāpūjā* in autumn. This, however, is the custom in Bengal and parts of eastern India, whereas in other parts of India – in northern and western India with particular vigour – the annual *pūjā* of Lakṣmī is held on a different festival day, which is the first *amāvasyā*, or new moon night after *Durgāpūjā*, known as *diwālī* or *dīpāvalī*, which is a festival of lamps. That same night, however, is dedicated in Bengal to the Goddess Kālī, who is worshipped in grand style, mostly as a public celebration, although private worship is not unknown. In several regions of Southern India, Hindus celebrate *dīpāvalī* as the occasion of Lord Kṛṣṇa slaying the demon Narakāsura.

One of the most widespread of Hindu rituals is *Śivarātri* or *Śivacaturdaśī vrata*, usually observed between late Māgha (mid-February) and early Phālguna (mid-March) depending on the position of the moon. The *vrata* begins on the fourteenth day

A woman performing worship of Śiva liṅga and Nandī on the bank of River Narmada.

of the dark fortnight and ends the day after the new moon, although some women observe this *vrata* for just one day, the day of *amāvasyā*, the new moon. At least till the mid-twentieth century many young girls, longing to be blessed with a good husband like Śiva, observed it, and in recent times it has again become popular. Married women also observe this *vrata* for the prosperity and good health of their husbands, and some men undertake it as well.[7] Currently, the observance of *Śivarātri* has expanded from its location at homes and temples to be celebrated in the public arena, and young girls are being encouraged to perform the *vrata*. Its importance is being emphasised by observing it as a three-day programme of worship that includes fasting, modified on the first day by restricting food to fruits and milk. The second day requires fasting without any water or food and the celebrant has to bathe Śiva by pouring milk over his *liṅga* form, usually once every four hours. On the third day she completes her vow after worshipping Śiva, concluding the *vrata* by offering lunch to (ideally) twelve Brahmins, or at least two, thereby earning the benefits of *brāhmaṇabhojana* (serving food to Brahmins).

The value of domesticity that traditional Hindu ethos associates with womanhood is well reflected in a ritual designed specifically for mothers to ensure successful and secure childbirth followed by the safety and good health of their children. This *vrata* is *Ṣaṣṭhīpūjā* or *Ṣaṣṭhīvrata*, aimed at winning the blessings of Goddess Ṣaṣṭhī (literally: 'the sixth', referring to ancient legends of her origin), who protects

---

7 A somewhat different and detailed description of this *vrata* appears in Samjukta Gombrich Gupta's essay, 'The Goddess, Women, and Their Rituals in Hinduism', in *Faces of the Feminine in Ancient, Medieval and Modern India*, ed. Mandakranta Bose (New York: Oxford University Press, 2000), 100. But the essential process is the same as here, drawn from my own experience.

children and looks after their welfare.[8] Till about fifty years ago it was a widely practiced ritual but is less so today, especially among younger people in the Indian diaspora. Its practice varies somewhat across India – as do most other religious observances and legends – and the account below is that of its performance in Bengal.

Ṣaṣṭhīvrata is observed by mothers on the sixth day of every other month in *śuklapakṣa* (the fortnight of the bright moon), that is, six times a year, for their children's well-being. Of these six occasions, an important and elaborate one is held in the month of *Jaiṣṭha* (mid-May to mid-June) and is known as *araṇyaṣaṣṭhī* (literally: Ṣaṣṭhī in the forest). The mother who performs it fasts during the early part of the day, goes through the usual tasks of purification by bathing, fasting, and cleaning the *pūjā* site, constructs a small make-believe forest by planting small branches of the banyan or pippal tree, cane, and other local trees on a lump of clay (ideally *gaṅgāmāṭī*, clay from the banks of the Ganges). A figure of goddess Ṣaṣṭhi is made with rice paste and placed on the clay at the foot of the little forest. She sits watching and protecting six babies, also made from rice paste, who were stolen by her two pet cats, one white (*dhali biḍāl*) and one black (*kālī biḍāl*). The cats too are there, at the goddess's feet, similarly made of rice flour paste, one white and the other painted black. The worship process is similar to that for Lakṣmī, which is common to most *pūjās*, with a pot of consecrated water, lamp, incense, sprays of mango leaves, fruits, and flowers. After the *ārati* the officiating mother recounts Ṣaṣṭhī's story to the audience. Its details may vary a little from family to family but the essentials remain the same, focusing on how the goddess saved six babies and restored them to their mother.

8 See Sukumari Bhattacharji, *Legends of Devī* (Hyderabad: Orient Blackswan, 1995), chap. 9.

Briefly, this is the story in outline: once there was a well-to-do family who lived in a village with their sons and daughters-in-law. The youngest daughter-in-law loved to drink milk, which she stole from the family pot but blamed it on two cats, one black and one white. They happened to be Goddess Ṣaṣṭhī's favourites, and becoming angry because of the woman putting the blame on them, they stole her babies each time one was born, placing them in the goddess's care. The daughter-in-law was distraught by her continual losses until she realised that her babies had disappeared because of her own fault. She prayed to Goddess Ṣaṣṭhi for forgiveness, offering her *pūjā,* which satisfied both Ṣaṣṭhī and her cats. The babies were returned to their mother, who thereafter observed *Ṣaṣṭhivrata* every year to show her gratitude and to receive Ṣaṣṭhi's blessings. The story ends happily and at the end everyone who listens to it is blessed by the officiant mother waving over them a hand-held fan with fruits and flowers tied to it. The mother who tells the story ends her fast after blessing her children. A special feast is arranged for everyone. Sons-in-law are invited as special guests to a big feast and they are presented with new clothes. This *vrata* is also known as *jāmāiṣaṣṭhī, jāmāi* (*jāmātā*) meaning son-in-law. The *vrata* ends by mid-day after the *pūjā* and *prasāda* distribution. Here again the story offers a two-fold moral lesson comprising the penalty of wrongdoing followed by penance in the form of a specific *pūjā* and absolution in the form of rewards.

A *vrata* performed specially by married women is the *Sāvitrīvrata,* which is performed by married women in Bihar, Jharkhand, West Bengal, and Odisha on the new moon day of the month of *Jaiṣṭhya,* and on the full moon day in western India. The ritual consists of a *pūjā* ceremony with the usual sacred objects and foods, such as lamps, incense, fruits, flowers, and so on, and by narrating the story of Sāvitrī and

Satyavān to a group of women. A greatly expanded version of the *vrata* in Bengal is initiated by a vow, which married women commit themselves to perform over twelve or fourteen years. In this expanded form, through the first eleven (or thirteen) years the *vrata* is performed once a year, when the woman performs rituals with the usual sacred objects and foods, such as lamps, incense, fruits, flowers, and so on, and by narrating the story of Sāvitrī and Satyavān to a group of women. In the twelfth (or fourteenth) year a much bigger ceremony is conducted by a Brahmin priest. The legend read out is that, after Satyavān's death, his wife Sāvitrī followed his body as Yama, the god of death, was taking him to the land of the dead, obtaining boons from him by her wisdom and devotion to her husband and his family, eventually tricking him into restoring her husband to life. A married woman undertakes this vow in the belief that she will be as lucky as Sāvitrī and never suffer widowhood. Performing the larger version of this *vrata* is a difficult commitment and few women have attempted to do it. It is not as popular any longer, at least not to the degree of elaborate and long commitment that was known in the past.

Vipattāriṇī vrata is another special ceremony performed by women once a year for averting any disaster or misfortune in the family. It is a three-day event held on any day between the third and the ninth day of the bright fortnight of *Āṣāḍha* (mid-June to mid-July) and must be initiated on either a Tuesday or a Saturday. The *pūjā* is offered to Durgā or Caṇḍī, the mighty Mother Goddess, and performed at home by a woman, usually with other women present. The number 13 serves as the magic number for this *vrata*. Fruits and flowers are offered but everything is offered in groups of thirteen, such as 13 types of fruits, 13 types of flowers, 13 leaves of *pāns*, 13 areca nuts, 13 strands of red threads bunched and threaded together with

13 knots and with a *kuśa* grass-tip. Thirteen small baskets are offered, with 13 of the special offerings bundled together. The woman who performs the *vrata* recites the *vratakathā* to her audience of women about the benefit of the observance. The three-day observance ends at noon of the third day with the eating of a fruit followed by eating the family's usual food afterwards. At the end of the *vrata*, the performer ties one of the red threaded bracelets on her right hand and offers the other bracelets to her family members.[9]

Vratas of North India

The popularity of *vratas* tends to vary regionally, which is well demonstrated in the observance of *Karvā Chauth*, one of the most widely practiced *vratas* of North India but of less influence in other regions, although it has gained adherents elsewhere in recent times. In North India, not only homebound housewives, but also professional women such as academics, doctors, and corporate executives take time off to observe this *vrata* to ensure the health and prosperity of their husbands. Celebrating the *vrata* on the fourth day of the dark fortnight in the month of Kārtika (mid-October to mid-November), women fast during the day, and break their vows and take food at sundown after watching the moonrise. The distinctive feature of this *vrata* is that after performing the standard rituals at home with lamps, incense, offerings of flowers and fruits, worshippers conclude the ceremony by watching the rising moon as reflected in an earthen dish or bowl filled with water. Husbands are offered special food and wives eat after their husbands have eaten.

9 For descriptions of more vows see Samjukta Gombrich Gupta, 'The Goddess, Women, and Their Rituals', 86–108; also see Mandakranta Bose, 'Sanctuary: Women and Home Worship', in *Women in the Hindu Tradition: Rules, Roles and Expectations* (London and New York: Routledge, 2010), 136–148.

Several stories about this *vrata* are told. One is about a queen called Vīravatī, who was tricked by her brothers to look at what she thought was the moon before the actual moon rose and thus broke her vow unknowingly. As a result, her husband died but was restored to life by Yama, who realised how devoted Vīravatī was to her husband. Another story is about Draupadī when Arjuna was away. At a particularly difficult time for her she was advised by Kṛṣṇa to observe this *vrata*, just as Pārvatī had done at some distant past, to resolve the crisis. By taking his advice she was indeed able to overcome her problems. A third story is about a woman named Karwa whose husband was killed by a crocodile. Through the power of her wifely devotion, she made Yama bring him back to life. Yet another story is about how the legendary Sāvitrī brought her dead husband back to life. Pleased to see her devotion for her husband, Yama was ready to give her any boon she asked for except the life of her husband, to which she agreed but asked to be blessed with a son. This trick succeeded because even though Yama realised that she could not have a son if her husband was dead and to grant the promised boon he would have to bring her husband back to life, he was pleased enough by her clever persistence to do so. Though told about different women and different issues, the argument of each is the same: in a dire crisis, a god or goddess is a woman's last resource, and they would indeed grant her favours but only if she could prove her selfless devotion to her husband or family.

Vratas of Western India

Moving to Western India we find the *Jaya Pārvatī Vrata*, which is observed by unmarried girls and married women of Gujarat and its neighbouring provinces. This vow can be observed for five, seven, nine, or eleven years successively in the month of Āṣāḍha (mid-May to mid-June). The legend behind this *vrata* describes a Brahmin woman who observed it to free her husband from any curse he might be under, which is averted when she worships Śiva and Pārvatī. The *vrata* is believed to give immense power to women who observe it.

Śiva Pārvatī Vrata is another *vrata* describing a legend about a childless Brahmin couple, devotees of the divine couple, who went to the forest when so directed by Śiva in their dream, to offer *pūjā* to a neglected statue of Śiva in his *liṅga* form. They had a few misadventures as a snake bit the husband while he was searching for flowers to worship Śiva. He died but was revived by Śiva because of the couple's devotion, and eventually all went well when they performed the *pūjā* as intended and were blessed with a son.

South Indian Vratas[10]

The *Tiruppāvāi* (also known as *Pāvāi*) vow is a Tamil *vrata* observed in Kṛṣṇa's praise by young girls in the month of Mārkali (mid-December to mid-January) in the hope of a happy marriage. The celebrants prepare themselves by self-purification, make clay images, and invite their desired one in the form of Kṛṣṇa wiṭh songs and poems of adoration. The *Nācciiyār Tirumozhi* vow is a follow-up of *Pāvāi*, and observed in the following month of Tāi (mid-January to mid-February) in anticipation of separation from the Lord, whose return the celebrants seek.

Varalakṣmī Nombu is a *vrata* to worship Goddess Lakṣmī, like *Lakṣmīpūjā*, for securing the well-being of the worshipper's husband, and is held on a special Friday before the full-moon of Śrāvaṇa (mid-July to mid-August). This is celebrated

10 Much of the information on South Indian *vratas*, except for Pāvāi, was provided by Nandana Nagaraj of the Oxford Centre for Hindu Studies during Trinity Term, 2019, for which I am grateful to her.

in Andhra, Karnataka, and Tamilnadu, being of particular importance in Tamilnadu. The same motive of seeking long life and prosperity for a husband drives the *Kārādāyan Nombu,* also known as *Sāvitrīvrata,* which is observed by married women of Tamilnadu. This *nombu* (*vrata*) is celebrated at the end of Māsi (mid-February to mid-March) and beginning of the following month of Pāṅguni (mid-March to mid-April). Sāvitrī, the icon of wifely devotion in the *Purāṇas,* fought with Yama, the god of death, and made him restore her husband to life. Women of Tamilnadu observe this vow in her honour. Anxious as married women are to secure the long life of their husbands and avoid widowhood, it is no surprise that *Sāvitrīvrata* is observed so widely all over India. Nor should it be a surprise that there are other *vratas* dedicated to the same end. One such *vrata* is the South Indian *Umā Maheśvara vrata* which is celebrated in Telegu, Tamil, and Kannada-speaking areas. It is claimed to be one of eight *mahāvratas* ('great' *vratas*) described in the *Skanda Purāṇa,* undertaken to win the blessings of Umā and Maheśvara for a happy married life, in which the husband does not die before his wife. Tamils observe it on the day of the full moon in the month of Bhādra (mid-August to mid-September) or Kārtika (mid-September to mid-October). In earlier days, this *vrata* was observed every year for twelve years in the month of Bhādra. Images of Umā and Maheśvara were made of either gold or silver for the adoration of worshippers. At the end of the observance of the *vrata* for twelve years, the images used in the *vrata* were donated to a Śiva temple of the devotee's choice.

Even the very brief overview given above demonstrates how much of Hindu worship is non-professional, that is, not performed under the authority of trained priests, traditionally Brahmin males. A great variety of worship practices are performed by women acting on their own, even though the ritual patterns they follow might have been set at some point by priestly initiative. Also to be noted is that the great majority of the *pūjās* and *vratas* is aimed at benefits for the families of the women celebrants, especially husbands and children (read 'sons'). But doesn't the power of rituals lie in the believer's faith? If so, then the performers surely come to possess personal power through their worship, especially as it is so often personally tailored. Part of that personalising occurs because these worship regimes are centred in the home, even when a part of them may require a temple visit or communal bathing in a holy river – for instance, the Chaṭ festival so popular among the women of Bihar.

An Aesthetic Dimension

As the theatre of women's religious life, their homes are sites of a subtle transformation of domestic geography into religious space.[11] This of course is the function of sanctifying the ground on which *pūjā* is offered by cleaning it and sprinkling it with holy Ganges water. But equally, indeed much more visibly, that space is given a special identity by women's art in the form of floor (sometimes wall) drawings. Perhaps the best known example of this art form of women is the *ālpanā* of Bengal. These are decorative designs drawn on auspicious occasions on the floor or on the seat of the deity with fine (uncooked) semi-liquid rice paste, applied free-hand with a fine piece of cloth held in the hand like a small bundle dipped into the rice paste, with the paste dripping down like paint along the middle or fourth finger, and a drawn with the finger like a brush. The designs may be

11 Though not directly or exclusively concerned with this form of women's art, Heather Elgood's *Hinduism and the Religious Arts* (London and New York: Cassell, 1999) offers useful insights into the religious aspects of Indian art.

large or small, simple or complicated, geometric or stylised representations of conch-shells, foliage, corn-sheaves, and flowers that are pleasing to gods and goddesses, and are usually symmetrical. Often a sacred pot of water is placed in the centre of the *ālpanā*. The designs remain for a few days until someone wipes them off.

Similar art forms, though none so elaborate, are found in many parts of India and now also in the Indian diaspora, executed by women for the same purpose of sanctifying their homes. One form of decorative design found at most traditional Tamil homes is *kolam*, but unlike *ālpanās*, these designs are drawn on the floor every day in expectation of ensuring an auspicious course of the day, rather than on special occasions. *Kolams* are not made of liquid paste but laid down with dry, finely powdered white rice by the mother or the wife of the family early every morning at the entrance of her home. Unlike Bengali *ālpanās*, *kolams* have to be drawn every morning because the dry rice powder scatters and the drawings disappear by the end of the day.

Ālpanā

Kolam

Rangoli

Yet another art form similar to *ālpanā* and *kolam* is *rangoli*, which developed in north and western India. *Rangoli* patterns are created on the floor or the bare ground using materials such as coloured rice, dry flour, coloured sand, or flower petals in combination to produce colourful designs. These designs are usually made during Diwali, Tihar, and other Hindu festivals, and have a similar celebratory intent as *ālpanā* and *kolam*, but different from them, as they are always coloured and the medium is different, although like them these too are freehand drawings.

The origins of this practice or of the designs can only be speculated: perhaps they are the fruits simply of women's instinct for art or derived from mystic designs of ancient religion, or even from Tāntric *yantras*. It is doubtful that they are so recognised by the women who create them but they are certainly prized as personal creations that turn physical space into sacred space.

Why Vratas?

Brief as is the view of the worship practices of Hindu women presented here, it does point at the value that the women attach to them. Why they do so is a question that would take us to the uncharted territories of both religious and social psychology, but the common and vastly extensive practice of *pūjās* and *vratas*, particularly by Hindu women, indicates some deep-seated need in the officiants. A matter of especial significance is, ironically, that practicing women often cannot pinpoint their reasons for their observance; blind faith, if such a term is at all fair, is at the very least a gesture towards sacred meanings. In this context it is also worth noting that many women, including those possessing high education, perform religious rites less out of devotion than an effort to claim a cultural identity. Considering that Hindu *dharma* is not only a spiritual regime but also an ethical system, a quest for identity through orthodox practices creates an area within Hinduism in which women can enjoy a degree of self-determination.

Validation

That is why, over time since the medieval era and the weakening of ancient Vedic ritual practices, *nitya pūjā* and *vratas* became more and more important in an ordinary Hindu woman's life, observed with strict maintenance of ritual purity to ensure her family's well-being and social prestige. At the same time she also considers her faithful observance as a way to enhance her own spiritual progress, while strengthening her prestige and power within the family. The combination of these motives, worldly and spiritual, is a striking feature of Hindu women's religious identity and aspirations, elevating them above the narrow range of worldly gain. The material interest of self and family do not shut out the hope of achieving *mokṣa*, or liberation from *saṁsāra* (the cycle of rebirth), even as she leads her life within the family, unlike a renouncer who seeks *mokṣa* by giving up worldly life and practicing austerity and self-restraint. A verse in the *Agnipurāṇa* makes it clear that, along with material benefits, a woman is also seeking *mokṣa*:

putraṁ dehi dhanaṁ dehi āyur ārogyasantatiṁ |
dharmaṁ kāmaṁ ca saubhāgyaṁ svargaṁ mokṣaṁ ca dehi me | |

> Grant me a son, wealth, long life, good health and progeny. Right conduct, pleasure, good fortune, heaven and liberation.
>
> (*Agnipurāṇa* 183, 17cd–18ab)

This prayer is part of the *Kṛṣṇa-janmāṣṭamī vrata* that celebrates Kṛṣṇa's birth and is observed by women in late August. Although the worshipper is asking mostly for the material gifts necessary for a fulfilling family life, she is going beyond that to pray for her entry into heaven, and going even beyond that, she is supplicating for *mokṣa,* that is, for her ultimate liberation from the cycle of time and materiality. An ambitious quest indeed! A similar cry from a woman is heard in the *Matsya Purāṇa* (54.5), where she is praying for *mokṣa,* which she fears is beyond the reach of a married woman immersed in *saṁsāra.* Clearly, these supplicants have enough religious knowledge and a high spiritual urge to value *mokṣa* above worldly goods. Practitioners of religious acts, who are at once pragmatic and selfless, Hindu women are indeed keepers of the Hindu religion.

Discussion Topic: Women's Worship

- Do you see any major, even fundamental, difference in the worship goals of Hindu women in the common run of social life and those of women saints and poets? Would you agree that for most Hindu women, worship aims at securing benefits while for women saints and renunciates the goal is spiritual elevation?

- Many of the *vratas* observed by Hindu women include obligatory recitations of legends. Do you see narrative patterns by which *vratas* could be organised into groups?

- Women's worship practices tend to be home-centred and their purpose that of bringing benefits to their families; do you see any spiritual value in such practices?

- To what degree would you say women are keepers of the religious tradition in Hindu families?

- Do you see in Hindu women's religious conduct a preference for ritualism over reflection?

VI
Women, Art, and Religion

Since almost nothing in life is left untouched by religious belief for the average Hindu, it should be no surprise to find gods and goddesses, religious themes and legends, and sacred imagery woven through the arts in the Hindu cultural world. It is an enterprise that is as social as it is devotional, and there are parts of it to which women's contribution is especially enriching, as we will see in the account that follows.

Gendering Art

Until the beginning of colonial times, the art of the Hindus in India was mainly oriented to their religion. Affirming and expressing reverence, devotion, and love for the Divine through all forms of art has always been an integral part of the religious life of Hindus, men and women alike. As late as mid-nineteenth century, the bulk of music, painting, and sculpture was either directly devotional in purpose or inspired by devotional themes and motifs. Even when works of art, such as bas-reliefs or songs, were not directly religious in intent, they were rooted in religious motifs and allusions. Let me emphasise here that by 'art' I understand all works of the human imagination, whether it is a formal product, such as the

Rāmāyaṇa or a marble image of Lakṣmī, or an informal one, such as a folk-song or a painted pot. The present discussion is not limited to erudite poetry or painting created or enjoyed only by a culturally trained minority but also includes instinctual expressions of thought, imagination, and feeling accessible to all. These are precisely the properties of art that make music, painting, poetry – indeed, all art forms – fertile fields for spirituality to take root. Moreover, the states of both art and spirituality are fundamentally states of freedom and for that reason they are open to those who are disempowered. No surprise, then, that the bond between women and the arts should be deep and strong. That bond exists at many levels, for women are not only consumers of art but also creators of art, not only receiving joy but also creating it. It is also important to bear in mind that gender does not determine – at least in theory – who produces or participates in music, painting, dancing, poetry, or story-telling, but in practice we see that some, though not all, branches of art have been mainly the province of women, such as dancing and decorative domestic arts. I must note here that in modern times, this gendering of art has lost its hard edge as a condition of identity in tandem with the reassignment of social roles across gender lines. The reason for this is that, for a long time now, Hindu women have been questioning their religion in sustained attempts to redefine their place in its ideology and practice and seeking unconstrained inclusion in their religious culture.1 The need to think of art as an inclusive human endeavour is important especially in the context of women's work because, for many centuries and in many social domains, the great majority of women have had little opportunity for acquiring the education and skills to participate in art for the privileged

1 See for example, Madhu Khanna, 'Here are the Daughters: Reclaiming the Girl Child', in *The Goddess*, Oxford History of Hinduism series, ed. Mandakranta Bose (Oxford: Oxford University Press, 2018), 173–198.

few. Fortunately, that has not stopped women across Hindu society's many strata from creating art of lasting value inspired by their religious thoughts and feelings.

Of the forms in which Hindu women's creativity has been expressed through the ages, poetry comes to mind as the earliest known genre to bear the stamp of femininity. The oldest poetry of the Hindus was predominantly religious, as the ṚgVedic hymns we have considered in Chapter 2 will have shown, one of the most moving being hymn 10.125 attributed to the female seer Āmbhṛṇī. The religious strain has never disappeared from poetry in India, including poetry by women. With time, poetry there began to flow in many channels, especially that of romantic love, epic narration, and courtly wit, but spiritual expression remained a constant. As we have seen in the discussion of women's writings in Chapter 4, the intensity of religious fervour reached and maintained an astonishing level of emotional and philosophical perception through the fourth century onward till the mid-nineteenth century. Through that long span of time religious poetry, both recited and sung, embodied women's greatest achievement in a genre of art, and in my view it still does. Often the line between poetry and songs was blurred, given the Indian tradition of reciting poetry in musical forms, even though it might not have been created primarily as music. Equally, musical compositions were created as complements to words, thus producing a vast storehouse of songs through the ages.

Music

As musical forms, the classical styles of India are wide-ranging, simple as well as complex, and often highly sophisticated in technique. They are also open to all who gain competence in them, irrespective of gender, social class, or religious affiliation. A great part of classical Indian music,

An Indian classical singer playing the tanpura.

though, is explicitly devotional in the Hindu tradition as the celebration of gods and goddesses or as prayers to them, performed by both women and men. But not all devotional songs are in classical styles and many – indeed the majority – of them are far less complex in their structure and musical grammar, thereby commanding vast audiences and encouraging performers at all levels of musical ability. The directness and simplicity of the lyrics allow the singer and listeners a sense of intimacy with the Divine, whether it be Śiva, Kṛṣṇa, or Kālī who is the song's subject. This type of song is especially popular with women although, again, they are not exclusive to women in any way. But the freedom inherent in them to express oneself draws women powerfully, whether on public platforms or in private, domestic, and solitary prayer. Given their intense and immediate appeal, devotional songs form an area in which women's engagement has always shone forth with particular intensity. Mīrābāī's songs are not the only exemplars of a woman's religious passion but perhaps the most often sung. These songs, not all of them composed by women, have the power to transport a singer, as we may see in their performance photos and videos, to a sacred space beyond the bounds of worldly life.

Situating women at the centre of songs of devotion is particularly noteworthy because the feminine persona is a crucial component of the culture of devotion, blurring the line between human and divine in many ways. Indeed, Hindu devotional songs, like devotional poetry, are largely testaments of surrender and mimic human relationships, in which love for the divine Beloved is expressed as love for a human lover, and the singer is a feminised person, identified by a cultural, not biological, gender.[2] When Kabīr (fifteenth century) entreats the

2 The trope of a feminised seeker of the divine is not particular to Hinduism but a common feature of other religious cultures as well; the metaphor of the Christian church as the bride of Christ is an example.

Beloved to come to him, he does it as '*tumhārī nārī*' (your bride) who cannot understand his lover's kind of love when they '*ekameka hvai seja na sovai*' (do not lie in bed as one).[3] This male poet's position is little different from the woman poet Mīrābāī's when she sings '*mhārā olagiyā ghar āyā jī/ tan kī tāp miti*' (my absent beloved has come home/ my body's heat has been quenched), a song made popular by Pandit Kumar Gandharva, a male singer. While Mīrā is the archetypal songstress devotee, uncountable numbers of Hindu women find spiritual solace and fulfillment in music, singly or in groups. Few Hindu worship ceremonies take place without music, usually songs in praise of deities, and music is often in itself an act of worship. For example, some years ago at Tirupati, one of the greatest Hindu pilgrimage sites in India, I met a woman scholar for whom singing before Lord Viṣṇu was an act of ceremonial worship shorn of rituals. For women in the Hindu diaspora, *kīrtan* singing, which is a call-and-response variety of religious music involving close audience engagement, has been for decades an engagement with their gods and goddesses at private homes and public venues, bringing them solace in lands away from their homeland. At Hindu temples and religious processions around the world, women are enthusiastic participants in sacred chants. For some time past an engrossing religious event in India has been the annual *Kabīr Yātrā* (Kabīr's Travels) in Western India, which has been drawing thousands of the devout, Hindus as well as people of other faiths. Hugely popular, this annual event largely consists of singing Kabīr's poems, many of the most admired

3 These words are from the following stanza:

bālama āu hamānrai greha re;
tumha bina dukhiyā deha re.
saba koi kahai tumhārī nārī mokauñ yaha andeha re;
ekameka hvai seja na sovai taba lagi kaisā neha re.

Kabīr Sāheb kī Śabdāvalī (Allahabad: Belvedere Steam Printing Press, 1913), Pt. 1, p. 9)

A woman sings during a festival in Manipur.

Manipuri women singing kirtan together.

singers being women, such as Shabnam Virmani of Bengaluru, Parvathy Baul of Thiruvanthapuram, and Gavra Devi of Bikaner.

Videos of the events show how complete their transport of joy is in their contemplation of the sacred.

For these women and their listeners, liberation comes from losing themselves in the music of adoration. In the theology of *bhakti*, surrender to the divine turns into a total submersion of the self in the godhead, a state of ecstasy often metaphorised as physical union, in which the devotee is imagined as a woman. That is why womanhood is a privileged state in the arts that *bhakti* has inspired.

Dance

As a religious medium, songs are especially popular with women because singing requires no special resources, not even any particular musical talent for a person's singing to be a fulfilling act of devotion. Far more demanding is dance, music's sister art: its indispensable requirements are physical competence, musical accompaniment, and a performing space, not to speak of the years of training that go into the making of a dancer. While dance is not exclusively a women's art, and although some of the greatest dancers in the Hindu classical tradition of dance are (and have been) men, most dancers are women. The tradition of dance is deeply steeped in Hindu religious culture, not only because most dance performances use Hindu legends as narrative platforms but also – more – because their goal is as much to expound and glorify gods and goddesses as to present the harmony of the human body in motion as an offering to gods and goddesses. Dance is a religious act for Hindus and in fact so signaled by the required practice of dancers to greet the dance platform as a sacred space before the dance begins. Like devotional music, dance too is a religious domain inhabited to a great extent by women.

Two aspects of the dance in India call for attention: first, traditional dance scholarship, initiated some time around second or third century BCE by Bharata Muni, traced the origin of dance to Śiva, the cosmic dancer, thereby legitimising dance spiritually (*Nāṭyaśāstra*, ch. 4, verse 13, verse 207). His text also tells us in the same section that dance was an essential complement to drama, and as such it was expected to reinforce religious faith, as drama was created to make sacred legends accessible to common people, especially *śudras* and women, that is, those who did not have access to formal education. This suggests that a woman's religious education could be accomplished through dance and drama. Bharata's views remained in force through centuries of classical scholarship, amplified forcefully in the thirteenth century by Śārṅgadeva in his *Saṅgītaratnākara*, in which he asserts that through dance and music one can attain to *Śivaloka*, Śiva's heavenly abode, that Śiva loves music and dance, Kṛṣṇa the

Young women dancing at a Rajasthani festival in Udaipur, India.

music of the flute, and Sarasvatī that of the *vīṇā*. He assures his readers that through music and dance one may reach all the four goals of life: *dharma* or righteousness, *kāma* or pleasure of the senses, *artha* or wealth, and finally, *mokṣa* or liberation (*'dharma-kāma-artha-mokṣadam'*, *Saṅgītaratnākara*, 1. 26–30). That dance is taken in the classical tradition of the Hindus as a sacred act is evident in the sacralising of the dance platform, which the dancer enters only after offering homage to the deity who commands the space. Secondly, the end product of dance has been held to be beauty and grace. Dance is thus valorised both spiritually and aesthetically, and has continued to be regarded by Hindus both as a sacred act and as a thing of supreme beauty. The sacred connotation of dance is clearly marked in the custom – banned by law in India since 1988 – of women being consecrated to the service of male deities at South Indian temples as *devadāsīs* (handmaidens of God), each woman ritually married to the deity, with dance set as one of their major duties.[4] Until the banning of the *devadāsī* custom, the Jagannatha temple in Puri, Odisha, had women dancers known as *māhārīs*, who were similarly married to the god worshipped in the temple and similarly responsible for dancing before their Lord. An inscription in the Oriya script above a door at the temple, dated 1499 CE, instructs the *māhārīs* to dance to the songs of Jayadeva's *Gītagovinda* in front of the image of Jagannatha every evening to entertain Him during His evening meal until He is put to bed.[5] Since beauty and grace are conventionally

4 See Saskia C. Kersenboom, 'The Traditional Repertoire of the Tiruttaṇi Temple Dancers', in *Roles and Rituals for Hindu Women*, ed. Julia Leslie (Delhi: Motilal Banarsidass, 1992), 131–147; and Frederique Marglin, *Wives of the God-King: the Rituals of the Devadasis of Puri* (Oxford: Oxford University Press, 1985).

5 Barbara Stoller-Miller, *The Gītagovinda of Jayadeva, Love Song of The Dark Lord* (Delhi: Motilal Banarsidass, 1984), Introduction, 6.

associated with femininity, dancers have been historically taken to be women, as the evidence of Sanskrit dance treatises tells us from the time of Bharata onwards. When Śārṅgadeva describes a dancer he refers to a female body and observes that the ideal dancer is female: '*pātraṁ syān nartanādhāro nṛtte prāyeṇa nartakī*' (*Saṅgītaratnākara*, 7. 1224. 1). Even though there is no bar to men taking up the art, descriptions of dances stretching back through the ages takes it for granted that they are performed by women, while musical accompaniments are left to men. Dancing figures carved on temple walls are those

Women dancers at Halebid temple.

of women, as in the following twelfth-century temple relief from Halebid, to cite only one of many instances.

Similar scenes of dancing female figures adorn Hindu temples of Southeast Asia, showing heavenly nymphs in dancing poses with a male musician in attendance.

Through its long evolution, the dance in India became an art principally for women in secular as well as religious contexts. One style that is well known for celebrating Kṛṣṇa is Manipuri, a style especially known for its graceful movements,

Women dancers at Halebid temple.

Manipuri dancers performing a Rādhā-Kṛṣṇa dance.

which is performed by women, including representations of male personae.

The repertoires of other classical styles of Indian dancing are similarly dominated by religious purposes, themes, and appeals for divine blessings and favour. Dances are also enactments of legends of gods and goddesses that glorify their power and love for humanity, and at the same time bring them into the dancer's and the audience's conceptual reach as part of their reality. As religious acts, formal dances in Hindu society were traditionally held within temple precincts, but in modern times dances, even on ceremonial occasions, have moved to public venues. Despite this shift and enlargement of the venue, the religious content has hardly changed and has in fact been reinforced by the dancers and their gurus as a matter of deliberate choice because of the rise of education among dancers.

The understanding of dance as a religious act underlies not only sophisticated dance styles such as Bharatanāṭyam or Odissi but also performances of faith keyed to everyday life. From as far back in history as can be traced, simple celebrations and propitiations of gods and goddesses through dance have been part of village life among Hindus, giving rise to a wide variety of folk dances. Some of such dance styles are relatively elaborate and practiced with great care and preparation as occasional presentations of joyous worship. A notable example is Garba, performed at the Navarātri festival of Western India in autumn to rejoice in the coming of the Mother Goddess to visit her earthly children. In a culture that has not traditionally provided for social dancing of men and women, Garba is a rule-breaker in valorising women's participation in dance with men as an act of worship. Women's performance of Garba is not only sanctioned by religious convention but also enjoined upon them as a sacred duty in which their delight signals their sense of affinity with the religious spirit of the occasion.

A group of young classical Bharanatyam dancers in South India.

A girl strikes an Indian classical Odissi dance pose in front of Brahmeswara Temple, Bhubaneswar, Odisha, India.

Garba is not the only community dance that forms a part of women's worship. The number of folk dances of India is great, and not all of them have religious connotations but many do, and quite a few are especially popular with women dancers, old and young. The list is long but one worth noting is the Phulpati dance of Madhya Pradesh, performed by unmarried girls to celebrate Holi.

From Tamilnadu comes another well-known folk dance called Karagattam, performed in praise of the goddesses Mariamman and Gangai Ammana. It has two branches, one of which is called Atta Karagam and is mainly danced by women.

Painting

Raṅgoli and Ālpanā

Women's religious self-expression in the arts is not confined to music and dance, though they command the most extensive public engagement because of their dynamic inclusiveness, pulling onlookers into the performance by their spiritual and emotional energy. This cannot be said of many other genres of art, which tend to be lonely occupations. Some show little participation by women, such as sculpture and architecture, which have not drawn many women to them. Even though both have been sites of religious vision, they are far more demanding with respect to time, finances, and technical training. Painting and the decorative arts, on the other hand, are heavily subscribed by Hindu women looking to affirm and define their faith. From drawing abstract or stylised designs on the floor to painting scenes from Hindu myths, countless women attempt to affirm their closeness to the sacred in lines and colours, some of them realistic portrayals of divine and mythical beings, nature and animals, while some are abstract designs. Known under different terms, one variety of this form of art is *raṅgoli*, achieved by drawing designs on the floor in colourful powdered grains and sometimes in flower petals, which can be seen in Hindu homes in many parts of India on festive occasions. A special genre of floor decoration is the *ālpanā* art of West Bengal, drawn similarly on the floor but using a thin, white paste made up of ground rice and water, as we have already noted in Chapter 5. *Ālpanā* and *raṅgoli* comprise an art widely practiced almost exclusively by women as part of the ritual preparation of the space consecrated for *pūjā* and the home in general. This is by no means a mechanical activity. Stephen P. Huyler has described in considerable detail how women employ these works as a means of communicating with gods and goddesses.[6] It is hard to know how self-conscious the women are in executing these designs as overt statements of faith but it wouldn't be an overstatement to say that the activity, in itself, is an engagement with their faith that brings them a distinct sense of closeness to whichever deity they hold in their hearts.

Paṭacitra

Ālpanā and *raṅgoli* are usually highly complicated floral or geometric figures that call for a fine sense of graphic design and considerable manual skill. They may or may not incorporate iconic elements, such as a stylised sheaf of rice or a lotus to symbolise Lakṣmī, the goddess of plenty, emphasising their religious intent. A very different form of art of folk origin is the *paṭacitra* of West Bengal and Odisha, which are pictorial narratives mainly of characters and events from Hindu myths such as the *Rāmāyaṇa*, life-events of Kṛṣṇa, or admonitory

---

6 Stephen P. Huyler, *Painted Prayers: the Village Art of India* (New York: Rizzoli, 1994). For an informative account of *ālpana* as a secular art, see *Alpana of Santiniketan School* (Calcutta: Chitrangshu Institute of Art and Handicraft, 1967).

A woman painter from Andhrapradesh working on a Chittara style painting.

An Indian craftswoman paints on colorful handicraft items in Kolkata.

scenes of divine justice in the afterlife. The *paṭacitras* of West Bengal are usually made in the form of panels arranged vertically as long scrolls that are unrolled, as the painter points at each panel and sings or recites that part of the story.[7] There are also stand-alone, single frame paintings of gods,

A contemporary display and recitation of a painted scroll.

7 For an illustrated critical account, see Mandakranta Bose, *The Rāmāyaṇa in Bengali* Folk Paintings (New Delhi: Niyogi Books, 2017).

goddesses, and mythical tales, such as *Kāliya Damana* (Kṛṣṇa's slaying of the snake demon Kāliya), particularly in the Oriya *paṭa* tradition. Till about mid-twentieth century, the *paṭas* were painted mainly by men with some help from the women of their families, but in recent years more women have taken up the art. Since the late 1900s *paṭacitras* have advanced to the front line of rural culture, especially in the southern districts of West Bengal, and at annual village fairs women are highly visible participants as *paṭuās* (*paṭa* painters).

This can be a modern performance in the public arena, as one of the photos above shows. At the same time, women artists continue to work in a non-public setting, immersed in creating figures and designs within their personal space.

Attracting large crowds, public demonstrations have now become part of the entertainment industry in India, even if a minor one that competes with other folk performing arts. This may suggest that the painters are now taking their art as a commercial career; but even casual conversations with them show that they value the religious content of their paintings, as emphasised in the following iconic image of Rāma with the Hindu trinity of Brahmā, Viṣṇu, and Śiva:

Rāma and the Great Gods.

Although systematic surveys of women *paṭuās* are yet to be done, I have found that women painters tend to be conservative in their choice of subject and stay within the religious framework, while contemporary social and political themes attract male *paṭuās*. Conserving the religious heritage does seem to be taken seriously by the women painters.

Madhubani

Among the domestic arts of India, one that shows the widest and most sustained participation by women is the Madhubani art of Bihar, also known as the art of Mithila. Folklore traces Madhubani paintings centuries back to the wedding of Rāma and Sītā, for which it is said to have been invented by order of Sītā's father, King Janaka of Mithila. Certainly of great age, Madhubani began as an art of wall and floor decoration in the Madhubani district of Bihar at village homes built with mud walls and floors, which women covered with paintings of gods, goddesses, mythical characters, birds, animals, plants, and flowers. The tradition has not changed much over the centuries except that now paintings are executed also on paper and fabric. The mud surface is plastered over with rice paste, and when it is dry, the image is drawn on it in bright colours. Each painting is tightly filled with figures and geometric designs to create a rich, crowded, ornamental composition.

Since the plaster and paint materials are derived from plants and earth elements, the paintings do not fare well from exposure to rain and sun, and the artists have to plaster the surface over after a while and start a fresh painting. Paintings done on paper or canvas are of course portable and not as vulnerable to weather. Here is a woman drawing an intricate design on paper, which is becoming increasingly common because of market demand for portable pieces that can be displayed wherever the purchaser wishes.

Sītā Devi, Madhubani painter.

Economic pressure is considerable in determining the kind of painting that these women produce today, but conventional subjects such as ancient legends and gods and goddesses still outnumber purely decorative patterns or scenes from nature. Madhubani art is not exclusively religious but Hindu religious ideas and motifs are a constant presence in the paintings, explicitly as central figures of adoration and implicitly as a framework for the lived experience of the painters. The painting below is of the wedding of Rāma and Sītā and can be taken as part of the painter's (or her client's) worship milieu.

Madhubani painting.

The paintings above can also serve as auspicious complements to marriage festivities, finding in hallowed tradition an echo and perhaps a valorising of the ceremony at which they are displayed. It is fair to note that the paintings might be taken by the viewer, and perhaps even by their maker, as objects entirely without religious or social significance, serving rather as purely decorative pieces of aesthetic, not ideological value. But it is unlikely that the religious association of the imagery would be lost on any viewer or that a painter would not have had that association in mind in the course of the painting. Madhubani paintings, like all other types of women's art we have surveyed in this chapter, are ambivalent in conveying their meaning because it is not possible to be certain about why their creators created them. It is only fair to concede that we do not know, and perhaps can never know, whether the artistic activity we have been considering here is planned self-consciously as statements of religious faith, or whether it is done for some other, perhaps commercial purpose. Is it not also possible that women (and men) create art for pure aesthetic satisfaction? Perhaps even playfully?

Why religion?

As the questions posed above imply, the 'why' of art is never quite certain and may even be irrelevant. In the traditional Hindu milieu, religion is all-pervasive and there is nothing within that milieu – we are talking about the traditional milieu – that does not bear some trace of religious beliefs and rules, from food to worship regimens. This is also true, perhaps especially so, of the vast Hindu diaspora which fervently nurtures its roots in the parent culture as all displaced people do. To label a particular art tradition as 'Hindu' is therefore not only legitimate but necessary, no matter how non-denominational or universal it may seem to be. In this chapter, I have been looking into that tradition to understand the ways in which women's participation in art may be regarded as a religious act, taking 'participation' in the widest sense of both creation and reception. It is highly doubtful that any branch of that tradition was ever deliberately designed exclusively by, or for, women but it is historically reasonable to identify some arts, such as dance, as a woman's art even though there is not, nor has there ever been, any barrier to men from taking it up. The decorative arts in the domestic setting on auspicious occasions are in the domain of women, as is the singing of devotional songs singly or in company of friends and relatives, but there are occasional exceptions even if few. Again speaking historically, Hindu women have gravitated to certain art forms rather than others – women are not known to carve statues of deities – but the reasons for those choices are not always clear, although the need to engage with one's community is a powerful motive for taking up this art rather than that. An art activity such as drawing an *ālpanā* may be taken on because everyone else is doing it and thereby to assert one's place in the community in a congregational sense: we pray together when we paint together. But obviously Hindu women's participation in art is not merely social but also devotional in the strictest sense of the word, art forging a link between them and the deity they worship.

Drawing upon Women's Art

Links are of course two-way routes. While women may find that art opens doors to religious peace and fulfillment, the Hindu religion on its part draws upon women's art for its enrichment, if only because it is seen to command devotion that is both passionate and persistent. Just by itself activity is affirmation and affirmation holds up the ideological edifice of religion. But on a deeper level, women's art, be it music or painting or dance, opens up ways of thinking about the whole notion of the relationship between the creator and creation, a relationship that is invariably defined by women's art as one of love and mutuality. This is not to say that such a relationship underpins only women's art, not men's. Kabīr's poetry is no less – perhaps much more – passionate in its foregrounding of love for God than Mīrābāī's. True, but consider this: doesn't Kabīr's passion take shape in the female persona? If you look at another great Indian poet, Nobel Laureate Rabindranath Tagore, you will find the same gender alignment in his spirituality, though in more restrained words and more oblique imagery. Women's art adds a special vocabulary to the dialogue between the human and the divine, broadening the meditative scope of the Hindu religion.

Discussion Topic: Art, Religion, and Gender

- If I showed you a painting that I know to be by a woman painter but you don't, would you be able to tell whether it is by a man or a woman? If you are able to do so, what would your explanation be for your identification? If you cannot, would you still think this chapter has been of any value? Why?

- In this chapter you have read lines from a poem by Kabīr who adopts a female persona; what do you think his reason for this might be? What is so special about a feminine position?

- Can every form of art be a vehicle of religious thought and feeling? Instrumental music is often played on religious occasions; would you call such music sacred? Why?

- Religious faith is said to be an emotional, intellectual, and imaginative experience; can it also be an aesthetic experience?

VII
Arriving at Modernity

The place of women in traditional Hindu religious thought and life may well appear ambiguous because women have been at once honoured and devalued. Since Hindu religious philosophy accords the Divine Feminine the highest adoration, one may expect at least a touch of it to be extended to women. The reality has been the opposite in general. Yet for the majority of Hindu women, their systemic disadvantage has not eroded their faith. In recent times, the liberalisation of Hindu social culture has alleviated gender prejudice, and Hindu women's devotion to their faith is recognised as one of the root causes of Hinduism's longevity. The great majority of Hindu women have always been deeply observant of religious rites, even orthodox in their practice. With advancing education and the pressure of secular needs, some women have questioned Hinduism's principles and practices without, however, abandoning the essential spiritual positions on which belief and practice are founded. Modernity has brought altered religious sensibilities and social relocation of Hindu women but has not eroded their faith.

Religion and Society

Our discussions through the previous chapters will have shown that Hindu women have not always had an easy time, either in religion or in society. That this has not turned women away from their faith argues for the potency of spiritual solace and personal comfort in the principles and practices of Hinduism. Looking closely at women's adherence to their faith is a particularly useful approach to understanding the longevity of the Hindu religion and the integrity of the social culture it sustains. Put simply, Hindu women's faith today remains as strong as in past times even as Hinduism has evolved to accord women a higher status than before. The causes of this development are two: the spread of women's education, which has heightened women's self-awareness, and the worldwide struggle for equality, justice, and human rights for all, especially women's social rights. As I noted at the beginning of this study, Hinduism is at once a religion and a social system, the two so closely interwoven that worldly life and religious life can hardly be separated. Yet it would be misleading to suggest that for Hindus, as indeed for all religiously inclined people, the life of the spirit is the same as life in the world. They are in fact different. The human instinct for aspiring to divinity, even when diffuse and undifferentiated as conscious thought, can be a heightened state of being, in which individuals may rise above material needs and social concerns. In their feeling for the sacred, women and men can rise above the circumstances of their worldly life, and many do so, no matter how difficult it may be. Sadly, the burden of social life everywhere has been historically far heavier on women than on men, and especially bitter for Hindu women because of the social constraints on them supposedly authorised by Hindu scriptures. But given that such scriptural authority in Hinduism is patently manmade, there is always room for questioning it, as indeed women as well as men have done through the history of the Hindus. We must also bear in mind that the same scriptures also elevate women to the highest spiritual level and that remains a permanent resource within the faith for claiming women's religious authority.[1] How else could there have been reform movements for women in Hinduism?

Let us note in passing that nineteenth-century reform initiatives by religious bodies such as the Brahmo Samaj and the Arya Samaj included women's liberation from customary social injunctions as part of their goal. Also important have been individual women's self-affirmation by rejecting the imposition of roles forced upon them by their social world. Note too that this is not a modern phenomenon but goes a long way back. The perfect exemplar of such an assertion of independent selfhood in religious faith is the poet Mahādevī Ākkā, who rejected all calls upon her to submit to the duties set for a woman of her time, and won an equal and independent place for herself in the community of scholarly devotion in her own time. As David Kinsley puts it, social duty is an 'inherited duty' for everybody, but individuals also have an 'inherent duty' to love the Lord;[2] for some, that love is all-consuming to the exclusion of social commitments. To the credit of the Hindu social system, it must be said that Hindu society has always accepted – indeed revered – women who have made single-minded devotion to their Lord their sole quest in life, even when they have transgressed against the gender roles set by their social world.

---

1 See Madhu Khanna, 'Here are the Daughters: Reclaiming the Girl Child', in *The Goddess*, ed. Mandakranta Bose, Oxford History of Hinduism series (Oxford: Oxford University Press, 2018), 173–198.

2 David Kinsley, 'Devotion as an Alternative to Marriage in the Lives of Some Women Devotees', *Journal of Asian and African Studies* 15 (1980): 1–2.

The Dictates of Dharma

These women are, however, unusual individuals who have carved out their own ethos, both religious and social. In comparison, the vast majority of Hindu women, like Hindu men, have had their religious life determined by their location in Hindu society, as set by gender, caste, and occupation, also to some degree by their economic class. As part of their social duties, women's *dharma* has been traditionally derived from the sacred texts of Hinduism and from the lives of revered individuals, which still exert considerable force in Hindu society. Since that *dharma* is a code of conduct rather than the expression of spiritual impulse, many Hindu women today, as in the past, have chosen to follow their personal spiritual needs on their own even if their quest may have taken them away from the duties prescribed by *dharma,* sometimes to the consternation of their families and even to outright persecution, as in the case of Mīrābāī, whom her husband tried to poison. But the more common response has been not to take such women's independence as transgression, but to accept – indeed to celebrate – it as the legitimate call of the spirit. In Chapter 4 we have noted how women such as Mīrābāī, Ākkā Mahādevī, and Āṇṭāḻ followed their personal spiritual quest within the Hindu faith as they set aside the domestic and gender roles ordained for them by conventional Hindu *dharma*. Even within their own lifetimes they came to be revered as holy spirits. This catholicity of Hindu society has proved to be an inexhaustible source of strength and one of the reasons of its survival through millennia of debate and assaults upon the social culture it created. As the charismatic nineteenth-century preceptor Ramakrishna Paramahamsa used to say, 'more opinions [open] more paths'. This twin accommodation of the world and faith is integral to Hindu social culture. Just as the world constantly encroaches upon areas of faith, so do articles of faith frame and form the social world of the Hindus. The religious history of Hindu women is thus their social history as well.

The Burden Women Bear

In tracing that history we must begin by acknowledging that for many centuries Hindu society has not been kind to women, not only denying them social equality but actively demoting the entire sex to a lower moral and intellectual order. Again, this denunciation was not universal, for there were, in the past, many influential voices extolling women's virtues. In general, though, women's subordination to men has been taken for granted through centuries well into modern times, taking the form of myriad rules locking women into narrow domesticity, especially in the form of self-denying service to husbands and other males of the family, for which support from scriptural authority was claimed, as we have seen in Chapter 3, and religion invoked to secure women's compliance. This religious validation of women's subjugation is now generally discredited and so is the disparagement of women as lesser creatures. But prejudice still lingers, in some instances even without the pretense of specific religious sanction, which has been replaced by an appeal to so-called traditional Hindu values in validating women's subordination to male self-interest.[3]

---

3 Among numerous studies, one especially helpful in its narrative spread is Steve Derné's article, 'Hindu Men Talk about Controlling Women: Cultural Ideas as a Tool of the Powerful', *Sociological Perspectives* 37 (1994), 2: 203–227.

Resistance

It took a long time for Hindu women to resist such dehumanising exploitation, passively at first with appeals to the sense of justice of the male rulers of society and government, later more actively denouncing male oppression. Since the second half of the twentieth century, Hindu women's demands for justice have drawn strength from feminist movements. Appropriately in the context of the Hindu faith, one strategy of claiming power and self-determination has been the invocation of the sacred tradition of the Divine Feminine.[4] Derived from the assertion of equality in faith is Hindu women's claim of religious leadership in the form of conducting priestly duties. While not common, women have been officiating and training as priests at formal rituals in many communities in India and abroad, as several online news sources report.[5] Formal training for priesthood is provided specifically for women at two Hindu religious schools, Shankar Seva Samiti and Jnana Prabodhini, in Pune, India. Practicing women priests are rare but not unknown today: two groups of female Sanskrit scholars and university professors in Kolkata are highly sought after as priests at Vedic wedding rites.

This assumption of leadership in the Hindu faith community by women is the positive aspect of Hindu women's battle to erase the religious sanction of gender inequality. In the backdrop to that struggle we may detect two social circumstances that have historically fostered Hindu women's awareness of the systematic injustice under which they lived:

---

4 See Ali Smears, 'Mobilizing Shakti: Hindu Goddesses and Campaigns against Gender-Based Violence', *Religions* 10 (2019), 6: article 381.

5 See Siobhan Heanue, https://www.abc.net.au/news/2018-04-11/meet-the-indian-housewives-studying-to-become-hindu-priests/9639760. April 10, 2018; and Lavina Melwani, 'Women Augment the Priestly Ranks', *Hinduism Today* (April/May/June 2007): 33.

education and India's struggle for independence from colonial rule. The spread of female education in India – as elsewhere in the world – not only made Hindu women critically aware of their place in society but also enabled them to voice their discontent in public. Secondly, turning our attention to the political platform of national affairs, we see that as the women of India, from the Hindu community and others, became involved in the struggle for India's independence, they began to realise that their nation's independence from foreign domination could not be full without women's independence from male domination. Education and politics thus became the twin liberating forces in modern women's life.

Freedom through Education

Education was the immediate instrument of women's awakening to their situation and their awareness of the ideals of self-determination and justice, which became persistent themes in women's periodicals that began to appear from about the second half of the nineteenth century. An influential Bengali monthly appeared in 1863, titled *Bāmābodhinī Patrikā* ('A Magazine to Raise Female Consciousness') and survived till 1922, exclusively devoted to urging and facilitating education for women from basic literacy to the post-secondary level, striving at the same time to persuade women themselves to seek education as the only means of elevating themselves in their personal and social life. Another periodical titled *Abalābāndhab* ('Friend of the Weaker Sex') was founded by the social reformer Dwarakanath Ganguly in 1869, with the express aim of advocating women's liberation from social bondage. Similar aims impelled other journals for women across India, such as *Kerala Suguna Bodhinī* in Malayalam, published from Tiruvantapuram 1884 onwards, *Sugrihiṇī* in Hindi, published from Allahabad 1888 onwards, and *Bhārat Bhaginī* in Hindi, also an Allahabad publication from 1889.

The push towards women's education was publicly initiated by influential men – not surprisingly because theirs were the voices heard – for instance, the early nineteenth-century social reformer Raja Rammohan Roy, whom we have encountered in Chapter 3 as the first campaigner against *satī*. In 1818 he challenged his orthodox compatriots:

> When have you tested women's intelligence that you term them slow-witted? If somebody who has been given education cannot comprehend it, you can call that person lacking in intelligence. You have never given women education; how then can you be so sure that they are lacking in intelligence? On the contrary, those women who were given the advantages of education, such as Līlāvatī, Bhānumatī, King Karṇāṭa's queen, Kālidās's wife – all to whom education was bestowed, earned fame as scholars in every field.[6]

Schools for girls had indeed been established as early as 1810 by British and American Christian missionaries, but since their primary aim was to spread Christianity in India, the education available there was not the liberating form of education that Roy and others had in view.

An Indian move in that direction came from Jayakrishna Mukhopadhyaya, owner of the vast, wealthy Uttarpara estate near Calcutta, who set up the Hitakarī Sabhā (Society for [Public] Benefit). A major aim of the Sabhā was female education, including vocational training, and although Mukhopadhyaya's wish in 1845 to found a girls' school did not receive government approval, the Sabhā ran education

6 Rammohan Roy, *Rammohan Granthābalī* (Collected Works), ed. Brajendranath Bandyopadhyay and Sajanikanta Das (Calcutta: Bangiya Sahitya Parishat, 1951), vol. 3, p. 45 [my translation].

programmes for girls and young women, eventually succeeding in establishing a school for them.[7] What was possibly the first school for girls established by Indians was one established in 1848 in the small Bengali town of Barasat by Peary Charan Sarkar, with help from Nabinkrishna Mitra and Kalikrishna Mitra, now known as Kalikrishna Girls' High School. This was so successful and innovative, in terms of its syllabus and teaching technique, that it encouraged the British educator John Elliot Drinkwater Bethune to found his Calcutta Female School for 'the daughters of native gentlemen . . . first of the kind in Calcutta',[8] in 1849. Financed by Dakshinaranjan Mukherjee, this school was later renamed Hindu Female School. In 1873, the Brahmo reformer Dwarakanath Ganguly and his associates founded the Hindu Mahila Vidyalaya, later

7 For a full account of the Hitakarī Sabhā, see Basantakumar Samanta, *Hitakarī Sabhā, Strī-śikṣā o Tatkālīna Baṅgasamāja [Hitakarī Sabhā, Female Education and Contemporary Bengali Society]* (Calcutta: Sāhityaloka, 1987).
8 H. E. A. Cotton, *Calcutta Old and New* (Calcutta: W. Newman, 1907), 957.

School girls in a rural village school in Maharashtra.

renamed the Banga Mahila Vidyala, which eventually merged with what was to become today's prestigious Bethune School and College in 1879. Close in time to its founding, in 1848, the Marathi couple Jyotirao (also known as Jotiba) Phule and Savitribai Phule founded a school for girls in Pune. Jyotirao's dedication and determination were remarkable. When he married Savitri, she was illiterate; so he first taught her to read and write, and then the two of them proceeded to dedicate their lives to teaching girls and women in parallel with their even harder task of working for the protection and rights of untouchable people around them. Another man of vision was Dhondo Keshav Karve, who founded a school for girls and women near Pune in 1896 and in 1916, a college in Mumbai for women. In 1920, this became the SNDT (Shreemati Nathibai Damodar Thackersey) Women's University, the first women's university in India and Southeast Asia.

Towards Politics

Education for women was a social movement that had a political edge to it, given that along with self-awareness, it also instilled in women some sense of the power relationships between rulers and ruled, which included not only men's rule over women but also that of the power the British exercised over the Indian people. Two women's periodicals of the first decade of the twentieth century in Bengali, *Bhāratamahilā* ('Women of India', 1905) and *Suprabhāta* ('Good Morning', 1907), had political leanings and took nationalist positions coloured by feminist ideas. Samples from *Bhāratamahilā* are worth pondering:

> Whose head would not bow in shame to call oneself human when one calls to mind the torment that the victorious white races of the world have

> always inflicted on enslaved dark-skinned people
> and still do?
> (*Bhāratamahilā,* part 4, no. 2, May–June 1908, p. 26)

The periodical's double motto was '*yatra nāryastu pūjyante ramante tatra devatāḥ*' (the gods are present wherever women are honoured, *Manusmṛti,* 3.56), followed by Tennyson's lines:

> The woman's cause is man's: they rise or sink
> Together, dwarfed or God-like, bond or free;
> . . . . .
> If she be small, slight-natured, miserable,
> How shall man grow?[9]

By the beginning of the twentieth century, women were actively participating in India's fast-growing nationalist movement for self-rule and a degree of independence from British rule. Women were in the front lines of the political agitation against the 1905 partition of Bengal decreed by Lord Curzon, the British Viceroy of India, their voice becoming stronger with time, as we see – to cite only one example – in the Bengali periodical *Suprabhāta*: the first page of volume 2 (1908) no. 2 of the magazine issues a short but fiery call to action by the pseudonymous 'Baṅganārī', a Bengali woman. The magazine's effort to link women's advancement through education was strongly echoed in the very next number of the same year, in a long speech by the leading physician of the time, Dr. Nilratan Sarkar, who declared that no nation could depend only on men for its advancement, which it could not achieve without women's education (*Suprabhāta,* vol. 2, no. 3, p. 85). Their fast-growing awareness of social inequity and their apprenticeship in political action was to

9 Alfred Tennyson, 'The Princess', in *The Major Works* [of Tennyson] (Oxford World's Classics. Oxford: Oxford University Press, 2009), Part 7, lines 3081–3088.

lead women to much greater participation in India's freedom movement through the first half of the twentieth century, leading to India's independence in 1947. It also brought more women with more commitment to the expanding political movements of the modern era, most notably those inspired by socialist ideals that came to include revolutionary action. Like women everywhere, Hindu women were politicised by global events and examples. Even though the Suffragist movement of England and America did not quite take root in India or elsewhere in Hindu communities, voices both female and male were raised in the early twentieth century to demand votes for women. In 1921, several provinces of India granted voting rights to educated women of property but that exclusionary requirement was set aside in Punjab by that province's dominant Sikh powers who granted all women the right to vote, whatever their social status. Full adult universal suffrage irrespective of social class, educational qualifications, and economic status did come for Hindu women, as it did for all women of India, after India's independence in 1947.

It may seem at this point that we have moved far from the subject of women's subscription to the Hindu religion. It is true that the move towards women's education was never aimed exclusively at Hindu women, shutting out women of other faiths, but in reality that move took for granted that education would – and should – entrench and enhance in women the virtues idealised in Hindu scriptures. For instance, an editorial in *Bāmābodhinī* concludes:

> Thus, providing more and more expositions of the principles of *dharma,* more and more instances of them designed to purify women's lives, should be the aim of women's education. That is what would best benefit individuals and society as a whole.
>
> (*Bāmābodhinī Patrikā,* summer 1870 [my translation])

The male editor arrives at this summation after explaining that education for women includes conserving the traditions of conduct that distinguished Hindu women from time immemorial. He also warns women readers that education without the cultivation of *dharma* would only lead to the ruin of their families and themselves, and counsels women to follow the chief principles of *dharma* as – to cite the main tenets – sincere faith in God, love for all human beings equally as God's children, truthfulness, charity, chastity, and so on. Although the principles invoked may fit religious ethics across most belief systems, the editorial seems to take for granted that the Hindu religion is the platform of *dharma*. Unexpectedly in that cultural context, one of the earliest numbers of the magazine, from 1864, printed a long appeal by a senior female student, Bibi Taheran Lecha, whose name does not place her within the Hindu fold. Invoking, in the overheated prose of school exercises of the time, the glory and compassion of God the Father, who has created men and women for the perpetuation of Creation, Lecha appeals to her countrymen to shake off their apathy towards female education. This, however, is the only hint of a non-Hindu (if that is what the writer was) contributor to the magazine.

Countering Orthodoxy

Although the movement seeking women's education was a social issue, it sought validation from provisions in Hindu religious texts and, more importantly, claimed that education was fully consonant with religion and virtually a religious duty. The drive to educate women drew sustained opposition from orthodox Hindus on the grounds that ancient authorities had declared the study of the Vedas and associated scriptures inadmissible for women, that women had no intellectual capacity for learning, and that parity with men would encourage women to abandon their domestic duties, rebel against male authority, and stray into licentious behaviour. Proponents of female education countered these fears by citing support for educating women in the same body of Hindu scriptures, and by reminding their opponents of historical precedence in the legends of learned women. Among ancient authorities, the *Bṛhadāraṇyaka Upaniṣad* provided evidence that the birth of a *paṇḍitā*, or scholarly daughter, was so highly valued that special rituals were designed to bring it about (*Bṛhadāraṇyaka Upaniṣad* 6.4.17). Legends of women philosophers such as Maitreyī and Gārgī were persuasive reminders of the value placed on women's education in early Hindu society. Above all, there was the constant reminder of the feminised deification of knowledge in the figure of the Hindu goddess of learning, Sarasvatī. The battle was thus fought very much on religious grounds.

That religious ideals must be conserved was never in question for women who voiced protests against female subjugation and seclusion through the nineteenth century, nor were accusations levelled against the laws that held together the Hindu religion as a spiritual and ethical system. What was under challenge was the body of Hindu customs, that is, the expedient practices that perpetuated the privileges of dominant men in the upper strata of Hindu society. To that end, selected parts of sacred texts were cited by orthodox Hindus, predominantly the Brahmin establishment, reiterating, for example, Manu's strictures on women and conveniently disregarding Manu's exaltation of women (see Chapter 3). Even great scholars and religious leaders stooped to devise forced interpretations of texts in their effort to deny women any advantage. A dismal example is the twisted interpretation of the term '*paṇḍitā*' in the *Bṛhadāraṇyaka Upaniṣad*, that is, a scholarly woman, by the revered eighth-century preceptor and scholar Śaṅkara, who takes it to mean a woman well-versed in domestic duties!

Religion was thus made to serve opposite ends of the same question. Efforts in the nineteenth century to sweep away biased uses of religious texts such as this were necessarily motivated by both the political need to restore women's rights and the religious need to discard misinterpretations to restore the Hindu faith to its fundamental spiritual and ethical principles. These twin needs were perhaps the strongest pillars of Hindu reform movements.[10] When Hindu women began to seek respect, consideration, and at least some measure of liberty, the enabling authority they looked for was a religion rescued from misinterpretation, scrutinising for that purpose Hindu scriptures and codes of law to question Hindu society's regulation of women's lives and the curtailment of their activities.

Liberal Ideology

Finding support in Hinduism's own resources undoubtedly strengthened women's aspirations for justice, freedom, and dignity but we must also note that the time was right for those aspirations. Culminating in the mid-1800s, the 'Age of Revolution', to use a phrase popularised by historian Eric Hobsbawm, was an era when the principles of equality and

10 A detailed account of movements to improve women's lives is given by Geraldine Forbes in *Women in Modern India* (Cambridge, UK: Cambridge University Press, 1996). See also: Spencer Lavan, 'The Brahmo Samaj: India's First Modern Movement for Religious Reform', in *Religion in Modern India*, 2nd edition, ed. Robert D. Baird (New Delhi: South Asia Publications, 1989), 1–25; Kenneth W. Jones, 'The Arya Samaj in British India, 1875–1947', in *Religion in Modern India*, 2nd edition, ed. Robert D. Baird (New Delhi: South Asia Publications, 1989), 27–54; and Kenneth W. Jones, *Socio-Religious Reform Movements in British India*, The New Cambridge History of India (Cambridge: Cambridge University Press, 1989).

liberty dominated political thought across the world. Liberal political thought and resistance to oppression had reached India as moral ideals of public life. Though these had not yet taken political form as demands for independence from colonial rule, the motto of the French revolution, 'Liberty, Fraternity, Equality', was by no means a distant star on the political horizon, eventually to be enshrined as the invocatory phrase of the 1950 Constitution of Free India. The growth of women's education in India exposed them to these political principles. The issue of personal freedom became eventually indistinguishable from the struggle for India's independence, in which women's participation and self-sacrifice constituted a phenomenon that was not only a matter of political choice, but also a moral one.

Politics in this context is obviously not party contest but a moral ideology. For almost 200 years now, the movement to secure Hindu women freedom in following the Hindu *dharma* has taken a political turn by drawing upon the dominant ideology of liberalism in modern times without, however, undercutting women's religious belief or practice. History tells us that Hindu women's religious life has been one of carrying out set religious rituals addressing deities worshipped in their homes and communities. In Chapter 5 on rituals and observances particular to women, we have seen how deep runs the belief in the necessity and efficacy of performing rituals in the hope of gaining divine favour. These observances are motivated not only by mundane self-interest but also, perhaps more, marked by devotion to the divine spirit, no matter in what form that spirit is conceived by the devotee. As in the past, so it is now: for many Hindu women, daily and occasional rituals and religious observances may be duties done by rote, as far as they are physical and social acts, but the impulse behind them arises from a deep-rooted belief in the divine spirit and desire for the peace it brings.

The Twentieth Century and After

This claim of devoutness can be made for the great majority of Hindu women with some confidence until the first half of the twentieth century. Closer to our time, that claim has become less certain because historical events through the past 200 years have reached into the farthest corners of society to shake the stability of social life as never before, exposing domestic life to public upheavals. Politically charged and market-oriented, modern public life provides little room for quiet religious reflection. It may not seem so when we witness the increasingly crowded and opulent public display of Hindu religiosity today in India and in the Hindu diaspora, but the issue is not how opulent and grand religious ceremonies are today but how deep runs faith. Over the past century, most religions in the world have experienced a falling-off of active practice. The rise and hold of rationalism and of compulsory universal education have led to systematic and universal scepticism about religion as a system impervious to objective scrutiny. In Hindu society today the number of educated women is very large and rising, even in rural India and in countries that host the Hindu diaspora, an important consequence being the entry of women into the higher levels of professional work, including academic positions. Not only has this heightened engagement within the world shortened the time and energy needed for religious tasks, but has also fostered disinterest or even disbelief in traditional Hindu rituals. This is not to say that religious belief and practice are withering away among educated and professional Hindu women; but they do seem to be devoting far less time to religious observances than, say, their grandmothers, although this is at best a general impression rather than a statistical conclusion. Traditional religious observances can be seen to thrive better among less educated women and women of lower economic status, who may not have time for much critical questioning of tradition. But even for conservative women, the religious sanction of gender inferiority may not command automatic acceptance, or the sanction, of *satī* and infant marriage, though disparate gender rights might still be accepted. A case in point is the Sabarimala Temple controversy of the recent past. This holy site was closed to women of menstruating age until the ban was lifted by India's Supreme Court in September 2018 in response to a petition made in 2006 by a group of female lawyers. The verdict caused fierce outrage among men, as well as many women, at what they considered a violation of sacred custom. Feelings have run high and women attempting to enter the temple have been turned away, occasionally with violence, by protesting mobs of men as well as women.

The issue demonstrates the contradictory values that characterise Hindu women's religiosity today: on the one hand, most Hindu women subscribe to Hindu religious ideas, including a strong belief in gods, goddesses, and their power to bestow boons or – if offended – their readiness to punish. But this trust in divinity comes today with a willingness to reject customs prejudicial to marginalised groups, such as women and persons of low-caste origin. In opposition to these liberal believers are women who cherish their devotion but also cherish every custom and convention of conduct that Hindu society has accumulated through millennia, whether such practices are directly supported by the sacred texts of Hinduism or by their expedient interpretations. The orthodox position taken by some women in the Sabarimala protest seems surprising in the modern milieu, in which women are usually on the side of demanding more, not less, social rights and freedoms. Infinitely more troubling is the minority – a very small minority but an active lot – of Hindu women who accept so tragic a custom as *satī*, of which a notorious twentieth-century example, cited in Chapter 3, was eighteen year old Roop Kanwar, who immolated herself on her husband's pyre in 1987. Although it is a matter of dispute whether she did so willingly or was forced into the act, there seem to be credible reports of many women, including her own mother, encouraging her to commit *satī*. If – and this is a very big if – Kanwar's *satī* was consensual or if other women were complicit in persuading her, that shows an extraordinary degree of female conservatism.[11] The tenacity of their subscription to inherited customs shows how strong a hold religion may have on Hindu women today. At the same time, when we turn to the recent conflict over conservatism witnessed in the Sabarimala issue, we must stress that the numerous Hindu women who continue to agitate *for* women's unimpeded entry into the Sabarimala, and all other Hindu temples, are impelled by a sense of their right to participate in the same religion, except that they want that religion to be divested of arbitrary rules. This forces us to face a conundrum: which is the 'true' Hindu religion? That is a perennial question not only for Hindus, nor is it limited to any particular historical period or culture or location in the world. It is a question that has dogged all religious cultures, fuelling intense debate that has inevitably, without exception, spilled over into political conflict. No answer seems within reach.

For Hindu women today, the question of the right way to worship a deity (or deities) may not be a vital issue, given that the Hindu religion has neither a single foundational doctrine nor a central authority to enforce it, which makes it possible to accept variations of religious conduct. In any case, faith and practice do not always go hand-in-hand and perhaps cannot in

11 Madhu Kishwar and Ruth Vanita reported in 1987 that on their visit to the memorial for Roop Kanwar, they found village women who were apparently proud of Roop's noble act; see Madhu Kishwar and Ruth Vanita, 'The Burning of Roop Kanwar', *Manushi* no. 42–43 (1987), 15–25.

the modern world under the compulsions of earning economic and social security. But if the power of religion is located internally and understood as personal subscription to the faith and observance of its rites, then Hinduism is doing well. In keeping it alive and forceful, women play a decisive role. Since there are no statistics of habitual temple attendance or of the performance of daily devotional rites, we have to fall back on what is no more than impressionistic and anecdotal views. But even so, the sheer number of women visibly engaged in public ceremonies and in keeping private worship integral to family life suggests the continuity of devoted female religious practice among Hindus.

Women's Activism

What that devotion means is a complex question. Lacking any hard facts, we can only go by what we see around us, and the current scene does suggest that women today have pressing concerns other than absorption in religious devotion. One measure – not reason – of this reorientation is the growing number of women's activist organisations working for women's social and political welfare, irrespective of their religious identities. The great majority of them are non-religious groups that work for women's civil and legal rights, education, health, security against domestic violence, sexual assaults, and exploitation. Bhumata Brigade of Pune fights for gender equality and against social injustice against women; Sanlaap (Dialogue) of Calcutta similarly protects women's rights; the Rahi Foundation of New Delhi helps women victims of incest and childhood sexual abuse; while the Sabala group of Bijapur works to empower women through political awareness and financial independence. All of India's major political parties have women's wings but their primary aim is to advance their party's cause, as the All India Mahila Congress does for the Indian National Congress, and on its part, the All India Democratic Women's Association for the Communist Party of India (Marxist). The women's wing of the Bharatiya Janata Party is called Durga Vahini, that is, the Army of Durga, founded in 1991 by Sadhvi Rithambara, an ascetic woman, which indicates the parent party's strong Hindu partisanship. In keeping with that, the Vahini promotes Hindu values and conduct suitable for women, including prayer.

Organisations for Hindu women driven primarily by religious purpose are few, although some do flourish as hubs for women's devotional engagement. An excellent example is Sri Sarada Math, the women's wing of the Ramakrishna Mission, an institution of marked achievement in promoting Hindu religious philosophy and devotional practice. Although Sri Sarada Math is energetically engaged in the social welfare of women, especially women's education, its main work lies in advancing women's spiritual aspirations. A greater global presence has been achieved by the organisation known as

Women government officers protesting in the street in Bhubaneswar, India.

the Brahma Kumaris. Founded in the 1930s in Hyderabad under the title Om Mandali, it renamed itself as the Brahma Kumaris World Spiritual University in the early 1950s, and now runs education programmes in spiritual awakening in most major cities in India and the rest of the world. While it does not exclude men from its membership or its work, over 80 per cent of the members of Brahma Kumaris are women. Its distinctive feature is that, though its roots lie in Hindu spiritual philosophy, it explores and promotes divergent spiritual ideas while upholding such characteristic Hindu notions as the indestructibility of the soul, the influence of *karma* and rebirth, though not transmigration of the soul across species, as orthodox Hindus believe.

Religion as Identity

Despite their cultivation of Hindu spirituality, the Brahma Kumaris remain on the margins of mainstream Hindu society and even though they are spread across the world, they have had little or no impact on the religious life of Hindus among predominantly Hindu populations, whether in India or in the Hindu diaspora. Self-conscious and assertive displays of religious observance have risen sharply among Hindus through the past half-century, especially in the large Hindu diaspora, as a declaration of identity. Diasporic Hindus, women in particular, lean in general towards orthodoxy, either continuing to practice inherited rituals and customs or mimicking the prevailing religious idiom of India. Emanating from India, pride in the Hindu identity is emphatically expressed by Hindu communities across the world in the form of increased participation in religious festivities and daily worship. Women's participation and public presence at religious occasions are important signifiers of their pride in being Hindu, of seeking parity with their sisters in India, the homeland of the Hindus, and of their affirmation of orthodoxy over and above their inner need for spiritual solace. For diasporic people, that affirmation is also an empowering declaration, as they face racial discrimination from host populations in countries where Hindus comprise a sizeable group, or even where they do not. Temples are potent expressions of Hindu self-assertion, and temple building is a major project of Hindus outside India. The USA, with a Hindu population of 2.23 million, has over 150 Hindu temples and more are on the way, almost all of them very grand. The UK has about 820,000 Hindus, who have built over 120 temples, with more than 30 in the London area alone. After the USA and the UK, the third largest Hindu settlement of Hindus outside India is Mauritius, with a Hindu population close to 700,000 out of a total population of about 1.3 million, and 20 Hindu temples. Another example is Fiji, an island nation with approximately 275,000 Hindus out of a total population of about 916,000, with 11 Hindu temples. Guyana, Surinam, Trinidad and Tobago, all have large populations of Hindus, with over 60 temples scattered across the islands. Canada, with fewer than 300,000 Hindus has over 50 Hindu temples. For diasporic Hindus today, temple building and temple worship are vitally important material signifiers, equally of devotion to their religion and of an empowering cultural identity, the core of which they understand as an unchanging set of beliefs and customs. In Fiji, the reform movement of the Arya Samaj has had little success in drawing adherents to its departure from orthodoxy, for instance, in its anti-idolatry platform, 75 per cent of Hindus opting for what is known there as Sanātan Dharma, that is, the eternal, unchanging way of faith. Similarly in the Republic of Mauritius, the 2011 Census shows 469,313 Hindus against 296 Arya Samaj followers. Traditional ways are followed by Hindus within and outside India, especially in understanding gender roles and caste duties. However, conservative as many Hindus may be in their religious observances, it can generally be said that they – Hindu men and women – no longer cling to the restrictive and oppressive customs that dominated pre-reform Hindu religious culture. Indeed, it is not unusual for Hindu women today to question the old dictates of *dharma* that arose from the gender prejudice inherent in the understanding of *dharma* in the past.

What this indicates is the accommodation that the Hindu religion has made with modernity, in response to the spread of education and the ideology of liberalism. Sustained scholarly scrutiny for almost two centuries has created a critical awareness of weaknesses and failures in the practices of the Hindu religion, especially in its dispensations regarding women and persons of the lower castes.[12] This perception of authorised prejudice and injustice has given rise to doubts concerning the worth of traditional Hindu customs, alienating some Hindus from the practical observances of their religion. But that perception, taken as a challenge to the core beliefs of Hinduism, has also prompted others to underscore the power of those beliefs to nurture bonds of mutual respect and support within Hindu society, by uncoupling gender and caste identities from personal and social worth. For Hindu women who observe daily and occasional worship practices faithfully, whether out of conscious devotion or as a matter of received custom, their faith is a resource in managing everyday life, especially in a world that still does not guarantee women security and equality, not to speak of confronting irresoluble

12 See Vanaja Dhruvarajan, 'Religious Ideology, Hindu Women, and Development in India', *Social Issues* 46 (1990); Prabhati Mukherjee, *Hindu Women: Normative Models*, revised edition (Hyderabad: Orient Longman, 1994); Susan S. Wadley, 'Women and the Hindu Tradition', *Signs: Journal of Women in Culture and Society*, 3 (Autumn 1977), 1: 113–125.

personal crises. For less committed believers, the faith into which they were born still holds value, if only as an anchor of identity. For most, though not all, Hindu women today, religious belief and practice cause no conflict with their everyday experience; on the contrary, religion brings both solace and hope.

Discussion Topic: Hindu Women in Modern Times

- Through the twentieth century, Hindu women have achieved a great degree of relief from the arbitrary and oppressive rules previously governing their lives. To what do you attribute this emancipation?

- What, in your view, is the connection between Hindu women's religious and social self-determination?

- Now that Hindu women have achieved considerable freedom from social dependency sanctioned by religion, is there a chance that their devotion to religious rituals may decline?

- How may women's social and political activism draw strength from Hindu beliefs available in scriptures and legends?

- How would you account for the fact that observance of religious rituals is especially prevalent among women in the Hindu diaspora? Is it due to a need for finding and asserting their cultural and political identity? Or is it due to their continued subscription to a tradition inherited from past generations, which has remained mostly unchanged?

AFTERWORD

Reading through the foregoing chapters that examine the place of women in the Hindu religious culture, you have, I hope, noticed one contradiction: on the one hand, women have been subjected to the strictest male control in every part of life, from personal relations to education to religious rites; on the other hand, the highest animating power of creation is imagined and revered by Hindus as female. Despite this baffling contradiction in social evaluation and the hurdles it presents, Hindu women in search of spiritual self-determination continue to earn independence and reverence against all gender handicaps. This contradiction defies all explanation save that oppositional stances are inherent in Hinduism, as much in its philosophical understanding of the world as in its efforts to organise social life. Recognising and accepting this opposition is an enduring strength of Hinduism; to do so is, in my view, as essential a task for Hindus themselves as it is for all who would understand Hinduism.

Understanding Hinduism poses a challenging methodological task because it is a world system comprising measurable and concrete worldly life as much as intangible and abstract spiritual perceptions. Even more complex is the interdependence of the two in the Hindu psyche. If charting the social and material life of a community is an uncertain undertaking, consider how much more difficult it is to put down on paper the nature of its religious life. The task becomes especially challenging when we are not talking about the entire Hindu community but about a part of it that is integral to the whole, yet separated from it by gender, a concept understood both biologically and socially. How may one ever know, let alone judge, what goes on in the minds and hearts of those who have been held to be different from their fellow human beings, merely on account of bodily particulars?

An absurd judgement indeed. Yet it is on that assumption, often explicitly stated, that women's lives, and the expectations from women, have been laid down in what is accepted as Hindu sacred law and social practice. Historically, women have been not only judged to be subordinate to men as their mental and physical inferiors, but also vilified as morally degenerate creatures so raucously that women's dismissal by men seems to hint at some deep fear of femininity. None of this vitriol is of course particular to Hinduism, nor would it be especially noteworthy, had it not been for its inconsistency with Hinduism's consistent elevation of womanhood to the highest level of adoration in the abstract and reverence for earthly women's procreative power as mothers. Hinduism also happens to be one of the rare belief systems that endow sexuality with mystical purity and power to the extent that an entire religious tradition, that of Tantra, holds it at its core as the key to spiritual liberation. With equal sophistication of philosophy and psychology, yet another Hindu tradition, that of Vaiṣṇavism, takes love extended to its erotic margins as a transcendental and liberating state for human beings. How could any of these sacred positions be conceivable without the recognition of spiritual agency in women?

Against the many strictures on womankind, the recognition of that agency has been part of Hindu consciousness even when it has not translated into women's social emancipation. But times do change: through the past two centuries, revaluations of religious discourse in the public sphere, the acceptance of personal freedom as an integral necessity of life, and Hindu women's ineradicable and expressed constancy to the sacred, often instinctive and undifferentiated, have reshaped women's life within the Hindu world. One aim of this short study has been to alert the reader that resources within the Hindu faith remain available to bring about that regeneration. It is the reader's task, an exciting and challenging one to my way of thinking, to put to scrutiny the extent and potency of those resources, as well as the reality of that regeneration.

References

Texts

Agnipurāṇa. Edited by pandits. Pune: Anandashrama Sanskrit Series, no. 41, 1900.

Aitareya Brāhmaṇam. Vol. 3. Delhi: Naga Prakashaka, 1991.

Ākkā Mahādevī. Menezes, Armando and S. M. Angadi, translators. *Vacanas of Akka Mahadevi*. Dharwar: Shri Manohar Appasaheb Adke, 1973.
Chaitanya, Vinaya, translator. *Vacanas of Akka Mahadevi*. Walnut Creek, CA: Altamira Press, 2005.

Āṇṭāl. Sundaram, P. S. *Poems of Andal*. Bombay: Ananthacharya Indological Research Institute, 1987.

Aśvaghoṣa. *The Saundarānanda of Aśvaghoṣa*, edited by E. H. Johnston. Delhi: Motilal Banarsidass, 1975 [1928].

Atharva Veda, edited and translated by Devi Chand. Delhi: Munshiram Manoharlal, 1990 [1982].

Ātukuri Mollā. Jackson, William. *Vijayanagara Voices*. Burlington, VT: Ashgate, 2005.

Bahiṇābāi. Abbott, Justin E. *Bahiṇābāi*. Poona: Scottish Mission Industries, 1929.

Bāmābodhinī Patrikā [Bengali periodical], edited by Umeshchandra Dutta et al. Calcutta, 1863–1922.

Bāṇabhaṭṭa. *The Harṣacarita of Bāṇabhaṭṭa*, edited by P. V. Kane. Delhi: Motilal Banarsidass, 1973 [1918].

Baudhāyana. *Baudhāyanadharmasūtram*, edited by Pandit Chinnaswami Sastri. Benares City: Kashi Sanskrit Series 104, 1934.

Bharata. *Nāṭyaśāstra*, edited by Bharatamuni. *Nāṭyaśāstra of Bharatamuni, with the commentary Abhinavabhāratī by Abhinavagupta*, edited by M. Ramakrishna Kavi. 4 volumes. Baroda: Gaekwad's Oriental Series, 1934–1964.

Bhāratamahilā [Bengali periodical], edited by Sarajubala Datta. Dhaka: Hemendranath Datta from the Bhāratamahilā Office, 1905–[unknown terminal year].

Bhattacharya, Raghunandana. *Aṣṭāviṁśatitattvam*, edited by Shyamakanta Vidyabhushan-Bhattacharya. Calcutta: n.p., *vaṅgābda* 1347 [1940].

Bṛhadāraṇyaka Upaniṣad, translated by E. Roer. Delhi: Bharatiya Kala Prakashan, 2000.

Bṛhaspati-smṛti, edited by K. V Aiyangar. Baroda: Gaekwar Oriental Series, no. 85, 1941.

Candrāvatī Rāmāyaṇa

Prācīna Pūrvavaṅga Gītikā, edited by Kshitish Moulik. Calcutta: Firma K. L. Mukhopadhyaya, 1970.

Maimansiṁha Gītikā, edited by Sukhamay Mukhopadhyay. Calcutta: Bharati Book Stall, 1970.

A Woman's Rāmāyaṇa: Candrāvatī's Bengali Epic, edited by Mandakranta Bose and Sarika Priyadarshini Bose. Translation with introduction and annotations. London and New York: Routledge, 2013.

Devana Bhaṭṭa. *Smṛticandrikā (Vyavahāra-kāṇḍa)*, edited by L. Srinivasacharya. Mysore: Government Branch Press, 1914.

Devī Bhāgavatapurāṇa Śrīmaddevībhāgavatam, translated by Swami Vijnanananda. [Reprint of Sacred Books of the Hindus, vol. 26, parts 1–4] New York: AMS Press, 1974.

Devīmāhātmya, edited and translated by Swami Jagadiswarananda. Mylapore, Madras: Sri Ramakrishna Math, 1953.

Dharmasūtras: The Law Codes of Āpastamba, Gautama, Baudhāyana, and Vasiṣṭha, edited and translated by Patrick Olivelle. Delhi: Motilal Banarsidass, 2000.

Gobhila Gṛhyasūtra with Sanskrit commentary of Pt. S. Samashrami, translated by Thakur U. N. Singh. Delhi: Choukhamba Sanskrit Pratisthan, 1992.

Jaimini.

[*Pūrvamimāṁsā*] *The Aphorisms of the Mimamsa by Jaimini, with the Commentary of Śavara-Svāmin*, edited by Paṇḍita Maheśachandra Nyāyaratna. Vol. 1, Adhyayas 1–VI. Calcutta: Asiatic Society of Bengal, 1873.

Jaimini. *Pūrvamimāṁsā*, edited and translated by Mohan Lal Sandal. Allahabad: Allahabad Panini Office, 1923.

Kabīr. *Kabīr Sāheb kī Śabdāvalī*. Allahabad: Belvedere Steam Printing Press, 1913.

Kālidāsa. *Abhijñānaśakuntalam*, edited by M. R. Kale. 10th edition. Delhi: Motilal Banarsidass, 1969 [1898].

Kārāikkāl Āmmāiyār

Pillai, S. 'Karaikkal Ammaiyar'. In *Women Saints of East and West: Śrī Sāradā Devī (the Holy Mother) Birth Centenary Memorial*. London: Ramakrishna Vedanta Centre, 1955.

Kaulajñāna Nirṇaya, edited by P. C. Bagchi. Calcutta: Calcutta Sanskrit Series, 3, 1934.

Kauṭilya. *The Kauṭiliya Arthaśāstra*. Part II. An English translation. R. P. Kangle. Bombay: University of Bombay, 1963.

Kenopaniṣad. Gorakhpur: Gītā Press, 1951.

Kṛṣṇayajurvedīya Taittirīyasaṃhitā. Haryana: Ram Lal Kapur Trust, 1982.

Kulārṇava Tantra: Readings and Text, edited by M. K. Pandit and T. Vidyaratna. Madras: Ganesh & Co. (Madras) Private Limited, 1965.

Lakṣmī Tantra: A Pāñcarātra Text, translated with notes by Sanjukta Gupta. Leiden: J. Brill, 1972.

Lāllā Yogeśvarī

Lāllā-Vākyāni, edited by George Grierson and Lionel D. Barnett. London: Royal Asiatic Society, 1920.

Mahābhārata

Mahābhārata, edited and translated by [Bengali] Haridas Siddhantavagish Bhattacharya. Calcutta: Siddhantavagish, [1338 baṅgābda] 1931.

Mahābhārata, edited by Ramnarayan Shastri. Gorakhpur: Gita Press, 1964.

Mahābhārata, edited by V. S. Sukthankar. Poona: Bhandarkar Oriental Research Institute, 1933–1966.

Mahābhārata, Southern Recension. 'Kumbhakonam', edited by T. R. Krishnacarya, Bombay: Nirnayasagar Press, 1906–1914.

Mahābhārata, translated by [English] Manmatha Nath Dutt. 18 volumes. Calcutta: H. C. Dass, Elysium Press, 1895–1905.

Mahānirvāṇa Tantra, edited by Baldeo Prasad Misra. Bombay: Srivenkateswar Steam Press, 1985.

Mahārthamañjarī, edited by Acharya Krishnanand Sagar. Varanasi: Krishnanand Sagar, 1985.

Manu. *The Laws of Manu*, translated by Wendy Doniger and Brian K. Smith. London: Penguin Books, 1991.

Manu-smṛti with the Manu-bhāṣya of Medhatithi, edited by Ganganath Jha. Calcutta: Asiatic Society, 1932.

Markaṇḍeya Purāṇa, translated by F. Eden Pargiter. Calcutta: Asiatic Society, 1904.

Matsyapurāṇa, edited by pandits. Pune: Anandashrama Sanskrit Series, no. 54, 1907.

Matsyapurāṇa. Volumes 1 and 2, translated by Sriram Sharma Acharya. Bareli: Samskriti Samsthan, 1970.

Medhatithi. *Manu-smṛti with the Manu-bhāṣya of Medhatithi*, edited by Ganganath Jha. Volume 1. Calcutta: Asiatic Society, 1932.

Milton, John. *Paradise Lost*, edited by Merritt Y. Hughes. New York: Macmillan, 1985.

Mīrā

Tiwari, Bhagwandas, editor. *Mīrā kī Prāmānik Padāvalī*. Allahabad: Sahitya Bhavan, 1974.

Sharma, Krishna Deo, editor. *Mīrābaī Padāvalī*. Delhi: Regal Book Depot, 1972.

Mitramiśra. *Vīramitrodaya*, Saṁskāra-prakāśa, edited by Jīvānanda Vidyasagara. Calcutta: [np], 1875.

Nārada. *Nāradasmṛti*, edited by Heramba Chatterjee Shastri. 2 volumes. Calcutta: Sanskrit College, 1988–1989.

Niruktam: Yāska's Nirukta, edited by Amareswara Thakur. Calcutta: Calcutta University, 1955.

Pañcatantram, edited and translated by Shri Shyamacharan Pandeya. Delhi: Motilal Banarsidass, 1975.

Parāśara. *Parāśara-smṛti*, edited by Alaka Sukla. Delhi: Parimal Publications, 1990.

Rāmāyaṇa

Śrīmadvālmikīrāmāyaṇam. Gorakhpur: Gita Press, Samvat 2056 [1999].

Vālmīki Rāmāyaṇa, edited by P. L.Vaidya. Baroda: Oriental Institute, 1962.

Ṛg Veda

The Hymns of the Rigveda, translated by Ralph T. H. Griffith [1889], edited by J. L. Shastri. Delhi: Motilal Banarsidass, 1973.

Ṛgveda Saṃhitā, with Sāyana's *Bhāsya*, edited by P. Venkata Rao. Mysore: Śrī Sāradā Press, 1955.

Ṛg Veda Saṃhitā, Volume 2, translation and commentary by T. V. K. Sastry and M. P. Pandit. Pondicherry: Aurobinda Ashram, 1967.

Ṛg Veda Saṁhitā. Maṇḍalas 1–10, edited by K. L. Joshi. Varanasi: Chaukhamba Orientalia, 2000.

Śāktānanda Taraṅginī, by Brahmanandagiri, edited by Rāma Kumar Rai. Varanasi: Tantra Granthamala Series 19, 1993.

Śaktisamāgama Tantra, Tārākhaṇḍa, Volume 2, edited by Benoytosh Bhattacharya. Baroda: Bhandarkar Oriental Research Institute, 1941.

Śārṅgadeva. *Saṅgītaratnākara*, edited by S. S. Shastri. Volumes I–IV. Madras: The Adyar Library, 1943–1953.

Śatapatha Brāhmaṇa, translated by Julius Eggeling. Volume 44 of *Sacred Books of the East*, edited by Max Müller. Oxford: Clarendon Press, 1900, reproduction. Delhi: Motilal Banarsidass, 1963.

Suprabhāta [Bengali periodical], edited by Kumudini Mitra. Calcutta: Suprabhat Karyalaya, c.1907–1914.

Taittirīya Saṁhitā, edited by A. M. Sastri and K. Rangacharya. Volume 9. Delhi: Motilal Banarsidass, 1986 [reproduction of 1897].

Tennyson, Alfred. 'The Princess'. In *The Major Works* [of Tennyson], Oxford World's Classics. Oxford: Oxford University Press, 2009.

Tharu, Susie and K. Lalitha, editors. *Women Writing in India, 600 BC to the Present. Volume 1, 600 BC to the Early Twentieth Century.* New York: Feminist Press, 1991.

Therīgāthā
Psalms of the Early Buddhists: I. Psalms of the Sisters. Translated by Caroline A. F. Rhys Davids. London: Pali Text Society, 1909.

Tryambakayajvan. *Strīdharmapaddhati*, translated by Julia Leslie as *The Perfect Wife*. Delhi: Penguin Books, 1995 [1989].

Vidyā Bhaṭṭārikā. *Kaumudīmahotsava*, edited by Sakuntala Rao Sastri. Bombay: Bharatiya Vidyā Bhavan, 1952.

Viṣṇu. *Viṣṇusmṛti*, edited by K. L. Joshi, translated by Manmath Nath Dutt. Delhi: Parimal Publications, 2006.

Yājñavalkyasmṛti, edited by K. L. Joshi, translated by Manmath

Nath Dutt. Delhi: Parimal Publications, 2005.

Yājñavalkyasmṛti, edited by Narayana Rāma Acharya. [Reprint of Nirnay Sagar Press, Bombay, 1949]. Delhi: Nag Publishers, 1985.

Critical Studies

Alpana of Santiniketan School. Calcutta: Chitrangshu Institute of Art and Handicraft, 1967.

Altekar, A. S. *Education in Ancient India*, 2nd edition. Benares: Nand Kishore, 1944.

Baird, Robert D., editor. *Religion in Modern India*, 2nd revised edition. New Delhi: South Asia Publications, 1989.

Beck, Brenda. 'Becoming a Living Goddess'. In Bose, editor, *The Goddess*, 201–227.

Bhattacharji, Sukumari. *Legends of Devī*. Hyderabad: Orient Blackswan, 1995.

Bhattacharji, Sukumari. *The Indian Theogony*. Cambridge: Cambridge University Press, 1970.

Bose, Mandakranta, editor. *The Goddess*. Oxford History of Hinduism series. Oxford: Oxford University Press, 2018.

Bose, Mandakranta. 'Śrī Lakṣmī: Goddess of Plenitude and Ideal of Womanhood'. In Bose, editor, *The Goddess*, 78–97.

Bose, Mandakranta. *The Rāmāyaṇa in Bengali Folk Paintings*. New Delhi: Niyogi Books, 2017.

Bose, Mandakranta. *Women in the Hindu Tradition: Rules, Roles and Expectations*. London and New York: Routledge, 2010.

Bose, Mandakranta. 'Sanctuary: Women and Home Worship'. In Bose, *Women in the Hindu Tradition*, 136–148.

Bose, Mandakranta, editor. *Faces of the Feminine in Ancient, Medieval and Modern India*. New York: Oxford University Press, 2000.

Bose, Mandakranta. 'Satī, the Event and the Ideology'. In Bose, editor, *Faces of the Feminine*, 21–32.

Christ, Carol P. 'Why Women Need the Goddess'. *Heresies: The Great Goddess Issue* (1978): 8–13.

Coleman, Tracy. 'Rādhā: Lover and Beloved of Kṛṣṇa'. In Bose, editor, *The Goddess*, 116–146.

Cotton, H. E. A. *Calcutta Old and New*. Calcutta: W. Newman, 1907.

Danielou, Alain. *Myths and Gods of India*. Rochester, VT: Inner Traditions International, c.1991.

Dasgupta, Mau. *Women Seers of the Ṛgveda*. New Delhi: D. K. Printworld, 2017.

Datta, Krishna. 'A Controversy over a Verse on the Remarriage of Hindu Women'. In Bose, editor, *Faces of the Feminine*, 7–20.

Dehejia, Vidya. *Āṇṭāl and Her Path of Love*. Albany: SUNY Press, 1990.

Derné, Steve. 'Hindu Men Talk about Controlling Women: Cultural Ideas as a Tool of the Powerful'. *Sociological Perspectives* 37 (1994), 2: 203–227.

Dhal, Upendra Nath. *Goddess Laksmi: Origin and Development*. New Delhi: Oriental Publishers, 1978.

Dhruvarajan, Vanaja. 'Religious Ideology, Hindu Women, and Development in India'. *Social Issues* 46 (1990), 3: 57–69.

Elgood, Heather. *Hinduism and the Religious Arts*. London and New York: Cassell, 1999.

Flood, Gavin. *An Introduction to Hinduism*. Cambridge: Cambridge University Press, 1996.

Forbes, Geraldine. *Women in Modern India*. Cambridge: Cambridge University Press, 1996.

Gombrich Gupta, Samjukta. 'The Goddess, Women, and Their Rituals in Hinduism'. In Bose, *Faces of the Feminine*, 87–103.

Hatcher, Brian A., editor. *Hinduism in the Modern World*. New York and Abingdon, Oxon: Routledge, 2016.

Hawley, John Stratton, editor. *Sati, the Blessing and the Curse*. Oxford and New York: Oxford University Press, 1994.

Heanue, Siobhan. www.abc.net.au/news/2018-04-11/meet-the-indian-housewives-studying-to-become-hindu-priests/9639760. 10 April 2018.

Huyler, Stephen P. *Painted Prayers: the Village Art of India*. New York: Rizzoli, 1994.

Jamison, Stephanie W. *Sacrificed Wife/Sacrificer's Wife*. Oxford: Oxford University Press, 1996.

Jones, Kenneth W. 'The Arya Samaj in British India, 1875–1947'. In Baird, editor, *Religion in Modern India*, 27–54.

Jones, Kenneth W. *Socio-Religious Reform Movements in British India*. The New Cambridge History of India. Cambridge: Cambridge University Press, 1989.

Kersenboom, Saskia C. 'The Traditional Repertoire of the Tiruttaṇi Temple Dancers'. In Leslie, editor, *Roles and Rituals for Hindu Women*, 131–148.

Khanna, Madhu. 'Here are the Daughters: Reclaiming the Girl Child'. In Bose, editor, *The Goddess*, 173–198.

Khanna, Madhu. 'The Goddess-Woman Equation in Śākta Tantras'. In Bose, editor, *Faces of the Feminine*, 109–123.

Kinsley, David. 'Devotion as an Alternative to Marriage in the Lives of Some Hindu Women Devotees'. *Journal of Asian and African Studies* 15 (1980): 1–2.

Kinsley, David. *Hindu Goddesses: Visions of the Divine Feminine in the Hindu Religious Tradition*. Berkeley: University of Los Angeles Press, 1988.

Kishwar, Madhu and Ruth Vanita. 'The Burning of Roop Kanwar'. *Manushi*, 42–43 (1987): 15–25.

Klostermaier, Klaus K. *A Survey of Hinduism*, 2nd edition. Albany: SUNY Press, 1994.

Kopf, David. *Brahmo Samaj and the Making of Modern India*. Princeton NJ: Princeton University Press, 1979.

Lavan, Spencer. 'The Brahmo Samaj: India's First Modern Movement for Religious Reform'. In Baird, editor, *Religion in Modern India*, 1–25.

Leslie, Julia, editor. *Roles and Rituals for Hindu Women*. Delhi: Motilal Banarsidass, 1991.

Leslie, Julia. *The Perfect Wife*. Translation of *Strīdharmapaddhati* by Tryambakayajvan. Delhi: Penguin Books, 1995 [1989].

Marglin, Frederique. *Wives of the God-King: the Rituals of the Devadasis of Puri*. Oxford: Oxford University Press, 1985.

Mcgee, M. 'Feasting and Fasting: the Vrata Tradition and its Significance for Hindu Women'. Unpublished Doctor of Theology dissertation, Harvard University, 1989.

Melwani, Lavina. 'Women Augment the Priestly Ranks'. *Hinduism Today*, (April/May/June 2007): 33. www.hinduismtoday.com/modules/smartsection/item.php?itemid=1542.

Mukherjee, Prabhati. *Hindu Women: Normative Models*, revised edition. Hyderabad: Orient Longman, 1994.

Nathan, Leonard, and Clint Seeley. *Grace and Mercy in Her Wild Hair*. 2nd edition. Prescott, AZ: Hohm Press, 1999.

Pandharipande, Rajeshwari V. 'Janabai: A Woman Saint of India'. In Sharma, editor, *Women Saints*.

Pauwels, Heidi R. M. 'Sītā: Enduring Example for Women'. In Bose, editor, *The Goddess*, 147–172.

Pauwels, Heidi R. M. *Goddess as Role Model: Sītā and Rādhā in Scripture and on Screen*. Oxford: Oxford University Press, 2008.

Pearson, Anne Mackenzie. *Because It Gives Me Peace of Mind: Ritual Fasts in the Religious Lives of Hindu Women*. Albany, NY: SUNY Press, 1996.

Pintchman, Tracy. *The Rise of the Goddess in the Hindu Tradition*. Albany, NY: SUNY Press, 1994.

Ramanujan, A. K. *Speaking of Śiva*. London: Penguin, 1973.

Roy, Rammohan. *Rammohan Granthābalī* (Collected Works), edited by Brajendranath Bandyopadhyay and Sajanikanta Das. Calcutta: Bangiya Sahitya Parishat, 1951.

Samanta, Basantakumar. *Hitakarī Sabhā, Strī-śikṣā o Tatkālīna Baṅgasamāja [Hitakarī Sabhā, Female Education and Contemporary Bengali Society]*. Calcutta: Sāhityaloka, 1987.

Saxena, Monika. '*Vratas,* Rituals and the Purāṇic Social Hierarchy'. In *Women and the Purāṇic Tradition in India*. Abingdon, Oxon. and New York: Routledge, 2019.

Sen, Subratā. *The Institution of Strīdhana in the Dharmaśāstra*. Calcutta: Sanskrit College, 1995.

Sharma, Arvind K. editor. *Women Saints in World Religions*. Albany: SUNY Press, 2000.

Smears, Ali. 'Mobilizing Shakti: Hindu Goddesses and Campaigns against Gender-Based Violence'. *Religions* 10 (2019), 6: article 381.

Smith, Frederic M. 'Indra's Curse, Varuṇa's Noose, and the Suppression of the Woman in the Vedic *Śrauta* Ritual'. In Leslie, editor, *Roles and Rituals*, 17–45.

Stoller-Miller, Barbara. *The Gītagovinda of Jayadeva, Love Song of The Dark Lord*. Delhi: Motilal Banarsidass, 1984.

Vanita, Ruth. 'The Self is Not Gendered: Sulabha's Debate with King Janaka'. *NWSA* [National Women's Studies Association] *Journal* 15 (2003), 2: 76–93.

Wadley, Susan S. 'Women and the Hindu Tradition'. *Signs: Journal of Women in Culture and Society* 3 (Autumn 1977), 1: 113–125.

SUGGESTIONS FOR ADDITIONAL READING

While the works listed below are not essential to make your way through this book, nor for grasping its argument, they will help to widen your understanding of women's place in Hindu religious culture. Since the authors are recognised authorities in their fields, they may lead you to further works of research on any particular themes or events that may interest you. An especially useful guide is the *Dictionary of Hinduism* (2009) in this list because of its wide coverage of Hindu thought and history.

Chitgopekar, Nilima. *Invoking Goddesses: Gender Politics in Indian Religion*. New Delhi: Shakti Books, 2002.
Presents detailed studies of hymns, prayers, and iconographic material to demonstrate the gender implications of imagining goddesses and of situating them in the power relationships of human society.

Desai, Usha, and Sallyann Goodall. 1995. "Hindu Women Talk Out." *Agenda* No. 25; Agenda Feminist Media.
Desai and Goodall explore Hindu women's perceptions of the roles that their religion prescribes for them, especially in the context of their subordination determined by gender.

De Souza, Eunice, and Lindsay Pereira, eds. 2002. *Women's Voices: Selections from Nineteenth and Early-Twentieth Century Indian Writing in English*. New Delhi & New York: Oxford University Press.

A varied and useful anthology of women's writings that supplements Susie Tharu and K. Lalitha's pioneering collection with more recent works by women.

Dhruvarajan, Vanaja. 1989. *Hindu Women and the Power of Ideology*. Granby, Mass.: Bergin & Garvey.
Detailing rural women's household roles set by traditional gender relationships, Dhruvarajan asks why it is that most women accept and even value their systemic subordination to patriarchy. The answer suggested by her detailed study of women's lives is that women have been persuaded into compliance by the ideology of *pātivrātya,* i.e., absolute devotion to the husband.

Goodall, Dominic, and R. C. Zaehner. 1996. *Hindu Scriptures*. London: J. M. Dent.
An anthology of the essential scriptures of the Hindus, these selections provide a solid base for understanding the rich variety of Hindu thought and worship practice from the earliest history of the Hindu religion.

https://www.hinduwebsite.com/hinduism/h_women.asp
Thematically grouped Hindu views about women as currently understood in the public sphere.

Hiralal, Kalpana. 2017. *Global Hindu Diaspora*. London & New York: Routledge.
A study of Hinduism in the modern, globalised world and the impact of changing social experience on belief and practice.

Johnson, W. J. 2009. *Dictionary of Hinduism*. Oxford and New York: Oxford University Press.
A comprehensive reference book that covers all important Hindu beliefs, deities, religious texts, worship practices, and festivals. Includes biographical notes on major Hindu thinkers.

Kabir. *Chalo Hamara Des*. 2008. Documentary film in Hindi, directed by Shabnam Virmani. Produced by Linda Hess. 98 min.
A journey of discovery of Kabīr's spiritual presence among a diversity of people, as expressed through Kabīr's songs.

Khandelwal, Meena. 2004. *Women in Ochre Robes: Gendering Hindu Renunciation*. Albany, NY: SUNY Press.
Khandelwal presents an analytical account of closely observed women renunciates, whose pursuit of an ascetic life reveals the tensions that are integral to a culture of gendered identities that continues into a life supposedly free of them.

McDaniel, June. *Making Virtuous Daughters and Wives: an Introduction to Women's Brata Rituals in Bengali Folk Religion*. New York: State University of New York Press, c2003.
Drawing upon extensive fieldwork in Bengal, McDaniel examines the domestic religious rituals (*vratas*) performed by Hindu women and girls to ensure the well-being of their families. Their observances, McDaniel shows, are expected to instill in them virtues idealised for women, such as devotion, humility, and compassion, which earn for them high regard as the keepers of traditional Hindu social and spiritual values.

Mitter, Sara S. 1991. *Dharma's Daughters: Contemporary Indian Women and Hindu Culture*. New Brunswick, NJ: Rutgers University Press.
Hindu women today are struggling with reconciling their inherited cultural values with the demands of a modern economy and politics. Mitter studies how their struggle is drawing upon Hinduism's inherent ability to absorb and use ideas and practices alien to its orthodox heritage.

Patton, Laurie L., ed. 2002. *Jewels of Authority: Women and Textual Tradition in Hindu India*. New York: Oxford University Press.
The common purpose of the essays in this collection is to discover how Hindu women relate to the worldly and spiritual authority of their religious heritage, as set both in religious texts and in the practice derived from them. Through close textual and ethnographic readings, the authors raise the possibility of alternative ways to interpret traditional sources of authority.

Pechilis, Karen, ed. 2004. *The Graceful Guru: Hindu Female Gurus in India and the United States*. New York; Toronto: Oxford University Press.

Gurus, or preceptors, held by Hindus to be essential guides to spiritual advancement have been traditionally men but modern times have seen a number of influential women in that role. Pechilis and her contributors present a historical account of the emergence of female gurus and locate their influence within the Hindu philosophical and worship tradition, a major source being Tantrism.

Pintchman, Tracy, ed. 2007. *Women's Lives, Women's Rituals in the Hindu Tradition*. New York: Oxford University Press.
Studying the relationship of Hindu women's ritual practices to domestic and familial concerns, the essays in this volume show the close dependency of women's religiosity on tradition. Yet it is also demonstrated that women's religious choices often go beyond, or even go against, received ideas to reconfigure the use of tradition to constitute an alternative spirituality.

Pintchman, Tracy, and Rita Das Gupta Sherma, eds. 2011. *Woman and Goddess in Hinduism: Reinterpretations and Re-envisionings*. New York: Palgrave Macmillan.
The essays in this volume examine Hindu views of the Feminine, divine as well as human, from theological as well as activist points of view to see how the idea of the goddess in Hinduism shapes belief and practice.

Polisi, Catherine E. "Universal Rights and Cultural Relativism: Hinduism and Islam Deconstructed." *World Affairs*. Vol. 167, No. 1 (SUMMER 2004), pp. 41-46

Radhakrishnan, Sarvepalli, and Charles A. Moore. 1957 [Paperback 1989] *A Source Book in Indian Philosophy*. Princeton: Princeton University Press.
These selections span the entire range of Indian philosophical thought and include excerpts from the Vedas, Upaniṣads, the epics, and treatises of later philosophical systems. Particularly useful are the introductions and interpretive commentaries.

Robinson, Catherine A. 1999. *Tradition and Liberation: The Hindu Tradition in the Indian Women's Movement*. Richmond, Surrey [UK]: Curzon Press.

Noting that women's status in India has been shaped by religious ideals and that opposition to women's rights has been justified by appealing to those ideals, Robinson cites material from 19th and 20th century women's movements to show how their struggle has, on the contrary, drawn upon traditional Hindu ethical prescriptions for promoting women's rights.

Sehgal, Meera. 2007. "Manufacturing a Feminized Siege Mentality: Hindu Nationalist Paramilitary Camps for Women in India." *J of Contemporary Ethnography*, 36, 2.
Sehgal examines the ideological messages and methods by which middle-class Hindu women are currently being politicised.

Sen, Kshitimohan. 2005. *Hinduism*. With a new foreword by Amartya Sen. London: Penguin.
A short but lucid survey and explanation of the basic tenets of Hinduism.

Sharma, Arvind. 1996. *Hinduism for Our Times*. Oxford: Oxford University Press.
Sharma's theme in this monograph is the urgent need for recognising within Hinduism an ever-present interplay between continuity and change. Recognising the capacity of Hindu belief and practice to respond to social reality in the age of globalisation, Sharma argues, is essential to affirm the centrality of Hinduism in the modern world.

Spina, Nanette R. 2017. *Women's Authority and Leadership in a Hindu Goddess Tradition*. New York: Palgrave Macmillan.
In this study of a particular religious community based in Toronto, Canada, the author emphasises the authority that women have gained as spiritual and organisational decision makers. Spina notes that these gains in the diasporic context represent no disjunction with the community's Indian counterpart but an innovative adjustment to its diasporic situation.

Srivastava, M. C. P. 2018 [1978] *Mother Goddess in Indian Art, Archaeology & Literature*. Delhi: Agam Kala Prakashan.
An illustrated survey of how the goddess figure has been

imagined and represented through time in images and words, with comments on how these representations have evolved.

Vemsani, Lavanya, ed. 2018. *Modern Hinduism in Text and Context*. London & New York: Bloomsbury Academic, Bloomsbury Publishing Plc.
The essays in this collection cover a wide range of themes and topics relating to Hindu spiritual ideologies as literary, performative, and political symbolism texts, viewed in modern historical contexts, with particular attention to the often contested role of gender in contemporary Hinduism.

Zimmer, Heinrich Robert. 1946. *Myths and Symbols in Indian Art and Civilization*. New York: Pantheon Books.
A critical and wide-ranging introduction to visual thinking and its expression in Indian art and thought, in which Zimmer finds correlations with universally recognisable myths and symbols.

Major Concepts and Terms

Goal of life

Mokṣa Liberation from *saṁsāra*

Paths to Mokṣa

Jñāna Knowledge
Karma Action and the fruit of action
Bhakti Devotion

Aspects of existence

Dharma: Duty, righteousness, religion, all moral qualities, choices, and action that hold life together
Karma Action and the fruit of action
Saṁsāra Cycle of birth, death, and rebirth

The four stages of life

Brahmacarya State of celibacy as a student of sacred knowledge
brahmacārī : a male student
brahmacāriṇī : a female student
Gārhasthya State of being a householder
gṛhastha: a householder

Vāṇaprastha	Retirement from active life to dwell in a forest
Sannyāsa	Renunciation *sannyāsī*: a renunciate

The four castes

Brāhmaṇa	Learned person/priest
Kṣatriya	Warrior
Vaiśya	Merchant
Śūdra	Serving person (*not* untouchable)

Rituals of worship

Arcanā	Worship
Pūjā	Worship ritual
Upavāsa	Fasting
Vrata	Ritual of fulfilling a vow
Prasāda	Food symbolically tasted by a deity

The six schools of philosophy

Nyāya	Logic
Vaiśeṣika	Physics
Yoga	Connection/Union with the Supreme Being
Sāṁkhya	Principles of creation
Mīmāṁsā	Questions and solutions
Vedānta	Exploring ideas beyond those stated in the Vedas

Sanskrit

Pronunciation Guide*

Vowels

a	like the *u* in b*u*t
ā	like the *a* in f*a*r
i	like the *i* in b*i*t
ī	like the *ee* in b*ee*t
u	like the *u* in p*u*t
ū	like the *oo* in p*oo*l
ṛ	something like the *ri* in *ri*g
e	like the *a* in g*a*te
ai	like the *ai* in *ai*sle
o	like the *o* in r*o*pe
au	like the *ow* in h*ow*

Consonants

k	like the *k* in s*k*ate
kh	like the *k* in *K*ate
g	like the *g* in *g*ate
gh	like the *gh* in bi*gh*ead
ṅ	like the *n* in si*n*g
c	like the *ch* in *ch*ill

*Adapted, with modifications, from Robert P. Goldman and Sally J. Sutherland Goldman (eds. and transl.), *The Complete English Translation of The Rāmāyaṇa of Vālmīki* (Princeton, New Jersey: Princeton University Press, 2021), xi-xiv.

ch	like the *chh* in mat*chh*ead
j	like the *j* in *j*ump
jh	like the *dgeh* in he*dgeh*og
ñ	like the *ny* in ca*ny*on
ṭ	like the first *t* in s*t*art
ṭh	like the *t* in *t*art
ḍ	like the *d* in *d*art
ḍh	like the *dh* in a*dh*ere
ṇ	like the *n* in ti*n*t
t, *th*, *d*, *dh*, *n*	like the five preceding sounds but with the tip of the tongue touching or extending slightly between the teeth
p	like the *p* in s*p*in
ph	like the *p* in *p*in
b	like the *b* in *b*in
bh	like the *bh* in a*bh*or
m	like the *m* in *m*ind
y	like the *y* in *y*ellow
r	like the *r* in d*r*ama
l	like the *l* in *l*ug
v	between the *w* in *w*ile and the *v* in *v*ile
ś	like the *sh* in *sh*ove
ṣ	produced with the tongue-tip further back than for *ś*, but giving a similar sound
s	like the *s* in *s*o
h	like the *h* in *h*ope
ṁ	a nasalisation of a preceding vowel
ḥ	an aspiration of a preceding vowel pronounced, almost like an echo, as an *h* followed by the short form of the preceding vowel. For example: *devaḥ* is pronounced *deva(ha)*, *muniḥ* is pronounced *muni(hi)*, and *devāḥ* is pronounced *devā(ha)*

INDEX

A

Abalābāndhab, 229
Abhang, 151
Abhijñānaśakuntalam, 95
activism, 242–244
  political, 232–235
Ādi Parva, 47, 71–72, 97
Adyapith temple, 35
Agastya, 59
Agni, 11, 52, 96, 126
Agnipurāṇa, 193
Aitareya Brāhmaṇa, 94
Ākkā Mahādevī, 78, 139, 226
Ālpanā, 191, 211–212
Amāvasyā, 180, 182
Āṇṭāl, 72, 79, 136–137, 146–147, 152, 156, 158–159, 161, 226
  Nācciyār Tirumoli, 138
  Tiruppāvai, 138, 188
Apālā, 60
Āpastamba, 115
Araṇyakāṇḍa, 48, 88
Arya Samaj, 109, 119, 225, 245
Aśvaghoṣa, 92
Atharva Veda, 93–94, 245
Atta Karagam, 211

B

Bahiṇābāi, 73, 151–152, 155, 159
bahu-vivāha (polygamy), 109, 111–112
Bali, 30
Bāmābodhinī Patrikā, 229, 234
Bāṇabhaṭṭa's Harṣacarita, 95
Banga Mahila Vidyalaya, 232
'Baṅganārī', a Bengali woman, 233
Baudhāyana, 84, 93, 96, 99, 107, 115
Bengal
  ālpanās, 191
  dāya-bhāga, 116
  Lakṣmī worship, 178–180
  shools, 231
  periodicals, 232–233
Bengal Sati Regulation, 230
Bethune School and College, 232
Bethune, John Elliot Drinkwater, 231
Bhadrā Kuṇḍalakeśā, 68
Bhāgavad-Gītā, 134
Bhairavī (Mahāvidyā form), 24, 29
bhakti, 38, 133–136, 139, 144, 152, 155, 157–158, 204
Bharata Muni, 105
Bhārat Bhaginī, 229
Bhāratamahilā, 232
Bharatanāṭyam, 105
Bhāskarācārya, 72
Brahma Kumaris, 244
Bṛhadāraṇyaka Upaniṣad, 63, 65–67, 95, 236
Brahmā, 12
Brahman, 15, 18, 52, 126–127
Brāhmaṇa, 59

Brahmavādinī, 61–62, 126
brahmins, 111, 131, 156, 164, 167, 182
Brahmo Samaj, 109, 119, 225
Bṛhaspati–smṛti, 115, 117
Buddhism, 67, 131–132

C

calendars, 44, 169, 172, 174
Candrāvatī, 151, 156–158
Chhath Puja, 166
Child Marriage Restraint Act, 112
Chinnamastā (Mahāvidyās), 24
Chittara style painting, 213
compassion, 94–95, 235
consciousness, 13, 24, 34, 36–37, 64, 128, 135, 229, 250
cow dung, 100
creation, 8, 10–11, 14, 17–19, 24, 54, 57, 59, 192, 219–220, 235
creative energy, 15, 55, 119
creativity, 103, 128–129, 160, 199
creator, 12, 15, 18, 77, 198, 219–220

D

daily worship routines, 177
dancers, 104, 206–211
dances, 207, 209
daughters, 67, 93–98, 111, 115, 176, 184, 231
Deity of knowledge. See Goddess Sarasvati
devadāsī custom, 206
Devi. See also Divine Feminine
  as great Goddess, 20, 30–31
  as mother, 26–30
  Mahāvidyās, 24–25

Mātṛkās, the 'Mothers', 26
philosophical speculations, 13–14
Devīmāhātmya, 15–19, 26, 44, 48
Devī Sūkta, 57, 127
devotees, 21, 27, 31, 36, 43, 134–135, 144, 156, 188
dharma
role of, 83–86, 226, 235
code of conduct, 226
dharma-śāstras, 67, 69, 73, 84–85, 92–93, 98, 104, 108
Divine Feminine
all-pervasive power, 57
Great Goddess, 14–19
identification of energy, 166, 228
in human life, 40–41
Mahāvidyās, 24
sacred knowledge as, 55
Sītā and Rādhā, 38–39
source of wealth and well-being, 30
unequivocal reverence in Hinduism, 56
divinity and womenhood
gender conceptions, 34–40, 42–48
in human Life, 40–41
philosophical theory vs worldly practice, 42
diwali, 180, 191
domesticity, 65, 131, 147, 182, 227
Durgā, 15, 18–19, 20–21, 24, 27, 34, 40–42, 44, 49, 169, 178, 185, 243

E

early Goddesses, 11–13
ekādaśī, 109, 172
energy, 8, 10–12, 15, 30, 41, 54–55, 59, 73, 119, 166, 168, 175, 211, 239

equality, 82, 92, 133, 224, 227–228, 237–238, 242, 246
exclusion, 39, 73, 101, 165, 225, 234

F

faith
  brahman as the Eternal Good, 154–155
  Buddhist, 133
  communities, 119
  divine presence, 144
  Hindu women, 1, 33, 106, 167, 190, 192
  hope, 176
  religious, 40, 45, 48, 122, 205, 219, 222
fasting, 108, 175, 179, 182–183
female education, 229, 235–236
femininity, 24, 30, 36–37, 39–40, 119, 151, 168, 199, 207, 250
festivals, 26–28, 35, 89, 169, 180, 190, 192, 203, 205, 209
freedom, 72, 103, 123, 130, 132–134, 198, 201, 237–238, 240, 247, 251
  through education, 229–232

G

Ganges water, 171, 175, 178, 190
Ganguly, Dwarakanath, 229
Garba, 209, 211
Gārgī, 62–64, 128, 236
gender
  art and, 197–199
  bhakti and, 134–135, 201
  Buddhist view, 92
  categories, 2, 61, 63–64
  characteristics and roles, 10–11, 42, 78, 102, 155, 225–226, 246
  equality, 242
  identities, 78

inequality, 228
parity, 73
prejudice, 68, 246
religious conduct, 3
ṚgVeda, 86
rights, 240
rules of conduct, 82
social life, 249–250
Tantric view, 34, 37, 165
girl child, 93–94, 108, 112, 170
Gītagovinda, 206
Gobhila Gṛhyasūtra, 68–69
Goddess Sarasvati, 11–12, 31, 33, 43–44, 47, 53–55, 206
gurus, 77, 209

H

Hindu culture, 5, 46, 60, 67, 72, 135
Hindu society
access to education, 58
authority of women, 60–61
convention of conduct, 240
ethical discourse on women's duty, 98–103
family and personal relationship, 47
formal dances, 209
intellectual elite community, 65
learned women, 67–68, 78, 236, 239
major goddesses, 43
Manu on remarriage, 108
oppression of women, 55
origin of existence, 7–8
polygamy, 113
punarvivāha, or remarriage, 106
religious ideology, 81–83, 237–242

role of dharma, 83–86, 226, 235
sacred knowledge, 52, 65
Sītā and Rādhā, 38–39
social life, women, 122–123, 128, 161, 227, 237, 246
social system, 225
woman as 'mother', 45
women's submissiveness, 38, 119, 131
Hindu thought, 2, 5, 10, 39, 42, 47, 52, 56, 94, 120, 265
Hindu women
changing need, 116–118
economic exploitation, 113–115
inner power, 120–121
liberation of, 118–120
in modern times, 122, 247–248
niyoga or levirate, 109–113
social world, 123
widow remarriage, 106–109
Hindu spirituality
religion as identity, 244–247
ideology of liberalism, 246
Hindu women
activism, 232–235, 242–244
demand for justice, 228
resistance to exploitation, 228–229
rules of conduct, 98–103
social equality, 92, 227
spirituality, 244–247
twentieth century, stability of social life, 239–242
Hitakarī Sabhā, 230–231
Huyler, Stephen P., 212

I

idiom, 138, 141, 152, 155, 159, 168, 244
illusions, 15, 136, 140
immortality, 12, 64–65
impurities, 96–97, 99–100
India
  freedom movement, 234
  independence, 229, 234, 238
  Northern, 109, 119, 147, 173, 180
  South, 134–135, 164, 188–190, 206
Indra, 30, 52, 60, 126
Indrāṇī, 60
inheritance, 83, 113, 115, 118
injustice, 118, 155–156, 228, 242, 246
intelligence, 17, 54, 92, 230
Ishwarchandra, Vidyasagar, 108

J

Jagannatha temple, 206
Jamadagni, 118, 153
Jānābāi, 151–152, 155, 158
Janaka, 63–64, 216
Jayadeva, 206
Jayakrishna Mukhopadhyaya, 230
Jaya Pārvatī Vrata, 187
Jnana Prabodhini, 228

K

Kabīr, 144, 147, 201–202, 220, 222
Kālī, 12, 15–16, 21–24, 28–29, 36, 41–42, 44–45, 133, 136, 169, 180, 200, 215
Kālidāsa, 92, 95
Kalikrishna Girls' High School, 231

Kāma, 97, 206
kāmalā, 24, 44
Kārādāyan Nombu, 189
Karagattam, 211
Kāraikkāl Āmmāiyār, 72, 136
Karṇa Parva, 85, 118
Kārtika (month), 186, 189
Kārtikeya, 26–27
Karve, Dhondo Keshav, 232
Kashmiri Śaivaite, 44
Kātyāyanī, 64
Kenopaniṣad, 52
Kerala Suguna Bodhinī, 229
Kaulajñāna Nirṇaya, 77
Kaumudī Mahotsava, 129
Kauṭilya, 84, 93, 115
kojāgarī pūrnīmā, 180
kolams, 191
Kṛṣṇa, 15, 38–39, 44, 118, 121–122, 137, 146–147, 151–152, 180, 187–188, 193, 201, 205–208, 212, 215
Kṛṣṇa Yajurveda, 94
kṣatriyas, 131
kṣetra, 110
kṣetraja, 110
Kubera, 30
Kularṇava Tantra, 34
Kumārī Pūjā, 34–36
Kuntī, 110

L

Lakṣmī, 11–13, 21, 27, 30–32, 36, 40, 43–44, 133, 169, 174, 177–183, 188, 198, 212
Lalitā, 36

learned women/women's education
legends of learned women, 59–61, 78–79, 236
orthodox view, 235–237
social movements, 232
voting rights, 234
political activism, 232–235
self-determination and justice through, 229–232
schools for girls, 230–232
first university, 232
in early Hindu society, 58–59
use of knowledge, 59–61, 65–68
Philosophical Discourse, 61–64
Sacred task, 68–72
public and private conduct, 72–75
religious culture, 75–78
liberal ideology, 96
satī and widow remarriage, 109
social culture, 223
public life, 237–238, 240
spread of education, 246
life, four goals of, 206
Līlāvatī, 72
Lopāmudrā, 56, 59, 127

M

Madhubani, 216–218
Mādrī, 104, 110
Mahābhārata, 16, 26, 47, 63–64, 69–72, 85, 88, 97–98, 104, 110, 118
Mahānirvāṇa Tantra, 34, 76, 120
Mahārthamañjarī, 77
Mahiṣa, 21
Maitreyī, 84–85, 78, 128, 236

Manasā, 14
Manu
Laws of, 74, 84, 89
condemnation of women, 90–91, 94
monthly menstruation, 97
wife's dharma, 101
self-sacrifice by a widow, 104, 111
Widow Remarriage, 106–108, 111, 116
eka-patnītva, or monogamy, 112
women's right to inheritance, 115–116
power relationships, 233
exaltation of women, 236
marriage
daughter's departure after, 94–95
in great epics, 69
inheritance laws, 83
saṁskāras, 74
sanctity of, 38–39
women's status, 101
Matsya Purāṇa, 95, 194
Medhatithi, 104, 112
medieval times, 75, 104, 111, 128, 132, 158
menstruation, 97, 99–100
Mīrābāī, 39, 47, 73, 79, 146, 148, 201–202, 220, 226
modern times, 79, 118, 123, 132, 157–160, 198, 209, 238
mokṣa, 4, 63, 145, 193–194, 206
Mollā, Ātukuri, 151, 156
Mukhopadhyaya, Jayakrishna, 230
music, 2, 12, 31, 34, 38, 43, 54, 59
bhakti and, 133, 158, 167
dance and, 204–207, 211
gender and, 198–203, 220
Hindusthani, 147

women's creativity, 103, 122
myths, 5, 21, 26, 39–41, 174, 211–212

N

Nārada, 84, 93, 107, 115, 117–118
Nārada–smṛti, 108
Nāṭyaśāstra, 205
Navarātri festival, 209
Nāyannārs, 134–135
Niśumbha, 21
nitya puja, 169–170, 193
niyoga, 109–111
non–Hindus, 38, 45

O

offering, 120, 167–168, 171, 173, 178–179, 182, 184, 186, 204, 206
orthodoxy, 48, 106, 154, 235–237, 244–245

P

Padmā, 44
paintings, 2, 178, 197–198, 211–218, 220
Pañcatantra, 88
Pāṇḍu, 104, 110
Pāṅguni, 189
Pāṇin, 61
Parāśara–smṛti, 107
Pārvatī, 21, 24, 187–188
Paṭacitra, 212–215
Phule, Jyotirao, 232
Phule, Savitribai, 232
poems, 60, 78, 129–130, 132, 135, 137–138, 140, 142, 144, 150, 155–156, 188, 202

polygamy, 105, 111–113
Prahlāda, 30
public life, 79, 131, 133, 238–239
purāṇas, 15, 152, 174, 189

Q

queen Śaibyā, 102

R

Rabindranath Tagore, 220
Rādhā, 37–39, 121–122, 158
Rāma, 37–38, 47, 71
Ramakrishna Paramahamsadeva, 79, 226
  Ramakrishna Mission, 243
Rāmānuja, 133, 135
Rāmāyaṇa, 37, 47–48, 69–71, 88, 156, 198, 212
Raṅgoli, 191, 211–212
religion
  art and, 211–218
  devotional purpose of art, 197–218
  feminine divine, 120–121
  modern worship, 163–165
  and Society, 224–225
  women's faith, 224
religious ideology, 81–83, 237–242
ṚgVeda
  condemning women, 55, 68, 87
  Devī Sūkta, 126–127
  elements of bhakti, 133, 157–160
  existence of gods, 8–9
  husband and wife, religious life, 164
  on divine feminine, 14, 52
  sūktas or hymns, 56–60, 126–127

women seers, 58
Roy, Raja Rammohan, 230
Ṛṣyaśṛṅga, 101

S

Sabarimala protest, 240
Śāktā theology, 77, 165
Sarasvatī (Goddess), 11–12, 27, 31, 33, 43–44, 47, 53–55, 206, 236
Sarkar, Peary Charan, 231
Satī, 103–106, 230
Sītā, 37–39, 46, 113, 156–157, 216–218
Śiva, 15, 18, 21, 24, 27, 133–136, 140, 145, 174, 177–182, 188, 201, 205, 215
śivarātri vrata, 176, 180, 182
social world, 225
Hindu women, 123
women's liberation, 120–121
Sri Sarada Math, 243
saṁskāras, 69, 75
self-determination, 7, 41, 47, 51, 92, 103, 128, 192, 228, 229
SNDT (Shreemati Nathibai Damodar Thackersey), 232
soma-yajña, 70, 164
Suprabhāta, 232–233
Supreme Being, 2, 9, 31, 54, 76, 133

T

Taittirīya Saṁhitā, 59, 94
Tamil language, 129
Tāntrism, 34, 36–37, 77, 145, 165, 192
Tharu-Lalita, 159
Tryambakayajvan, 99–101, 167

U

Umā Maheśvara vrata, 189
Upadhyāyā, 61
Upādhyāyī, 61
Upanayana, 74
USA, Hindu population, 245

V

Vāk or Āmbhṛṇī, 52, 56–59, 126, 199
varṇas, 74
Vasiṣṭha, 85–86, 93, 96, 99, 107–108
Vāyu, 52
Vedas, 11–12, 61, 70, 72, 74, 82, 94, 152–153, 235
Vengamamba, Tarigonda, 159
Vratas
  goal and purpose, 172–177
  for Lakṣmī and Śiva, 177–186
  of North India, 186–187
  of Western India, 187–188
  South Indian, 188–190
  Ṣaṣṭhīvrata, 182–183

W

widow remarriage, 106–108, 111, 118
women's art, 190, 204
  dance, 204–211
  music, 199–204
  painting, 211–218
women's life
  attitude towards daughters, 93–96
  category of rules, 86–88
  dharma, role in, 83–86
  duty, 98–103

gender bias, 88–93
in modern times, 122–123
inescapable conditions, 116–118
inner power, 120–122
niyoga or levirate, 109–113
religious ideology, 81–83
rule bound suffering, 81–83, 118–120
Satī, 103–106
wealth, 113–116
widow remarriage, 106–109
women's periodicals, 229
women's regeneration, 122
female creativity, 129–132
women's worship
nitya pūjā and vratas, 170–171, 185–190, 192–194
aesthetic dimension, 190–192
belief and action, 166–168
brāhmaṇabhojana, 182
eight mahāvratas ('great' vratas), 189
jaya pārvatī vrata, 187
kārādāyan nombu, 189
karvā chauth, 186
kolam, 191
pāvāi nombu, 188
routine, 168–170
śiva pārvatī vrata, 188
tāntric yantras, 192
Umā Maheśvara vrata, 189
Varalakṣmī nombu, 188
Vipattāriṇī vrata, 185–186
women's writings
creativity, 129–130
cultural milieu, new wave, 132–134

elements of bhakti, 134–135
heritage, 125–129, 150–155
modern, 157–159
Mutta, 130
poets and poetry, 135–156
Sumanā, 130
vedic civilization, 125–129

Y

Yājñavalkya, 62–65, 84, 93, 99, 101, 107–108, 115
Yama, 74, 185, 187, 189
yoginis, 77–78

MANDALA
An Imprint of MandalaEarth
PO Box 3088
San Rafael, CA 94912
www.MandalaEarth.com

Find us on Facebook: www.facebook.com/MandalaEarth

Follow us on Twitter: @MandalaEarth

ISBN: 978-1-64722-916-0

Publisher Raoul Goff
Associate Publisher Phillip Jones
Editorial Director Katie Killebrew
Acquisitions & Publications Coordinator Amanda Nelson
VP Creative Chrissy Kwasnik
Art Director Ashley Quackenbush
VP Manufacturing Alix Nicholaeff
Sr Production Manager Joshua Smith
Sr Production Manager, Subsidiary Rights Lina s Palma-Temena

Designed by Anupama dasa

Images courtesy Mandala Foundation (Pages 23, 25, 32, 46, 53, 62, 114, 116, 169, 203); Mandakranta Bose (Pages 20, 22, 28, 33, 179, 215); Shutterstock (Pages 35, 66, 148, 166, 173, 181, 200, 205, 207, 208, 210, 213, 217, 218, 231, 243); Rituparna Dasgupta (Page 27); and Biswarup Ganguly (Page 214).

Manufactured in India by Insight Editions
10 9 8 7 6 5 4 3 2 1

ROOTS of PEACE REPLANTED PAPER

Insight Editions, in association with Roots of Peace, will plant two trees for each tree used in the manufacturing of this book. Roots of Peace is an internationally renowned humanitarian organization dedicated to eradicating land mines worldwide and converting war-torn lands into productive farms and wildlife habitats. Roots of Peace will plant two million fruit and nut trees in Afghanistan and provide farmers there with the skills and support necessary for sustainable land use.